COUNSELING COPS

Also from Ellen Kirschman

I Love a Fire Fighter:
What the Family Needs to Know

I Love a Cop: Revised Edition:
What Police Families Need to Know

For more information, visit Ellen Kirschman's website:
www.ellenkirschman.com

COUNSELING
COPS

What Clinicians Need to Know

Ellen Kirschman
Mark Kamena
Joel Fay

Foreword by Ellen Scrivner

THE GUILFORD PRESS
New York   London

To the men and women of law enforcement
and their families
You deserve the best.

Library of Congress Cataloging-in-Publication Data

Kirschman, Ellen.
  Counseling cops : what clinicians need to know / Ellen Kirschman, Mark Kamena, Joel Fay.
     pages cm
  Includes bibliographical references and index.
  ISBN 978-1-4625-1265-2 (hardback)
  ISBN 978-1-4625-2430-3 (paperback)
  1. Police psychology.   2. Police—Job stress.   3. Police—Family relationships.
I. Kamena, Mark.   II. Fay, Joel.   III. Title.
  HV7936.P75K57 2014
  363.201′9—dc23
                                                          2013022755

ABOUT THE AUTHORS

Ellen Kirschman, MSW, PhD, is a clinical psychologist in independent practice in Redwood City, California, and a volunteer clinician at the West Coast Post-Trauma Retreat. She is a recipient of the Award for Outstanding Contributions to Police and Public Safety Psychology from the Police and Public Safety Section of Division 18 (Psychologists in Public Service) of the American Psychological Association (APA). Dr. Kirschman presents workshops worldwide and is the author of the bestselling self-help guide *I Love a Cop: What Police Families Need to Know* as well as *I Love a Fire Fighter: What the Family Needs to Know* and the mystery novel *Burying Ben*. Her website is *www.ellenkirschman.com*.

Mark Kamena, PhD, ABPP, is Director of Research and Co-Founder of the First Responder Support Network, a volunteer, nonprofit organization that operates the West Coast Post-Trauma Retreat and a separate program for first-responder spouses and significant others. He has a private practice in Marin County, California, where he specializes in first-responder posttraumatic stress injury. Dr. Kamena is a recipient of the Award for Outstanding Contributions to Police and Public Safety Psychology from APA Division 18. He is President of the California Psychological Association (CPA) and serves on the CPA Foundation Board.

Joel Fay, PsyD, ABPP, is a psychologist in private practice who works with emergency responders and provides crisis intervention training for numerous agencies throughout California. He served as a police officer for over 30 years before retiring in 2011. Dr. Fay is a recipient of the Humanitarian Award from the California Psychological Association and the Award for Outstanding Contributions to Police and Public Safety Psychology from APA Division 18. He serves on the Psychological Services Committee of the International Association of Chiefs of Police, is Clinical Director of the First Responder Support Network, and teaches and presents workshops widely.

FOREWORD

The world of law enforcement is facing new challenges that affect the roles of mental health professionals who work with police officers and their families. Crime is taking new directions that add complexity to what the police officer faces on a daily basis. While the need for cops on the beat remains as strong as ever, we are now seeing more incidents of violence, both lethal and nonlethal, that are fueled by increasingly sophisticated digital-age technology. Such phenomena as "flash mobs" and rampage shootings, both of which can escalate via social media, lend an immediacy and unpredictability to crimes that once took more time to carry out and where police had the decided advantage. In addition, there are increases in home-grown terrorist threats, while the growth of cybercrime has made the intersection of gangs, guns, and drugs far more sophisticated and creates the capacity for criminals to outthink the police. A prime example includes the new trend of hackers raiding bank accounts rather than risking their lives in bank robberies or street holdups. Furthermore, the growing trends in prescription drug abuse add a new element to the types of criminals peddling drugs. Drug trade is no longer solely the domain of armed gangs doing exchanges on city street corners. Rather, we now see comparable behavior from kids in suburbs who have raided medicine chests to engage in similar transactions with equally harmful substances.

Just as crime is changing, there are also changes in the methods and strategies used to fight crime. There is a growing dependence on DNA analysis, geospatial analysis that supports "hot-spot" policing, conducted energy devices, and a range of high-tech surveillance technologies, including drones, cameras mounted in police cars, and even cameras on uniform lapels. All of these new methodologies generate concomitant concerns about protecting civil liberties, and they bring new levels of scrutiny to police and public safety in an era where "transparency" has become a public safety watchword.

While many of these changes came about in response to the attacks on September 11, 2001, they have led to strategic approaches frequently defined as "hyphenated policing." Building upon earlier success of community- and problem-oriented policing strategies, the newer strategies include intelligence-led policing, predictive policing, and smart policing, each with its own unique twist in the pursuit of crime control and crime prevention. Whatever the approach, however, they add new stress factors and challenges to the cop on the beat—and thus also can affect the work of the mental health practitioners who provide services for cops on the beat and their families. The need for well-functioning officers may be greater than ever, so hiring officers capable of functioning in the new environment is critical, as is ensuring that they are appropriately trained and that they have services available to help them and their families cope with what is being referred to as the "new normal." Within that context, there is a greater emphasis being placed on the need for officer wellness programs and interventions that promote resiliency and strengthen mental health.

Despite all these changes, the culture of law enforcement has not changed dramatically, and that is why this book is so important. Starting with chapter titles that pique the imagination and invite the reader to delve further, Drs. Kirschman, Kamena, and Fay cover the broad spectrum of police roles and their effect on individual officers and their families, as well as on their respective departments. Moreover, the authors make it acceptable to talk openly about these roles and their related impacts. Their treatment of law enforcement professionals reflects their professional and personal beliefs that police officers have a very difficult job, one more difficult than many, particularly their critics, realize. Though many do not think about psychology and policing as being compatible, the authors show how a respectful relationship has evolved over time, which continuously needs to be nurtured and sustained, while also maintaining the independence of the role of the mental health professional.

The publication of this book comes at a time when police psychology has achieved great strides in being recognized as a professional specialty by the American Board of Professional Psychology, with identified domains of practice and related guidelines that define and strengthen the practice of psychology in police and public safety agencies. Accordingly, the time is right for the type of literature that supports the specialty and that synthesizes important issues practitioners need to be aware of when providing services to police and public safety personnel.

In essence, Drs. Kirschman, Kamena, and Fay have turned out a great book demonstrating their in-depth understanding of the psychology of human behavior as related to police and public safety. It is a "must read" for anyone who evaluates or treats cops, or who counsels their families. I also recommend it as important reading for social science researchers who are studying policing issues from both an individual and an organizational perspective; police officers from the rank of recruit up to those who occupy positions as chiefs; and students of mental health and criminal justice.

ELLEN SCRIVNER, PHD
Executive Fellow, Police Foundation
Washington, DC

PREFACE TO THE PAPERBACK EDITION

A lot has happened since we first published *Counseling Cops: What Clinicians Need to Know* in 2014. Several high-profile police shootings of unarmed citizens exposed smoldering resentments in communities across the nation. There were protests and riots. It was as though hot lava poured through fractures in the surface of society, scalding everyone it touched. The Internet lit up. Battle lines were drawn across cyber-space. Voices of reason and nuance were hard to find. The president convened a special task force with public hearings to investigate the state of modern policing (*http://www.cops.usdoj.gov/pdf/taskforce/TaskForce_FinalReport. pdf*).

Traditional practices were called into question. Were cops warriors or guardians? Why does the emphasis on physical confrontation exceed the emphasis on problem solving and de-escalation in police training? Has the broken window theory, a well-intentioned effort to utilize police to stop neighborhood deterioration, failed in its promise, forcing cops into confrontations over minor violations and leaving citizens feeling as though they live in occupied territory? Why do police departments need tanks? What about community policing, citizen oversight, racial equality, and fairness?

In the midst of all the debate, cops on the street, despite feeling under assault from the public, kept working. And looking over their shoulders. Afraid to make a move, worried about using force for fear of being pilloried in the press or betrayed by their departments. Equally afraid of hesitating a moment too long and getting killed. Reluctant to stop suspicious people for fear of being labeled as racist. Hoping their children will find another way to make a living.

In response to the bad press, as the actions of a few spread a shadow over the entire profession, law enforcement agencies and organizations initiated public relations campaigns attempting to balance the relentless bad news about cops. The efforts ranged from humorous to dignified. There was a proliferation of positive YouTube videos: cops singing in patrol cars, playing with little children, walking down the streets they patrol with signs offering free hugs. The International Association of Chiefs of Police began a campaign, #WhyIWearTheBadge, to show the diversity and commitment of the law enforcement community, one cop at a time.

As we write this preface, the debate about police/community relations continues to gain traction. Solutions will be slow to emerge because the problems facing our society are complex and many. It is a difficult time to be a cop, especially for those who feel unsupported by their communities, their departments, their governments, and, on occasion, each other. And it is not an easy time for police families, who feel the brunt of negative publicity as deeply as their loved ones in law enforcement. It is families who face the taunts of classmates and friends. Families who are confronted by unanswerable questions. Families who read the headlines describing the people they love as bigots with badges.

The clinical approaches described in this book still stand, although creating a therapeutic alliance may be even harder than before. Cops are going to be reading you, waiting to see if you will take sides or stereotype them. At the same time, more than ever, there is a need for culturally competent clinicians, peer support personnel, and chaplains who can listen with compassion, and understand the challenges facing law enforcement and how it feels to have one's dedication and hard work tarnished by the actions of a few. The culture of law enforcement, like other uniformed professions, rests heavily on tradition. Change doesn't come easily or quickly. Hence the need for patient listeners who can empathize with a cop who feels caught in a maelstrom of societal change or feels blamed for institutional problems like poverty and racism that are way beyond his or her control.

How do you develop this empathy? You don't have to be a cop to understand the shame they feel when someone in their profession betrays the public trust. You don't have to be a cop to sense the subtle shift in how people in their communities look at them. Or to intuit the unasked questions, the skepticism, the lack of trust. Of course, no matter how good you are at empathizing with clients, you cannot know how it really feels to take risks with your safety, perhaps your life, for people who appear not to care about you or respect what you do for them. As you gain familiarity with the culture of law enforcement and increase your competence in working with cops, you'll be better able to access feelings and experiences that will help you identify with an officer and challenge any judgments you might hold.

We have no special strategies to add to what we've already written. We only want to emphasize the need for compassion and understanding. Morale is low in law enforcement. We advise officers and their families to avoid reading contentious blogs and other incendiary material and to search, instead, for balanced, informed reporting. We suggest the same to our readers. We also emphasize the need for patience and taking the long view—officers should avoid precipitous decisions about quitting the force in reaction to recent events. We believe policing is an honorable profession and that the current national conversation, while painful, holds promise for major improvements that will benefit our communities and those who serve and protect them.

Redwood City, California
June 2015

ACKNOWLEDGMENTS

We owe a huge debt of gratitude to our clients who have trusted us with their stories and their struggles, and to our mentors and colleagues who have generously shared their experiences and their expertise: Anne Bisek, Emily Brucia, Dave Corey, Mike Cutler, M. Michael Fagan, Emily Keram, Jo Linder-Crow, Robin Matthews, Jeni McCutcheon, Gary Olson, Louisa Parks, Mike Pool, Jocelyn Roland, Steven Sultan, Phil Trompetter, Bryan Vila, John Violanti, and the volunteers at the First Responder Support Network. Our special thanks to Al Benner, who literally started it all; we wish he had lived to see how far we've come.

Our hats are off to the staff at The Guilford Press, especially our hardworking editor, Jim Nageotte, and his able assistant, Jane Keislar.

Our own first responders, Steve Johnson, Paula Kamena, and Ann Buscho, deserve the highest honors for their support, patience, and love.

CONTENTS

INTRODUCTION

Police officers and their families make up a unique subculture. They do what most of us couldn't or wouldn't. The complex and sometimes overwhelming challenges they face are piled on top of the commonplace problems we all share. They are both the same as and different from other clients. As therapists dedicated to serving law enforcement officers (LEOs),[1] we have repeatedly heard stories about how first responders overcame their natural resistance to asking for help, only to be turned off by well-meaning, and occasionally not so well-meaning, clinicians who didn't understand the law enforcement culture and had nowhere to learn about it. We hope this book will fill that gap in the clinical literature and provide clinicians with practical advice about working with law enforcement so that first responders and their families can get the culturally competent treatment they deserve.

Caveat emptor: We want to be clear about our biases. We like cops, respect them, and have a great deal of compassion for the complex, sometimes impossible, work they do. Our goal is to return officers with psychological injuries to work and, when that is not feasible, at least restore them to healthy, happy, and productive lives.

We appreciate that LEOs represent domestic authority in a democratic society and are caught in the middle between majority rules and individual

---

[1]We use the terms LEO, police officer, law enforcement officer, public safety officer, and cop interchangeably throughout the book. Unless rank is specified, LEO refers to a line-level officer.

rights, enforcing laws they didn't create. Policing is a difficult and complex job requiring an amalgam of skills suitable to a team of lawyers, athletes, priests, counselors, enforcers, and judges. Society asks a great deal of law enforcement professionals, and we see, firsthand, how much they give in return—and what it costs them. This is the reason our book emphasizes clinical interventions over assessment, as well as treatment over screening.

Much of what has been written about treating law enforcement officers and their families has been written by and for police psychologists. Membership in police psychology organizations has nearly doubled in recent years, and the American Board of Professional Psychology has just approved board certification for police psychologists, most of whom specialize in assessment. But there is little written for the community therapist, the employee assistance program (EAP) provider, the chaplain, or the peer supporter, who may be the best and most available personal resource for troubled cops and their families. Without specific understanding of the culture in which LEOs work and the jobs they are mandated to do, it is easy to make clinical errors based on misinformation, stereotypes, personal bias, or even worse, television cop shows.

This is a practical book. Cops distrust what they call psychobabble, so it is written in plain language. Much of the material is illustrated by vignettes drawn from our files and the files of our colleagues. Unless we have been given permission to reveal parties' identities, all quotes, examples, and names are disguised, and some scenarios are composites. Our focus is on police officers and their families, but many sections will be relevant to treating other emergency responders as well (see Chapter 19).

Because we often work and teach together, we approached this book as a team. We collaborated on its structure and content, wrote chapters individually, and then reviewed each other's contributions.

The book is divided into six parts.

- Part I covers the basics of becoming culturally competent to work with law enforcement.
- Part II drills down into line-of-duty issues.
- Part III moves to treatment tactics.
- Part IV describes common presenting problems.
- Part V is about working with police families.
- Part VI considers other first responders and how to get started.

The Appendix has information about the West Coast Post-Trauma Retreat (WCPR), a residential treatment center for emergency responders. The Resources provide information about websites, conferences, organizations, and recommended reading for clinicians to use and recommend to their clients.

Part I

THE BASICS OF CULTURAL COMPETENCY

Part I is basically the heart of this book. We look at the similarities and differences between cops and clinicians and how they affect the formation of a strong therapeutic alliance. We ask you to look at the world from an officer's perspective. We introduce you to some cops with whom we have worked, and hope that we have done so skillfully enough for you to see the person behind the badge. We ask that you consider the narrative arc of a cop's life rather than a single trait or a single incident. As you read, think about whatever stereotypes you may have, perhaps based on personal experience, perhaps not, and how they might affect your work with law enforcement clients.

I

WORKING IN THE LAW ENFORCEMENT CULTURE

> If we civilians are to see the policeman [*sic*] as a human being rather than as the embodiment of virtue or evil, we must recognize and understand those forces in us that make us see him as either superman or less than human. If police officers are to view themselves as human rather than as superheroes or society's victims, they must also recognize and understand those same forces that make them see themselves as different from everyone else.
>
> —PHILIP BONIFACIO, *The Psychological Effects of Police Work* (1991, p. xii)

Cops are not eager clients. It takes a lot for them to seek help and very little to turn them off. Therapists who make mistakes with cops don't get second chances. The number one error clinicians make treating cops is failing to understand what they do, why they do it, and the culture in which they operate. The clinician who works with a police officer or a police family is like a sociologist or an ethnologist who is entering a closed culture with high levels of distrust for outsiders (see Chapter 2).

It is understandably difficult for many therapists to approach a police client or a police family with therapeutic neutrality. What other profession is so mythologized in the movies, on TV, or in books? What other profession carries so much power over people's lives and civil liberties? Who hasn't gotten a traffic ticket they didn't think they deserved or read about someone who was abused by the police?

By the same token, law enforcement officers hold distorted attitudes about mental health professionals. It was a psychiatrist, after all, who invented the abuse excuse, allowing criminals to abdicate responsibility for their actions because Mommy and Daddy didn't love them. It's "shrinks" who call 911 when they can't control their patients, and it is "shrinks" who designed those weird questions that cops have to answer during preemployment screening. These mutual perceptions represent, for lack of a better term, transferential hazards. The heart of this chapter lies in highlighting these biases and bringing them into awareness.

> Tracy was looking for a therapist. The first therapist he consulted teared up and didn't think she could bear listening to the kinds of challenges he encountered at work. The second therapist reassured Tracy that he understood the impact of carrying great responsibility because many of his clients were CEOs of large organizations. Tracy responded in anger. "When a CEO makes a mistake, the company loses money. When I make a mistake, someone dies." The therapist Tracy finally chose was a combat veteran who knew firsthand what it meant to put your life on the line and knew the costs of doing it year after year.

People who become cops and people who become therapists seem to represent two distinctly different groups with differing demographics, personal characteristics, mindsets, and occupational hazards. In attempting to tease out these differences we may be justifiably criticized for engaging in dueling stereotypes or generalizations. This is not hard science. Our observations are just that, observations. We lay them out in broad brushstrokes, knowing that there will be exceptions to every description. We do so because, when things go wrong in therapy, this is often where it starts.

WORLDS APART: DEMOGRAPHICS, SIMILARITIES, DIFFERENCES, VALUES, MINDSETS, AND OCCUPATIONAL HAZARDS

Demographics

In general, cops come from working-class backgrounds and therapists come from middle- or upper-class homes. Therapists usually have graduate degrees. While there's wide variance in the requirements, many law enforcement professionals need only a high school diploma. Therapists are more likely than their officer clients to have delayed starting a family and a career into their late 20s or early 30s. Cops are more likely than clinicians to have military backgrounds and to be politically conservative. Therapists are older than most cops and less likely to have encountered violence in their lives. They may also be less physical and more intellectual.

Similarities

This may surprise you: the primary reason police officers say they chose police work was to make a positive difference in the lives of others. That is the same answer most clinicians would give. Clinicians relieve suffering psychologically; cops relieve and prevent suffering by putting bad people in jail. That's not all they do, of course, but it is a primary objective. Cops and clinicians are both problem solvers who are guided at work by ethical principles. We both hold positions of public trust. Like police officers, most clinicians work within managed bureaucratic structures and are subjected to organizational stress. All of us are exposed to people in pain and are at risk for burnout and compassion fatigue. All of us are objects of stereotyping and derisive humor. And based on our observations, cops and clinicians alike frequently have a history of conflict or mistreatment in our families of origin that has influenced our choice of career (Kirschman, 2007).

Differences

Cops are action-oriented people who value variety and excitement. They hate being confined to an office. They are comfortable giving and taking orders and are generally intolerant of law breaking regardless of the circumstances. They are decisive, assertive, and willing to do their job in front of others. They value conformity, tradition, teamwork, structure, and predictability because these are the things that keep them safe. They set great store in emotional self-control, particularly in stressful situations, and can become emotionally guarded as a consequence. They are comfortable in a crisis and cherish humor as a way to manage stress and express affection.

   Therapists, on the other hand, are generally nondirective and contemplative. We are careful not to impose our views on our clients or give them advice. We work behind closed doors and are confined to our offices and our desks for hours on end. We tend to value individuality, spontaneity, and emotional expression in ourselves and our clients, especially when under stress. We prize self-actualization and attach great importance to our clients' feelings. We encourage reflection before action and view behavior, even illegal activity, in context, with special consideration to its historical antecedents.

   Cops live in a world of probabilities based on past experiences. Therapists, like other civilians, live in a world of possibilities (K. M. Gilmartin, presentation, January 9, 2012). Once a cop is lied to, and it happens frequently, he or she assumes it will happen again and is determined not to be fooled a second time. Even "white lies" are unacceptable. This leads to the presumption that almost everyone lies—or as one officer said, "If your lips are moving, you're lying." Clients lie to clinicians too, but rather than make that assumption a priori, we generally think it's possible, but not likely. When it happens, we are often surprised and dismayed.

Values, Mindsets, and Occupational Hazards

> Bill had been in two shootings that resulted in his killing two suspects. He was having nightmares and seriously considering quitting police work in order to avoid the possibility of a third deadly encounter. His department EAP referred him to a local clinician who had a lot of experience, none of which involved law enforcement. This was Bill's first-ever counseling session. The therapist listened to Bill's story carefully. When Bill was finished talking the therapist asked him, "So, are you ready to stop killing people?" Bill left the session very upset. It wasn't until he talked to some of his friends who had been in therapy that he learned how inappropriate and untherapeutic this question was and accepted another referral to someone familiar with the police culture.

This therapist made a mistake of the first order, confusing Bill's social mandate with a personality disorder. There certainly are cops with personality disorders, but they're rare. Unlike most clinicians, cops have been so thoroughly screened before they get their jobs that they constitute a hardy, healthy worker population, at least when they start their careers (see Chapter 4). Bill did not kill two people because he wanted to; he had no other choice. His shootings were lawful, meant to protect his life and the lives of citizens. As we said earlier, cops become cops because they want to help people, not because they enjoy killing them. We don't know Bill's therapist, but we do know Bill. We can only assume his therapist was ignorant about what cops do; at worst, he stereotyped Bill as badge-heavy, aggressive, angry, and impulsive.

In their professional socialization, cops undergo what Philip Bonifacio (1991) calls a "moral inversion." The values they hold before joining the force are altered as a result of their experiences on the job, and this change sets them apart from most civilians. It is important for therapists to understand that this transformation is a learned adaptation, not necessarily an expression of innate pathology. Certainly, such transmuted values can be harmful when misapplied, for example, to a cop's personal life. What is important is to respect the officer's mindset and understand how the following values, mindsets, and occupational hazards make sense in the context of police work.

The Touchy-Feely Stuff: Emotional Sensitivity

As a rule, cops are rather contemptuous of emotional sensitivity. They make lots of jokes about therapists who sit around singing "Kumbaya." Expressing feelings for their own sake seems wasteful and inauthentic. Cops spend much of their time controlling their own reactions to what they see and what they do. In fact, the stress of their job often comes from the effort it takes to hide the stress.

No one wants to see a cop burst into tears when delivering a death notification, tremble visibly at the sight of a broken window, or slap someone who has just spit in his face. Police work is about control: control of self, control of others. The public calls cops when control has been lost. This may be one of the reasons cops are apprehensive about therapy. In the therapy session, the clinician is in control.

Cops are also apprehensive about revealing feelings because, in their world, doing so can be a prelude to trouble. Cops would never get a confession if they disclosed their real feelings to a child molester. To show fear to a violent criminal is to invite an attack. Your cop clients will be reading you as intensely as you are trying to read them. Do not push for feelings or visibly overreact to what you hear. You may have to reassure your clients that you can handle hearing the bad stuff they encounter. Stephanie Cress, MSW, routinely tells her cop clients that they can't "gross her out" because, as a former nurse, she's seen it all herself.

> One of us was attending a psychology conference at a federal law enforcement agency at which a federal agent made a presentation about sexual torture, including very disturbing videos of victims pleading for their lives. Several psychologists got up and left before the presentation was over and later complained that the videos were inappropriately graphic.

Be prepared. Cops see a lot of gory things, including unimaginable cruelty and tragedy. They need to talk about what they see with someone who can "hold" the emotions and contain their own reactions. We're not suggesting keeping a stone face, but rather responding calmly with a simple expression of empathy such as "That must have been tough." The kind of content a therapist can tolerate is an individual decision. If you feel uncomfortable with this kind of material, you may not be the right therapist for a police officer. Cops have the same range of emotions that we all have, but compassion is their Achilles' heel. Their hearts may be breaking for a victim, but usually they cannot allow their feelings to surface because emotions might slow them down. As we mentioned earlier, like therapists, cops are at risk for compassion fatigue and burnout. Keeping social distance is how cops protect themselves from overwhelming despair. Identifying with victims eliminates the needed social distance and makes the officer's job much harder. (This is one of the reasons dealing with child victims is particularly challenging.)

The Victim's Error: Kindness, Empathy, and Trust

Kindness, empathy, and trust may appear to cops as preludes to victimization. In an officer's experience, people who open their doors to strangers are just asking for trouble. Cops, not therapists, are the first people on scene after someone has been knocked down and robbed because she stopped to give a panhandler some money or pulled over to help a motorist in distress. It is a mistake, no doubt, to judge all people based on the small sample a cop encounters, just as it would be a mistake to judge all people by the troubled clients who show up in our consulting rooms. But rather than label or argue against an attitude of distrust, be curious about your client's experiences that confirm it. Explore how they affect the officer's personal life. Self-inflation—thinking that cops are the only people who know what's going on, and that civilians are naive about people—is an occupational hazard that you can and should challenge, albeit gently.

Another occupational hazard of law enforcement is cynicism, expecting everyone, including you, to have an agenda. It doesn't pay to argue with a cop's cynicism because, in a funny way, cynicism provides a gloss of protection for him and his family. If you trust no one, you avoid trouble. If you check your daughter's dates for criminal history, she won't be beaten and raped, as happened with the case you just finished.

Navel-Gazing

Therapists value introspection, contemplation, meditation, and other forms of self-knowledge. Our consulting rooms are designed to give our clients a safe space to slow down and think. In contrast, police officers value action over contemplation. Of course, there are many junior and senior officers who plan operations in advance or develop intricate problem-solving strategies. But, for the most part, the rank and file operate in a time-driven, crisis-response mode. They are called upon to make life-altering decisions in a split second, in the dark, in the rain, with inadequate information. That's why cops train and train and train. When a crisis occurs, they have to act, so they go on automatic pilot and fall back on their training. There is no hesitating when decisive action is needed (Benner, 1993). The ability to act quickly saves lives. Cops view people who can't make decisions as wishy-washy and dangerous to work with. If introspection and identifying emotions are skills your clients need to develop; you may need to present a convincing case about why this is valuable.

Perfectionism

Many cops are perfectionists and are intolerant of making mistakes, in a job where the potential for mistakes is great. Society, understandably, has little acceptance for police errors because the stakes are so high. When it comes to police work, "One sin is worth a thousand good deeds." Because their work is public, there is no place for cops to hide when they do err. Every encounter has the potential to turn into a headline-making event, or a video gone viral. Cops are under constant scrutiny by the public and by their administrators. As clinicians, unless we do something egregious or present our clinical mishaps for consultation, our mistakes are made behind closed doors.

For a cop, admitting vulnerability, helplessness. or error is tantamount to admitting a weakness. Rather than addressing these concerns directly, officers may cope by working harder and faster (see Chapter 3). For example, over the years, we have worked with many officers who had been abused as children. In fact, early trauma is what motivated some of them to be police officers. These officers are secretive and ashamed about the abuse they suffered, often blaming themselves rather than their abuser. This is also true of civilian victims of childhood abuse, of course, but in the law enforcement culture, admitting any kind of weakness comes with a high price. No one trusts weak cops or wants to work with them. The unrealistic expectation many cops hold of themselves and each other is to be superhuman and have a bulletproof mind. To admit to being a victim feels to them like an admission of failure and inadequacy.

Navel-Gazing Redux

Therapists are more apt to endorse being cautious and patient and taking the long view of things rather than reacting. For a cop, being cautious at work is generally taken as an indication of fear. Hesitation costs lives. This doesn't mean that real police officers are like their TV counterparts, busting through doors with no backup and no information about who or what is on the other side. But when someone is screaming for help, a cop must respond. She cannot hesitate when someone is being aggressive toward her, or she risks being hurt or killed. The ability to be decisive and take action in a crisis is a special skill that not everyone possesses. It is different from being impulsive. (Preemployment psychological screening does a good job of flagging applicants with impulse control problems.)

Vigilance

Don't be surprised if a police officer client checks out your office, looking for hidden microphones or video cameras. Vigilance is what keeps cops safe. It exists on a continuum from attention to detail to a state of hypervigilance, in which an officer cannot relax because he or she is constantly scanning the surroundings for threats, seeing lethality where it doesn't exist (see Chapter 13). Hypervigilance is pathological, causing biochemical changes in the brain. Vigilance is better controlled and gives the officer a sense of safety by knowing what's in the environment. It's why cops always face the door when they eat in a restaurant so they can see who is coming and going. That might seem silly to a civilian, but when officers live in or near the same town with people they've arrested, who may be carrying a grudge, it is more understandable. Consider cops to be like physicians or paramedics—field ready and on the alert—willing to step in and help when and where they are needed, on and off duty.

Command Presence

Cops are used to giving and taking orders. They work in paramilitary organizations that are structured along rigid chains of command. They can be stiff and formal at times. A key occupational technique for cops is to present themselves as commanding and decisive. This persona is a tool to gain respect on the street and display confidence to the citizens who rely on them. It involves posture, eye contact, speech, and grooming. Command presence can become second nature when it is overlearned or overpracticed. The problem with overlearned behavior is that it becomes so automatic that it can be inappropriately used with friends and family (see Chapter 18).

Cop Humor

Cops are funny people. Humor is one of their favorite and most effective ways to de-stress, blow off steam, and get a little distance from whatever misery they've encountered. This is gallows humor, strong, crass, with more than a touch of mockery. Civilians often don't understand it. One of the reasons incidents involving children are so difficult to bear is that using cop humor to defuse emotions is clearly inappropriate. When the victim is a child, no one jokes around (see Chapter 5). Humor is also how cops express their affection to one another. If a cop doesn't kid you, he or she probably doesn't trust you.

Don't be offended by the humorous shorthand cops use to label various calls for service. A pedestrian hit by a car is called a "ped spread," a person burned beyond recognition is a "crispy critter," and an "ahvahnhi" incident stands for "asshole versus asshole, no humans involved," usually signifying something that occurred between crooks or gang members. Civilians understandably tend to be shocked and repelled by these labels. Still, therapists who challenge this language or accuse an officer of being callous do so at their own risk. Remember, cops are constantly testing you before they will trust you with deeper confidences. To dismiss them as callous may signal to them that you discount the underlying pain they are feeling.

KEY POINTS

- Be clear about your personal biases, positive or negative, toward law enforcement. Don't judge, ask for clarification.

- Take time to learn about the history, values, behavior, and customs of your client's department, the relationship between the department and the community, and the way history has shaped contemporary life for the officer and his or her family. Has there been a recent scandal, lawsuit, or officer-involved shooting (OIS)? Even events taking place thousands of miles away can influence your client's everyday life.

- Beware of idealized transference.

- Avoid "psychobabble." Instead, talk in terms that are familiar to cops. But be careful not to come across as a "wannabe cop" or a "lookey-loo" who is more interested in the gory details of an incident than in the officer's reactions.

- Encourage skepticism, not cynicism.

- Police work is an identity, not just a job. It can be all consuming in a way that few other professions are.

2

MANAGING THE
THERAPEUTIC ALLIANCE

> Clinicians have to realize that part of our job description is
> to be the psychological toxic spill dispersant who can absorb
> and empathize with the guilt and pain [officers feel] without
> getting enmeshed. We sometimes have to be the one person
> who is willing to listen without evasion or dismissal. Only
> then will our efforts to provide a therapeutic reality check be
> taken seriously.
> —LAWRENCE MILLER, PhD, police psychologist
> (personal communication, June 3, 2010)

Our colleague, the late Dr. Al Benner, used to say that creating therapeutic alliance with law enforcement clients is like building a
three-legged stool: Therapists should be transparent, competent, and familiar with the police culture. We would add that the glue that holds the stool
together is confidentiality and ethics. This chapter will address transparency, guns in your office, confidentiality, ethics, and some legal issues. The
various components of clinical competency will be discussed in Part III.

TRANSPARENCY

Cops have "shit detectors" that are miles wide; it's what keeps them safe.
They are trained and rewarded to look for what is wrong or out of place

before they look for what is right or good. That's because what's right or good won't hurt them. Reading people is their stock in trade. This is especially true of your initial session. From the minute you open your office door they'll be sizing you up, looking to see if they can trust you, if you can tolerate what they have to say. It is important to be more open and transparent than you might be with other clients. It isn't necessary to tell stories about your life, unless they have some relevance to the client's presenting problem. The first responders we work with generally know who we are from reading our online biographies. We tend not to spend much time, if any, discussing our backgrounds unless it is germane to the topic at hand. However, it is important to be transparent in the immediate context of your counseling relationship. Answer questions when asked rather than putting the question back on the client. If you don't know the answer to a question, say so; they will respect you for that. Try to anticipate what questions a cop might ask you, then think about what you are willing to disclose. If you pause to think about whether or not you are going to answer a question, your client may think you are lying or hiding something.

When it is reasonable, give advice. When appropriate, confront. Cops will be looking to see if you can call them on their "B.S." A nondirective style may not work for most of them. Cops are trained interrogators and can spot interrogative techniques because they use them at work. They may turn the tables and start interrogating you, unwilling to "give anything up" without knowing who they're talking to. How you answer their questions, and to what degree of transparency, may determine if they return for a second appointment.

Transparency, or self-disclosure, is essential in working with cops. Be as open and forthcoming as possible. When asked a question, answer it directly. Get used to more self-disclosure than you would give in a typical therapy session. Psychotherapy research suggests that revealing nothing about yourself, acting as a blank slate, is not optimal for a therapeutic outcome. Disclosure has been shown to increase the perception of similarity between clinicians and clients, model appropriate behaviors, increase the therapeutic alliance, normalize client experiences, offer alternative ways of thinking and acting, and allow clients to feel less defective (Edwards & Murdock, 1994; Fay, 2002; Geller & Farber, 1997; Goldfried, Burckell, & Eubanks-Carter, 2003; Simon, 1990). Feminist theorists state that self-disclosure fosters an egalitarian relationship and increases solidarity between therapist and client (Simi & Mahalik, 1997). Humanistic/phenomenological therapists believe self-disclosure allows the client to feel a sense of equality rather than inferiority, and that honesty is fundamental to therapy (Bugental, 1987).

Group psychotherapists credit self-disclosure for allowing clients to reveal personal feelings, articulate the reasons behind their behaviors, acknowledge blind spots, and demonstrate respect for the group, at the same time reducing both the guilt and shame that group members may experience (Mallow, 1998; Vinogradov & Yalom, 1990). The evidence continues. In one study of lesbian, gay, bisexual, and transgender (LGBT) clients seeking therapists (Liddle, 1997), 63% of therapists surveyed indicated they were asked about their own sexual identity during the first contact. Therapists who failed to self-disclose were seen as guarded, mistrustful, or paranoid. Similar reactions have been observed in ethnic minority populations, where flipping a question back to the client may be perceived as insulting or patronizing (Hays, 2008; Sue & Sue, 2008).

There are times, of course, when self-disclosure is inappropriate: if it is done for the therapist's own needs, moves the focus away from the client and onto the therapist, interferes with the flow of material presented by the client, is perceived as burdensome or confusing, feels intrusive, undercuts the uniqueness of the client's experience, blurs boundaries, or contaminates the transference (Edwards & Murdock, 1994; Geller & Farber, 1997; Simon, 1990).

Transparency is a two-way street. We are transparent in the service of making officers feel safe so they can be transparent in return. As a veteran officer succinctly put it, "If you show me yours, I'll show you mine." Keep in mind, though, that some of what officers want to share is hard to hear.

> Juan was a captain and a 17-year veteran with a metropolitan police department. He had been called to supervise the investigation of a suicide-filicide of a father and two children. The bodies had been in the bathtub for several days. The father had slit his children's throats before drowning them. He then slit his own wrists and throat and stabbed himself 16 times in the chest and abdomen. Juan described the bodies in detail and stated that he was having nightmares and hadn't been able to sleep through the night for several days. He has two children who are the approximate ages of the victims.

It is important to not be overwhelmed by these stories. Tears may be appropriate in some therapeutic instances, but certainly not in the first session. You are being tested, plain and simple. Juan wants to know if you can tolerate the smells, the visions, the sounds, and the tastes of being an LEO. He wants to know if he can trust you, if you can witness his pain and bear his suffering. He wants to be able to share his experiences and not feel that he has to rescue you. He is a first responder, so his inclination is to rescue people. As a psychotherapist, you are no different from any other person he may meet on the street. If your reactions indicate that you are overwhelmed, his instinct will be to comfort you and save you from the horror of what he has experienced.

Stepping into the role of rescuer is also a way Juan can distance himself from his pain. He may unconsciously think, "If I can attend to you, I don't have to talk about myself." Avoidance, regardless of the defense mechanism that is employed, is a key characteristic in first responders and leads to isolation, depression, anger, and burnout. We investigate the many forms avoidance can take in the next chapter.

GUNS IN YOUR OFFICE

To be successful working with the first responder population you will need to come to terms with having guns in your office.

> A new clinician was participating in a role-playing exercise as part of an assessment for a job consulting with a police department. The scenario required that she mediate a conflict between two angry police officers. As a first step, she asked the officers to leave their weapons in their cars. They refused to comply and stonewalled her for the rest of the exercise. As soon as the scenario ended, she was challenged to explain why she had made such a request. "Would I ask you to take off your glasses before doing therapy?" someone asked. "Guns are part of our uniforms. If you're afraid of guns, you shouldn't be working with cops."

It was a beginner's mistake. While there are rare times when it is appropriate, even necessary, to take an officer's weapon—during a depressive episode, for instance (see Chapter 12)—for the most part, cops and guns go together. To separate a cop from her gun is to remove an essential part of her identity. While it is customary to remove an officer's weapon for ballistics tests following a shooting, standard procedure is to return the gun immediately (or to provide a substitute weapon if that is not possible) so the officer feels safe, and not like she is being treated as a criminal.

Many clinicians are afraid of guns. It isn't necessary to overcome this apprehension to treat cops, but you do need to understand how attached officers are to their guns. Cops see their guns as the last resort when their lives are in danger. In the academy they spend hours improving their shooting ability. They practice gun retention—keeping a suspect from taking their weapon. They practice how to stand when talking to people so as to minimize the risk of losing their gun. Some officers are more interested in guns than others, and may own a number of weapons. Other officers see the gun as a work tool and only have a duty weapon and an off-duty weapon, one that is generally smaller and more easily concealed. Some officers routinely carry more than one weapon because it gives them a tactical edge should their first weapon malfunction or be lost in a skirmish.

Some officers carry a weapon off duty because they are required to do so by their departments; others choose to do so voluntarily. Some officers always have a gun with them; others only carry when they are concerned about where they are going. So it is a mistake to assume all officers feel the same way about guns, or to overreact to the presence of guns in your consulting room.

> In Bob's first session the therapist asked him to put his weapon on top of an armoire in his office and not to bring it back during future sessions. Bob said, "I guess he didn't want me shooting him if I lost control of myself. . . . I thought that if he didn't trust me to talk about emotions without killing him, he wasn't the right therapist for me."

While there are risks associated with carrying a weapon off duty, some officers view their weapons the way doctors and paramedics view the medical bags they carry in their cars in case of an emergency. In the same vein, cops don't want to be caught in a situation where they are unable to protect their families or their friends. To be unable to act in a crisis runs counter to police officers' professional dedication, their identities, and the social mandate to protect and serve. Occasionally, the need to carry a weapon off duty has a more personal urgency. Some officers and their families live in the same communities where they work, so just taking the kids out for ice cream can bring an officer face to face with someone he has recently arrested.

> Ed and his children were in the supermarket when he spotted a wanted parolee in the same aisle. He was unarmed—after all, he was just shopping for groceries. He grabbed his children and moved to the far side of the store. Ed wasn't concerned about the parolee avoiding apprehension. He was more concerned about what would happen if the suspect recognized him from previous encounters and pulled his own weapon to avoid arrest.

These types of scenarios are rare, but they happen frequently enough to raise officers' concerns. The level of concern is easily seen in the nearly universal experience cops report of a dream they have throughout their careers. The dream starts simply—the dreamer is confronted by a suspect and needs to use his or her gun—and has several frightening endings.

- The officer tries to pull the gun out of the holster, but it won't come out.
- The officer pulls the gun out but is unable to pull the trigger back.

- The officer shoots the gun, but the bullet doesn't reach the suspect.
- The officer shoots the gun, and the bullets hit the suspect but have no apparent effect.
- The officer shoots the gun, and the bullet dribbles uselessly to the floor

It is important not to overinterpret officers' attachment to their weapons or overinterpret their dreams.

> William told his therapist about a dream in which he was confronted by an armed suspect. When William tried to fire back, his gun barrel melted like a wax candle, and the bullets dropped to the ground. The therapist told William that his dream demonstrated fears that he was sexually inadequate and unable to achieve or sustain an erection. Erectile dysfunction was not part of William's presenting problem. The therapist's interpretation was off base and inaccurate, and it bypassed William's true concerns, which were about his safety and his ability to defend himself. When William protested, the therapist offered another interpretation: that William was ambivalent about needing to use deadly force. Wrong again. Officers take the use of deadly force very seriously and would do anything possible to avoid using it. But they are not ambivalent about staying alive. Needless to say, that was William's last session with this therapist.

Carrying a gun isn't all power and fun. There is risk associated with having a weapon on your person. Off-duty officers will have seconds to decide if they should turn over their wallets or pull their weapons when they're held up. If they see a robbery in progress, should they try to stop it? Should they be good witnesses to a crime or actively intervene? When officers choose to use their weapons in an off-duty encounter, they face public scrutiny, possible criminal or civil charges, and administrative discipline including termination. Officers who are required to carry a weapon off duty face the weight of these concerns 24 hours a day.

We recommend that a clinician interested in working with law enforcement learn to shoot a gun. Not only will your understanding of the police culture increase, you will make yourself known to local law enforcement as someone who understands firsthand the complexities of police work. Many police and sheriff's departments have a firearms training simulator (FATS). Trainees are given a laser gun and placed in front of a large video screen. Several different scenarios are projected on the screen, each involving a shoot/don't shoot decision. The scenarios change dynamically according to the trainees' responses—their voice commands, shooting decisions, and firing accuracy.

The ultimate firearms reality training is Simunitions, in which students and instructors engage in gunplay using real weapons that have been modified to shoot paintball projectiles.

CONFIDENTIALITY AND ETHICS

Dual Relationships

Dual relationships are a fact of life in the police culture. Don't be surprised if while you're on a ride-along, working with a countywide crisis intervention team, consulting on a criminal case, or teaching at the local academy, you're approached by an officer who is seeking therapy for herself or her family. Expect spontaneous hallway encounters in the gym or the bathroom. A lot of officers tend to think if they're talking to you while standing up or moving, it isn't therapy. Clients will invite you to weddings, parties, funerals, and graduations. We have stood by deathbeds and christenings. We've gone to retreats, Alcoholics Anonymous (AA) meetings, and management off-sites with people who are, have been, or will be clients. Once you have the respect and trust of the first responder population, they will want to bring their problems to you, rather than turn to a stranger.

There is nothing inherently harmful about such a dual relationship unless, according to the Code of Ethics of the American Psychological Association, it "could reasonably be expected to impair the psychologist's objectivity, competence, or effectiveness in performing his or her functions as a psychologist, or otherwise risks exploitation or harm to the person with whom the professional relationship exists" (3.05[a]). Obvious violations include having sex with a patient, using your patient to clean your house or office, or requiring your patient to attend your church services.

Complex or dual relationships with cops can be tricky, and often there is really no right or elegant way to navigate them. Consider peer-driven residential treatment, for example, where therapists and their clients may work and live side by side, sharing meals, restrooms, shower facilities, and so on. Or consider the growing phenomenon of "cop-docs"—police officers who are also licensed therapists or counselors and may be assigned or transferred to a supervisory position over one of their clients. What happens when the therapist is a crime victim and the responding officer is his client? Or when a therapist's child gets arrested for driving drunk by an officer she is seeing for family therapy? In responding to such complex situations, therapists must anticipate and prioritize the client's needs. Some risks can be minimized by establishing clear office policies and procedures and by emphasizing informed consent for clients regarding dual relationships. These procedures are especially important when therapy is conducted outside a normal office setting.

On initial contact with a client discuss the possibility of multiple relationships, and then follow up by talking about the nature and risk of such relationships in your initial session. When encounters occur outside the office, make sure to bring this up at the next session if your client does not mention it. There is no way to eliminate potential risk, but by warning everyone involved you can minimize it.

Boundary Issues

Dealing with public service agencies while simultaneously treating their employees is a hazardous situation for therapists, who must maintain clear boundaries and distinct roles. By the same token, it is also an opportunity to educate well-meaning, sometimes cash-strapped administrators.

A therapist's first contact with a local police agency often follows a request for debriefing services. While it is beyond the scope of this book to teach clinicians how to conduct debriefings (see the Resources), we endorse debriefings as highly effective interventions. Yet the following example illustrates a common hazard the responding therapist may face.

> The chief of a local department asked Dr. Gibbons to meet individually with his officers following a critical incident in order to determine if the officers involved were psychologically sound and able to return to work. What he was asking for was a de facto fitness-for-duty evaluation (FFD). FFDs are lengthy, complex, and often litigious procedures that should be done only by specially trained psychologists or psychiatrists (see the Resources). Dr. Gibbons pointed out that an FFD requires an identifiable, observable, and articulated work-related problem. While he was sympathetic to the chief's concerns for his officers, he made it clear that the only information he could provide would cover attendance; nothing could be released concerning the content of the debriefing sessions. Dr. Gibbons informed employees of this limitation at the beginning of each debriefing session.

Therapists should also guard against being lured into substituting for a lack of strong supervision. It is not your job to deliver performance feedback, impose discipline, or make decisions regarding officers' careers. These are administrative and supervisorial duties. However, there is nothing to prevent you from suggesting to your client that he or she might benefit from additional training, therapy, medication, and so forth.

What should you do if you judge that the officer you are seeing is not fit to return to duty because of a mental disability? Your course of action will be determined by several factors: state law, whether the injury is work related, and whether the officer concurs with your assessment. In some instances, it will be the officer who first raises the issue of fitness. In all instances, we recommend consulting with a knowledgeable colleague and an attorney who is familiar with both workers' compensation and the law enforcement culture.

> Carter was suffering from what he labeled job stress, exacerbated by a lifelong anxiety disorder that was evidently missed during his preemployment screening. To compensate for his deep feelings of inferiority and low self-esteem, he became an overachiever, working 16 hours a day until he was exhausted. His therapist suggested he use some of the vacation and sick time he had accrued over the years to take a break and attend an outpatient treatment program to deal with his anxiety. Carter rejected this suggestion and declared that he was capable of returning to work. His therapist did not agree. They discussed the potential negative consequences of working in a state of high anxiety and exhaustion. The therapist then asked Carter if he would feel safe working with a partner who was in a similar emotional state. Carter had not considered things from this angle and was forced to admit that he had become a liability to himself and others. This was a turning point in the discussion, and Carter actually felt relieved to have both help and permission not to return to work until he had his anxiety and his health under control.

What would have happened if Carter had refused to take a voluntary leave? When you and your client disagree about your client's ability to return to work, this *does not* trigger an exception to confidentiality. The therapist cannot disclose his or her concerns unless the situation meets the local state standards for duty to warn (see "Legal Issues," below). We try to get officers to participate in their own treatment decisions because an involuntary commitment may lead to an officer having his gun removed, effectively ending his career (see Chapter 12 for further discussion about the consequences of involuntary commitment). The therapist's job is to help the client investigate alternatives and weigh the consequences of his or her decisions. Be prepared to have some sleepless nights—we all do. First and foremost, seek consultation.

Trust

If you want to spread the word, tell a secret to a coworker. It will be out on the street before you are.
—POLICE OFFICER

Confidentiality is the foundation of managing the therapeutic alliance. LEOs are often cynical, expecting that no one can be trusted. Often their biggest worry is that if others find out they are having psychological problems they will be rejected, seen as incompetent, untrustworthy, and worst of all, weak. As a result, they are reticent to seek psychotherapy and may delay treatment until their symptoms are so bad that they can't work. On the other hand, they understand confidentiality because, like us, they are mandatory reporters. The only difference is that therapists are not required by law to report domestic abuse or criminal activity, while police officers are.

In addition to discussing the limits of confidentiality (and giving your clients written copies of your office policies on this issue), take a look at your office setup. Arrange things so that you keep your patients from running into each other in the waiting room or the parking lot. The optimal setting has separate doors for entering and leaving. Be careful not to schedule cops in adjacent hours; leave time between your enforcement clients. Even in a large department where officers may not know each other personally, LEOs may come to appointments in their uniforms and do not want others to identify them.

Protecting clients' identities is a special challenge in small rural communities where therapists may run into clients at libraries, restaurants, school functions, supermarkets, places of worship, and so on. We routinely tell officers that when we meet them outside of the therapy office, we will not acknowledge them unless they acknowledge us first. Police officers are trained to be nosy, and if they see the "shrink" greeting a coworker, they will find it hard not to ask what's going on.

LEGAL ISSUES

There are a number of legal issues to be considered in any clinical practice, but especially when dealing with law enforcement because of the frequency with which officers are themselves mired in legal difficulties: civil and criminal lawsuits, court testimony, adverse relationships with their administrations or workers' compensation, the citizens' complaint process, and media scrutiny that could lead to legal issues. Furthermore, the treating therapist may well become involved in any of these difficulties. So it makes sense to be fully prepared. Start by knowing both the state and federal laws that may affect your practice. In California, where we practice, we are governed by the following codes and regulations, as well as licensing laws and the Department of Consumer Affairs: the Business and Professions Code, Code of Regulations, Penal Code, Welfare and Institutions Code, Civil Code, Evidence Code, Family Code, and Health and Safety Code. Our colleagues who perform psychological evaluations of police officers' mental status or fitness for duty are also governed by Section 2960.2 of the Business and Professions Code and Section 1031 of the Government Code.

Federal laws that impact our profession include the Health Insurance Portability and Accountability Act (HIPAA; 1996); the USA Patriot Act (2001); and the Americans with Disabilities Act (ADA; 1990) and its progeny found in the ADA Amendments Act (ADAAA; 2008) and related case law. *Jaffe v. Redmond* (1996) extends the psychotherapist–patient privilege to master's-level clinicians.

Of the panoply of codified laws and case law, the ones that most inform our therapy practices are those related to confidentiality, privilege, and records. Statements of understanding, also known as informed consent (Serafino, 2010), and keeping and maintaining records (and their confidentiality) are crucial (for California, see the Confidentiality of Medical Information Act, 2012, and the Business and Professions Code, Sec. 2919). Clients may be treated only after giving their permission. Records must be kept and maintained in an appropriate fashion for at least 7 years after termination of treatment and may be released only with the consent of the patient, by subpoena, or by court order. HIPAA protects the privacy of patients' health information.

It is our practice to provide every client, at the first session, with written documents concerning HIPAA and our general office policies and procedures. We explain in lay terms what we mean by confidentiality and the limits of confidentiality. We further discuss development of a treatment plan and the need to periodically assess the patient's progress as therapy continues. In addition, we discuss the possibility of contacting other providers or family members and clarify why we might need such information, as well as the extent of our inquiry and limitations for use.

Through HIPAA, patients have federal protections for personal health information and an array of rights with respect to that information. The Privacy Rule of that act provides a balance so that some disclosure of personal health information is permitted when needed for patient care and other important purposes. The HIPAA Security Rule outlines the steps a clinician must take to protect confidential information from unintended disclosure through breaches of security. As of 2010, HIPAA now applies to "business associates," that is, organizations or persons outside of a practice to whom protected health information (PHI) is sent in order to provide services such as billing.

The law regarding records is pertinent in the practice of police and public safety psychology and is inextricably intertwined with the rules of confidentiality and privilege. In California, confidentiality is mandated by psychologist–patient privilege (Business and Professions Code, Sec. 2918, and Evidence Code, Sec. 1010 *et seq.*). The privilege must be upheld not only as it relates to conversations, e-mails, and general communication but also to subpoenas and court orders. All patients must feel comfortable in sharing their innermost thoughts and concerns with a therapist, but police and public safety officers may have a higher threshold of concern in doing so. In general, they fear that what is revealed in treatment will somehow cause them to lose their jobs, since they are held to such a high standard. We therefore make an extensive effort to assure cops we treat that confidentiality is of highest priority. We clearly go over what we cannot keep confidential or have to report, and what we can maintain in confidence.

> Roy mistakenly thought if he divulged that he had been sexually abused as a child, his therapist would be mandated to report him. Fortunately, his therapist was able to clarify Roy's concerns and let him know that he would not be reported if, in fact, a report needed to be made.

A unique issue arises regarding peer supporters. Peers are public safety personnel who have been trained to assist their fellow officers with personal and professional problems but who, in most states, do not have privileged communication. Guidelines exist for peer supporters (see the Resources), and departments with peer support programs generally have explicit written policies about how peer supporters are to be utilized. At the West Coast Post-Trauma Retreat (WCPR; see the Appendix), we require each volunteer to sign an agreement to maintain confidentiality. Although this is unenforceable, it has never been problematic because our peers, most having been former retreatants, understand the value of confidentiality.

Therapist–client privilege relates not only to conversations, e-mail, other communications, and court testimony but also to records provided under subpoena. Privileged records must never be released without permission of the client. A court may order release of records, but you should always seek legal advice before complying. Read court orders carefully. Often a court orders the release of records only to the court for a relevancy review and will not release the information to the opposing party. The Patriot Act of 2001 is a major exception to this rule. Under Section 215 of the act, the FBI can require access to any information that is relevant to an investigation. If federal authorities suspect a public safety officer is engaging in illegal activity, the psychotherapist must comply with the request for records, and he or she is forbidden to tell the client that the records have been subpoenaed.[1]

Another critical aspect of law that informs our practice is the duty to warn established by case law in *Tarasoff v. Regents of the University of California* (1976), later codified in the California Civil Code, Section 43.92. Be sure you read up on the duty to warn case law in your state. In

---

[1]In 2006 the law was amended to allow the record holder to consult with an attorney and file a challenge to the records request with the United States Foreign Intelligence Surveillance Court (or FISC).

California, the duty to warn mandates that psychotherapists make a reasonable effort to communicate to a victim and a law enforcement agency when a patient has made a serious threat of violence against a reasonably identifiable victim or victims. Progeny of this case expanded the requirement to include family members of the client. For example, if the father of a patient reports to the psychotherapist that his son has threatened harm against a person, the psychotherapist must now assume the responsibility of notifying that victim and the police (*Ewing v. Goldstein*, 2004). This places the psychotherapist in the difficult position of having to evaluate the credibility of a person he or she may have never met. In this case, the client's father.

The Police Officers' Bill of Rights in California is codified in Government Code Sections 3300–3312. This bill outlines the rights and protections to which police officers are entitled when they are the subject of a personnel investigation. Investigations that are concerned with behavior or performance often include an FFD. Because our focus is on treatment, not assessment, we do not conduct FFDs. We make it clear to officers and their administrators that the work we do is separate from the police department's administrative concerns. We are careful to preserve the confidentiality of any officer's attendance in therapy. We only release files or get involved in workers' compensation claims (see below) when we have a written request from the officer. Because of ongoing trust issues and officers' concerns that they will be found unfit for the job, we offer to share any of our reports with our clients and discuss our rationale for what we have written.

Workers' Compensation

Cops get involved with the workers' compensation system because they are frequently injured on the job. Dealing with this system often creates significant stress for LEOs and their families. The workers' compensation system was created to support workers and avoid confrontations, but it seems to have failed on both scores (Kirschman, 2004). Expect to offer support to any client who is involved; they will need patience, encouragement, and sometimes anger management. Workers' compensation also covers emotional issues. Unless your client has predesignated you as his or her mental health clinician, the employer controls the injured worker's treatment choices for the first 30 days post injury, after which the officer may request a change of clinician.

If you are designated by the injured officer as the primary treating clinician, then it is your responsibility to submit the Doctor's First Report and Medical Treatment Plan to the workers' compensation claims administrator within 5 days after the officer's initial visit. We work in conjunction with the injured cop's attorney to ensure claims are filed for all work-related injuries. It is also useful to reassure officers who are applying for workers' compensation disability that there is no need to maintain or exaggerate their symptoms to win their cases. Explain that symptom reduction is part of normal healing, and the courts anticipate that symptoms will ebb and flow over time.

> Dr. Morse was seeing an officer for depression related to chronic pain from an injury sustained during a physical confrontation with a suspect. He found the officer to be suffering from posttraumatic stress disorder (PTSD) and, with his client's permission, asked the client's attorney to file an additional claim related to the incident that likely triggered the PTSD.

For more information on the intricacies of treating patients with work-related injuries who have filed claims with their workers' compensation insurance carriers, clinicians should familiarize themselves with their state's statutory compensation law and seek consultation from colleagues who may specialize in workers' compensation cases.

KEY POINTS

- Keep treatment and assessment functions separate. A therapist who provides therapy or debriefings should never conduct FFDs. Unlike therapy, there is no confidentiality for the officer in FFDs.

- There is no guarantee of confidentiality for group debriefings. We always ask participants to agree that "what is said here, stays here," but we have no way to enforce this agreement.

- It may be prudent to have employees sign a form indicating that they understand the limits of confidentiality and agree to participate in the debriefing process.

- In terms of required reporting, some consider debriefings to be education, not therapy. This may vary. Encourage your clients to ask about their department's reporting policy regarding medical treatment.

- Make a list of local attorneys who are familiar with both workers' compensation issues and law enforcement. Get to know them before you need them.

3

THE EMERGENCY RESPONDER'S EXHAUSTION SYNDROME

> At my worst, I could tell you what my pistol tasted like after
> firing a test round into the dirt. I truly believed without a
> shadow of a doubt that I was weak and going crazy. I thought
> that absolutely no one could begin to comprehend what I
> had seen. I thought I was alone, and because I was alone,
> I thought that asking someone, anyone, for help would be
> about as effective as yelling for help into a jet engine.
> —POLICE OFFICER

The concept of the emergency responder's exhaustion syndrome (ERES) was developed in the mid-1990s after Dave Nagle, a retired sergeant and trained peer supporter, noticed that some deputies in his agency were feeling burned out, having difficulty with their spouses and children, and experiencing trouble at work. The symptoms he noticed most were depression, isolation, and exhaustion—the unfortunate acronym for which is DIE. Sgt. Nagle shared his observations with Fay, Kamena, and others. After some discussion, the group realized that what Nagle was observing could not be accurately classified as individual pathology but was, instead, a compendium of individual and social factors. The factors included critical incident stress, a common set of false beliefs, childhood experiences, and maladaptive coping strategies, all of which were complicated by interactions with peers. The group named this cluster of factors the *emergency responders' exhaustion syndrome*. They later expanded the concept to include anger, changing the acronym from DIE to AIDE. The ERES concept, presented in a psychoeducational format using everyday language, can help officers and their families understand their reactions to critical events and cumulative stress.

We begin our discussion of ERES with a brief overview of three different types of stress and then go on to discuss the key characteristics of ERES, including common maladaptive coping mechanisms and barriers to treatment.

CATEGORIES OF STRESS

Acute stress or trauma has a clear beginning and end. When it's over, it's over. It is usually a significant event, and most people would agree to its traumatic nature. In police work such events include shootings, horrific homicide scenes, the violent death of a child, and so on.

Chronic stress is a state of ongoing arousal without specific acute events to provoke it. For police officers, chronic trauma could come from working in a high-crime, high-risk area or working a sex abuse or domestic violence caseload. In high-crime areas there is always the possibility for something to go wrong, and an officer must maintain a state of alertness that perpetually activates his or her neurological alarm system. With sex abuse or domestic abuse caseloads, the officer is repeatedly exposed to traumatized victims.

Cumulative stress/trauma is a combination of acute and chronic factors, micro and major traumatic events. In our experience, cumulative trauma is the most difficult to treat when officers have adapted to the ongoing events, often causing serious difficulties in their lives due to their maladaptive coping strategies.

How ERES Works: Mary's Story

> Mary worked for the traffic division of a large urban department where she handled a lot of serious crashes. The more crashes she observed the more worried she became about her family's safety. She developed a theory that the person with the most "lug nuts" wins in any crash, meaning that the bigger the tire, the bigger the car, the safer the occupants. Mary bought her family a large SUV. One day at work she responded to a fatal accident. A drunk driver in a small car had

crashed into an SUV and killed several people. It was the same model SUV that Mary had just purchased for her family, and the child in the backseat was wearing the same pajamas that Mary's son was wearing when Mary left for work.

Mary, like many in law enforcement, used adaptive denial to minimize the physical and emotional risks of her job in order to be able to do it (Barlow & Freyd, 2009; Kirschman, 2007; Rudofossi, 2007). But at that moment, her adaptive denial failed. Mary could no longer say, "This can't happen to me or mine."

Mary became obsessed with her family's safety, creating arguments with her husband and alienating her children for being too restrictive. At work she tried to catch all the drunk drivers. Every time there was a crash involving alcohol, she was either too aggressive to the driver or berated herself endlessly for failing to stop the accident from occurring.

Mary's perceived sense of failure caused her to fall into a depression. None of the other officers seemed to be having a problem with calls to fatal accidents. Mary began alienating herself from friends and coworkers in the belief that they could tell she was a failure and a fraud. She used so much energy to keep going that she was exhausted, yet unable to sleep well. She tried drinking in the hope that alcohol would ease her depression and stop the nightmares. Finally her husband confronted her about her behavior, and she agreed to seek help.

In therapy Mary recognized that her life was out of control, but she didn't understand why she was so troubled. "Nothing bad happened. I didn't get into a shooting or anything," she said in the first session. "I have been to 50 fatalities, why would this one bother me?" Her therapist responded, saying, "It bothers you because you have been to 50 fatalities. This one was one too many."

Using the ERES concept, Mary and her therapist were able to see how and when her adaptive denial failed. They were able to identify the maladaptive coping strategies, including alcohol abuse, that Mary used in her frantic effort to regain a sense of normality. The therapist helped Mary examine her tactical thinking errors (see Figure 9.1, pp. 104–105) and rewrite a childhood script that had led her to be super-responsible. At termination, Mary was able to hold the thought that she was a good officer even though she was unable to predict or prevent every crash.

THE KEY CHARACTERISTICS OF ERES

There are five core elements to ERES: depression, isolation, exhaustion, anger, and maladaptive coping. These factors arise occasionally for many

LEOs, but for some they combine and intensify to the point of making the officer unable to perform the job safely or effectively, unhappy at home, and convinced this state of mind will never end.

Depression

Although the level of depression varies for each responder (Breslau, 2002), it is not uncommon for responders to report suicidal ideation, active planning, and actual attempts. Violanti and Drylie (2008) found that depression was reported among 12.5% of female and 6.2% of male police officers, compared to 5.2% of the population at large. Situational events, critical incidents, and life stressors do not lead to police officer suicide, but depression does (Hackett & Violanti, 2003). It is important for cops to understand that depression is a correctable chemical imbalance that can create feelings of helplessness and hopelessness. When combined with poor judgment, difficulty concentrating and making decisions, poor impulse control, and substance abuse, it significantly increases the potential for suicide (Hackett & Violanti, 2003). Responders who are depressed have selective perception that "proves" their presumed insufficiency (Furr & Funder, 1998; Moffitt, 1994) or validates their problematic stories. This cycle of depression, negative self-appraisal, and a reluctance to accept positive outcomes further isolates and exhausts the responder.

Isolation

Cops have a strong need to conform and be a part of the team. They rely on each other for emotional and physical survival, and motivate one another to confront and handle danger. The best compliment an officer can receive is for another officer to say "I would go with you on any call" or to be known as a "cop's cop." Officers overcome their own very human fears because they don't want to let their fellow officers down. They must protect their image of reliability because to lose it would mean they could lose acceptance within the team.

At times, responders may believe that they are not worthy of the respect and trust of their peers, but few will leave the job voluntarily. Furthermore, leaving the job may not alleviate symptoms. In fact, there is evidence that separation from police duties increases vulnerability to symptoms (Paton, Violanti, & Schmuckler, 1999). So what do officers do when they can't control their emotions or fear they may not be functioning well on the job?

> Ron worked for a small municipality and responded to a 911 call that involved a stabbing with multiple victims. When the suspect confronted the officers, he was shot and killed. Ron came into treatment

so upset that he was shaking. He saw the suspect, but he didn't see that the suspect was holding a knife, and therefore he didn't shoot. Because he failed to see the suspect's weapon, he felt that he could no longer trust himself. He couldn't tell anyone else about his feelings because the word would get out that he was "losing it." His solution was to cut himself off from the other officers so they wouldn't discover he was a fraud.

Isolating himself meant that Ron lost the very support he needed to continue doing the job.

Eileen spent months investigating a difficult case involving unthinkable child abuse. She suffered greatly during her lengthy exposure to the cruelty and pain the perpetrator had inflicted on his victims. When she received an award for her investigative abilities she felt like a fraud because no one knew how bad she felt inside and how much the case had affected her emotionally.

Social support from colleagues reduces the effects of critical incidents, but cops learn early on that certain emotions are not acceptable. The taboo surrounding such emotions leads to a sense of separation, isolation, secrecy, resistance, and, in some instances, avoidance of thoughts and feelings (Brown & Campbell, 1994; Lowery & Stokes, 2005). Avoidance involves attempts to escape or minimize heightened emotionality (Asmundson, Stapleton, & Taylor, 2004). Emotional distancing makes it unlikely that cops will receive the help they need. It is an effective strategy during an ongoing incident, but after the event emotional distancing becomes maladaptive (Lowery & Stokes, 2005).

Several officers responded to a motor vehicle accident where a number of people, including children, were killed and several others severely injured. There was some joking and small talk at the scene, but no one talked about the incident or how it was affecting them. On his way home, one of the officers came across a dog that had been recently hit by a car and was dying. Alone in his car, he broke into tears and sobbed. He irrationally believed that his callous joking at the accident scene somehow was responsible for the dog's death. He felt terribly guilty and asked himself over and over, "What kind of a person have I become who can laugh at such a tragedy and cry over the death of a dog?" He had no way to tell his peers how badly he felt because they all seemed to be doing OK with it. At work no one mentioned the accident during the following shift, and he never mentioned the dog.

Judging one's insides by other officers' outsides is a common mistake. All cops have a game face. Almost everyone looks great at work and no one talks about emotions, so the affected cop believes he or she is the most messed-up police officer in the agency. What the officer doesn't know is that two of the other cops on scene take antidepressants, another is drinking heavily every night, and the third is so withdrawn at home that his wife is about to leave him.

It is not only the shame attached to depression or anxiety that leads officers to isolate. Officers associate these negative feelings with weakness and with the emotionally disturbed citizens they have placed on involuntary psychiatric holds. Within their professional culture, officers see themselves as solving problems, never having them.

Exhaustion

We define exhaustion as the depletion of an officer's normal ability to cope. It can be manifested in many ways: insomnia, suspiciousness, hypervigilance, chronic fear, panic attacks, disengagement, emotional constriction, depersonalization, derealization, memory disturbance, exaggerated startle response, agoraphobia, and so on (Briere, Weathers, & Runtz, 2005). As coping resources diminish, adaptive coping—physical exercise, peer support, hobbies, spirituality, relaxation, and family support—decreases, while maladaptive coping—engaging in high-risk activities, substance abuse, and multiple sexual relationships—increases. The officer may make a few halfhearted attempts at getting help or compensate for perceived failures by working harder and faster, but nothing changes. Family members and bosses become more demanding. Stresses from the job carry over to the home, making it difficult to restore oneself and recover from the demands of the job (Peeters, Montgomery, Bakker, & Schaufeli, 2005). Increasing stress at home and work can lead to burnout, which has, at its core, exhaustion and cynicism (Peeters et al., 2005) and is closely associated with maladaptive assumptions, negative beliefs, excessive demands, and unmet expectations (van Dierendonck, Gaarssen, & Visser, 2005).

Anger

In the law enforcement culture, anger is the one acceptable emotion. It is OK to be angry with suspects on the street, or with the way a judge mishandles a case. Anger follows an officer home: you will hear officers claim they don't bring the job home, but if you talk to their spouses, you'll get a different story.

> Judy would wait to see if Tom had "the look" when he came home. If he did, she and the children would stay away from him. Sometimes she had to tell him, "Don't talk to me like a suspect," which made him mad.

Officers are trained to react at work. Identifying a threat and reacting quickly is what keeps cops safe. It is drummed into them in the academy, day after day, month after month. "What are you going to do when the suspect has you on the ground and is beating the crap out of you?" their self-defense instructor will demand. "I hope like hell you get angry." Anger becomes a friend, a valuable asset to rely on during the working day. And yet, the more overwhelmed officers feel, the more likely they are to bring the anger home (see Chapter 16). Anger can also be problematic at work: too much anger or inappropriate anger can lead to citizen complaints. By the time he sees a therapist, an officer likely feels the one tool he thought he could rely on is now causing problems across all dimensions of life.

Maladaptive Coping: Strategies That Are Doomed to Fail

LEOs commonly use maladaptive coping strategies in an attempt to recover and rebalance after acute or chronic stress. Officers may console themselves by thinking they've at least tried, but it is cold comfort to themselves and their families. The most common maladaptive coping strategies are alcohol abuse and sexual acting out, including addiction to pornography (see Chapter 11).

Counterphobic Behaviors

These kinds of behaviors have a reckless, rogue-like quality. They are dangerous in their own right and often in violation of accepted practices. Some examples include failing to wait for backup, not wearing protective equipment, or deliberately engaging in risky stops without using proper officer safety procedures.

> Karl's best friend was killed in an on-duty crash. Karl told his therapist, "If two wheels don't leave the ground when I am driving, then I am not going fast enough."

Avoiding Treatment

There are culturally held beliefs—some of which we described in the preceding sections—that delay or impede officers from seeking help, for instance, the belief that needing help is tantamount to being weak or that emotional reactions are incompatible with being an effective cop or that letting your guard down is a prelude to danger. Sometimes officers don't even realize they hold such beliefs until someone points it out.

The Myth of Uniqueness

One of the most common fears a cop may have is that he or she is the only person experiencing negative symptoms. This belief is closely associated with shame. "Since I am the only one feeling this bad, I must be a bad person."

Many police agencies have peer support teams staffed by peers who are psychologically healthy and altruistic, capable of dealing with countertransference and validating others' experiences while maintaining confidentiality (Loo, 1999). Many have recovered from their own traumas and act as a model of hope for the responder who is currently experiencing significant distress. They are invaluable in dealing with the myth of uniqueness because they have "walked the walk and talked the talk." They have credibility and respect that therapists, who are not cops, will never have (see Chapter 9).

> Joe was a big guy and a tough cop, the survivor of numerous critical incidents. He had been brutally abused as a child but never told anyone, including his wife, because that history and the scars it left didn't fit his image of who he should be. As the years went by, events from his traumatic past began connecting to current events. He had bouts of feeling helpless and then exploding in a rage. Finally in an act of desperation, Joe told a peer supporter about his abuse. The peer support officer shared his own experience with abuse, and Joe found out that he was neither alone nor unique. The peer supporter referred Joe to therapy. After treatment Joe began speaking out about abuse to his fellow police officers, encouraging them to get treatment. He has since become a peer supporter himself.

A correlate of the myth of uniqueness is an officer's concern that no one but another officer can understand what he or she is going through. (This points to the value of peer support.) Of course, this is not true, any more than a therapist needs to be alcoholic or suicidal to treat clients with those problems. Believing only another officer will understand is often a defense against talking about difficult things, especially to one's family (see Chapter 16). Challenge this gently and respectfully, but never pretend to know more than you do. Reading this book will help, but it is not a substitute for going on a ride-along and observing cops at work.

Since most officers feel responsible for others' well-being, they often further isolate themselves because they don't want to burden other people with their problems or contaminate other people by talking about the gruesome or horrific things they've seen and done. This is a major problem in families.

Finally, some officers are simply embarrassed to admit they have the normal range of human emotions. It is humiliating to throw up at a crime scene or cry or pass out, especially for women officers. Even when the officer carries on with his or her duties, exhibiting human emotions and reactions can be seen as shameful and weak.

Incident Envy

LEOs dealing with traumatic incidents frequently believe their incidents were not as bad as those experienced by others, and thus they are less deserving of treatment.

> During group treatment, Jake, who had been stabbed multiple times, apologized to another officer. "You were in a shooting," he said, "I was only stabbed."

> Judy responded to a horrific homicide scene involving the brutal murder of several children. She told her therapist, "It's not like it happened to me. Why am I making such a big deal out of this?"

While it is important for officers and for all first responders to distinguish between trauma and tragedy—tragedy happens to other people, trauma happens to you—Judy, like so many others, was minimizing her symptoms and denying that she was suffering from vicarious trauma.

The Curse of Omnipotence

In *Imaginary Crimes*, Engel & Ferguson (2004) discuss how children develop a sense of omnipotence, feeling responsible for the behaviors of others. When something goes wrong, they blame themselves for not controlling the other person's behavior. Police officers engage in this practice as well. You will often hear an officer say, "If only I was working that day . . . " or "If I got there a couple of minutes earlier, it would have changed things." Officers assume tremendous responsibility when something goes wrong. They can display an irrational disregard for their own human limitations. The shattering of illusions is painful, particularly the illusion that one is always in control (Kirschman, 2007).

Many of our clients are like Frank, abused in childhood, and trying to master old experiences by never again feeling helpless.

> Frank worked sex crimes. He received a call about a young girl who never came home from school. Forensics showed that by the time Frank received the call, the girl was already dead. When her body was discovered, Frank blamed himself for her death. He started on a litany of if-onlys: If only he had identified the suspect before he committed the crime, if only he had had the information that she was missing sooner. Over and over, Frank found a way to convince himself his negligence had contributed to the girl's death. His guilt and his need to believe that he had the ability to stop sex crimes was so great that it nearly drove him to suicide. It was only when he connected his own childhood abuse to his current situation that he began to heal.

Rescuing Others

The belief underlying the impulse to rescue is that the officer can't share information with anyone else. To do so would be a burden on others or pose too great a risk for the officer.

Unfortunately some treatment modalities support this belief. While group therapy is an effective treatment for trauma, it can be problematic for LEOs. Cops don't feel they can discuss what they have seen and done with civilians. They don't want to further traumatize the other people in attendance, and they don't feel safe discussing their experiences with a group of people who don't understand police work. Group therapy will not be helpful if LEOs repeatedly need to explain themselves or defend their actions.

The fear of burdening others is a crucial dynamic in psychotherapy, one we address several times in this book. A therapist must be able to handle an officer's stories. Officers are rescuers, and if a therapist shows too much emotion, the officer will shut down.

> Within 10 minutes of arriving at the retreat, Lizzie cornered the lead therapist and bombarded him with her history of abuse. As she talked, he wondered about possible borderline traits, rare for a police officer. When Lizzie was done, the therapist said, "Sounds like we have a lot to do this week. I am looking forward to working with you." Later on, Lizzie confessed to the clinician that she had been testing him, wanting to see if he could hold the information. If not, she wouldn't have said much else during the week.

KEY POINTS

- Workers' compensation adjustors like to see acute events, something that they can look at and say, "I get it." For officers with cumulative trauma, it may be difficult to point to one event and say this is why the client is having trouble. This can cause problems with workers' compensation claims and lead officers to feel betrayed (see Chapter 2 for more information on workers' compensation claims).

- Don't pretend to know what an officer is experiencing if you haven't experienced it yourself. Book learning isn't enough. It's OK to say that you don't know about some things firsthand but you are willing to listen and learn. Be honest about your lack of specific experience. Don't pepper your client with questions, but make it clear that if the officer is willing to explain and maybe answer some questions, you would be honored to work together and hear his or story.

4

GROWING OLD IN A
YOUNG PERSON'S PROFESSION

> The developmental trajectory of a police career moves from
> idealism to realism to pessimism to fatalism.
> —BARRY J. KOCH (2010)

Police applicants face a daunting array of hurdles: preemployment psychological screening, polygraphs, background checks, medical examinations, and a raft of other measures of suitability. Barely 2 out of 100 will get the job. The profile of a successful candidate is an emotionally stable individual who is action oriented, honest, intelligent, usually extroverted with good impulse control, a desire to make a difference in the world, and a predilection for job security. Yet the profile we see of officers after the wear and tear of the job is often different. In a 2012 presentation, Kevin Gilmartin, psychologist and retired sheriff's deputy, found it ironic that law enforcement agencies recruit from a pool of applicants based on their positive traits and then train them in street survival skills until they become negative, suspicious, distrustful experts in abnormal behavior.

Police work changes people, not overnight, but in incremental stages. It is our hope and our job to see that it doesn't also damage them. Change, which can be positive as well as negative, starts during the application process and continues through retirement (Fagan & Ayers, 1981); Paton, Violanti, Burke, & Gerhke, 2009). Some officers will stay positive about

policing throughout their careers, but many will become jaded and cynical. The reality for most will fall in between the two extremes (Burke &
Mikkelsen, 2006). Officers progress through several distinct career stages,
each one posing a different developmental task. There is variation among
theorists concerning the length of each stage and the relationship between
age and stage. The specifics and labels are not as important as the concept.
Every officer is unique. How each negotiates these changes depends on
many personal, social, and organizational variables, as well as a little luck.

Police officers receive thousands of hours of training during their
careers, most mandated, some voluntary. The short list of subjects covered
in training includes law, driving skills, firearms handling, human relations,
defensive tactics, homeland security, and physical conditioning. What they
are not taught is how to manage a stressful career that is expected to last
two or three decades. Police departments could do a lot to help but rarely
have the resources to do so. This chapter presents research and theoretical
ideas about the career trajectory of a police officer and offers suggestions
about ways in which clinicians can help officers and their families navigate
through the many good times, as well as the bad.

AT THE ACADEMY AND ON PROBATION

The beginning of a career as an LEO is a time of great exhilaration, great
stress, and accelerated change. Officers have won a long-sought job, and
now they must prove themselves to keep it. They have no job security, are
under constant scrutiny, and are evaluated on every aspect of their performance—from attitude to appearance, academic achievement to physical ability. Nothing they do seems good enough for their training officers
(Kirschman, 2007). Regardless of their background, they are at the bottom
of the heap, depersonalized and disempowered. They have more demands,
personal and professional, than they can possibly satisfy. New officers'
families are getting their first taste of how it feels to play second fiddle to
the job and how much their lives will be affected by a career they didn't
choose for themselves. Paton and colleagues (2009, p. 17) label this period
one of "abrupt resocialization." The demands to fit in are high, and young
officers have to trade in their prepolice selves to assimilate into this new
culture (Koch, 2010). For them, policing is no longer just a job, it is fast
becoming an identity.

This is a time to build new competencies, to become more confident,
more organized, and better time managers. It is a time to learn to adapt to
the authoritarian, paramilitary nature of police organizations and develop
new systems of social support with fellow rookies. Loyalty to each other
and to the job will be repeatedly reinforced as critical to survival on the

street. Most important, rookies are learning to control their emotions, which will prove to be both a benefit and a detriment in their future.

On an interesting side note, Paton and colleagues (2009) report that some rookies felt academy training imposed meaning on their past traumatic experiences and increased their sense of well-being, probably through mastery over their emotions and increased physical prowess. We have observed that many officers, especially those who later on struggle with PTSD, seem to come from dysfunctional families and have a history of neglect and physical, emotional, or sexual abuse. As one of our clients joked, "Without dysfunctional families, we wouldn't have cops or fire fighters."

The exhilaration of academy graduation is short lived as officers move from the classroom to the field training program, a move that resembles a novice scuba diver leaving the swimming pool to dive into the ocean. No more scenarios or practice drills, this is the real deal—real bullets, real bad guys, real victims. Violanti (1983) calls this the alarm or reality stage, where new officers' expectations may or may not match the reality of the job. For many, this is their first exposure to a side of society they didn't know existed: domestic violence, poverty, human malevolence, unbearable tragedy, and unimagined cruelty.

> Jack had led a sheltered life. He came from a loving middle-class family who supported his choice to be a police officer. He had never before seen a dead body. During his first week of field training he saw three, including a baby who had been suffocated at birth by her teenage mother. Where he expected grief and outrage from the baby's grandparents, he encountered only indifference. He had more downtime than he expected and many tedious tasks to complete. Rather than the excitement of catching bank robbers, he spent several shifts sorting out a dispute between neighbors who each complained that the other's gardener was in violation of a leaf-blower ordinance. He found a great contrast between public expectations, probably based on TV cop shows, and what he could actually do to catch long-gone burglars and recover stolen property. The contrast between Jack's expectations and the reality he encountered made him question for the first time whether this was the right job for him. But there were high points too: the day Jack returned a missing toddler to his frantic parents, the compliments he got from veteran officers over his handling of traffic control around a serious vehicle accident, and the letter of appreciation he received from the family of an Alzheimer's patient who had wandered away from home.

Helping people, working as a team, the excitement of responding to emergencies, and putting bad guys in jail were what Jack and his fellow rookies expected out of the job, along with a secure position and decent pay. As he recalibrated his expectations to meet this new reality, he was still under constant surveillance, and would be until his probationary year was over. Rookies have no job security and can be fired without cause. Every mistake, every less than satisfactory performance rating, has major consequences. Some 25–30% will fail to pass muster and lose the job they have worked so long and hard to get.

Competency and fitting in are the major challenges of this phase. Rookies need to learn more than tactical skills and the formal, written policies of their agency. They are also, for good or bad, soaking up the informal, unwritten ways that veteran officers behave, think, and manage their emotions.

THE HONEYMOON PHASE

The 5 or so years following probation are a time of utter intoxication, novelty, and continued change. Young officers learn something new and see something new every day. They carry levels of responsibility and authority they may never have experienced, unless they served in the military. Early-career officers report more favorable work outcomes, greater social support, less exhaustion, lower levels of cynicism, and better overall health than do mid- or late-career officers (Burke & Mikkelsen, 2006). They feel invincible, perhaps as an adaptation to the perceived dangers of the job (Kirschman, 2007), and may take unwise risks. Some show signs of arrogance and self-inflation, thinking they know more and are more important than others, including their friends and family (Laguna, Linn, Ward, & Rupslaukyte, 2010). These eager officers, sometimes called "hot dogs," are consumed with police work 24/7, often in inappropriate circumstances and frequently to the dismay of their families, who don't want or need cops at home. Dinners out and trips to the mall become extensions of work; officers insist on sitting facing the restaurant door, carry their weapons off duty when not required, or spend their shopping time scanning the mall for shoplifters and gang members. The enthusiasm for work takes priority because nothing else, even family, seems to consolidate their identity and give them greater personal validation (Miller, 2007). Contextually, such high levels of dedication are viewed as positive attributes and rewarded by the officer's superiors, who, too often, value productivity over family and personal well-being.

Such high levels of devotion to the job do not go over well at home, as families learn that, with few exceptions, the job comes first. If there are small children in the family, sleep deprivation and sharing child care responsibilities can become major challenges (see Chapter 15), especially for couples with two wage earners and no extended family in the area.

Socialization forces are strongest at the patrol level, where there is a shared mission and safety depends on solidarity. By now, officers have developed an occupational persona, a public face (Kirschman, 2007) that serves to obscure individual differences, suppress emotional expression, and hide the stress of the job (see Chapter 16). Some will have difficulty turning this persona off when they are at home. Many become more black and white in their thinking—you have either broken the law or you haven't—because shades of gray slow them down. Their sense of humor becomes darker. Some will be caught in a cycle of hypervigilance (see pp. 162–164) where they feel exhilarated at work and bored at home. Others will have started living beyond their means, dependent on overtime to support their lifestyle. Those who have had children no longer look at child victims the same way or are unwilling to take the same risks they did before they became parents. Seeing a dead or abused child packs an unimagined emotional wallop. As one officer told us, calls involving children left him "emotionally defeated." He couldn't shake the feelings off, and he would break into tears when he got home.

THE EARLY MIDDLE YEARS

Kirschman calls the years between 5 and 10 a time of "settling down" (2007) or decelerated change. Violanti (1983) calls this phase "disenchantment." Officers are likely now in their 30s with young families and significant financial debt. They have confidence in their street skills and the job is still appealing, but the novelty has worn off and the learning curve has flattened. Youthful idealism is now tempered by a more realistic appraisal of the limits of law enforcement to affect crime and of one's own limited abilities to make a difference in the world. More attention is paid to the boring and frustrating aspects of police work: report writing, politics, flaws in the judicial system, and distorted media reports about police actions. Administrative policies, authoritarian practices, and petty criticisms become harder to take the more confident the officer becomes in his or her own judgment and competence. There is a dawning realization that the officer has invested time and energy into a career over which he or she has little control.

During these first 10 or so years, many cops have become more invested in work and less emotionally invested at home. Some have been divorced and are now single parents. Their perspective on life may have narrowed considerably. The world is a "felony in progress," and they have grown accustomed to judging 97% of the world by the 3% they encounter

(K. M. Gilmartin, presentation, 2012). A moral inversion has occurred (Bonifacio, 1991); trust now equals naiveté and distrust equals safety. Only innocent victims like children warrant much compassion. Officers who once had several roles and a range of interests beyond law enforcement now have only their cop role left. Gone are their civilian friends, personal goals, spiritual pursuits, sports activities, family activities, and hobbies. With all one's financial and social resources dependent on the job, despite any regrets an officer may have, leaving police work is rarely an option.

Gilmartin called overinvesting in police work a problem of singular identity and declares that officers who are so overly identified with the job suffer from "usta syndrome." They are no longer the person they "usta" be and no longer engage in the activities they "usta" love. Koch (2010, p. 92) asserts that when the police role overtakes all other roles, an officer's sense of self narrows and rigidifies so much that the officer may "no longer be able to access any part of himself that is not a cop, even when off duty." Mental inflexibility and the loss of diversity in roles and relationships undermines resilience and diminishes an officer's options for coping adaptively with critical incidents. It's a vicious circle. The more an officer identifies exclusively with the police role, the more risk factors he or she has for maladaptive coping, such as escape or avoidance through drinking, gambling, blocking feelings, rugged individualism, and emotion-based rather than problem-focused reactions (Paton et al., 2009). Maladaptive coping is positively related to work stress in older officers, and work stress is significantly associated with anxiety, depression, somatization, posttraumatic stress, burnout, and inappropriate aggression (Gerson, 2002).

At this stage of an officer's career, we see a shift from police goals to personal goals. Individual comforts, such as shift assignments, pay raises, and retirement benefits, take precedence over organizational needs. Officers may begin to look around for new challenges such as specialty assignments or promotions. The time and money involved in getting promoted, often requiring a return to college or a long period of intense study, means the family must, once again, postpone its own needs for the promise of future rewards in money and status.

Officers and their families are usually poorly prepared for the anxiety and disappointment that accompany getting ahead. There is approximately one supervisory position for every eight patrol officers. Only 5% of middle managers will be promoted to an executive rank. Promotional opportunities and specialty assignments are scarce in small departments, and departments of 50 or fewer officers make up almost 90% of all police agencies.

PLATEAUING: THE LATE MIDDLE YEARS

The period between 10 and 20 years on the job is a time of continuing disillusion and growing disenchantment for many (Violanti, 1983). Cynicism and many other "isms" abound. Crooks appear to have the advantage. Neither the community nor the department seems to understand or appreciate the police. The new rookies look younger than ever at the same time that one's parents are aging and one's children are entering adolescence. There may be a pileup of negative life events like divorce, illness, or financial problems. It's getting harder to chase down suspects, and the person in the mirror now has some gray hair and wears glasses. For many senior officers, the cumulative results of years of chronic work stress, sleep deprivation, and episodes of dysregulated cortisol output have taken their toll, leading to weight gain and an elevated risk for diabetes, cardiovascular disease, and premature death (Joseph et al., 2009; Toch, 2002; Violanti et al., 2006).

Officers who have been promoted and those who were not now begin to view their careers differently. Those passed over may be frustrated and bitter as they watch younger people being promoted above them. They continue to do the job but complain about politics and blame the agency for failing to see their merits. A career that once promised years of fulfillment has run out of steam. Job satisfaction is the lowest in an officer's career. Pushing a patrol car at age 45 has little status, despite the fact that patrol work is the backbone of policing (Burke & Mikkelsen, 2006). Even those who maintain a positive attitude express dissatisfaction with supervision, the promotional process, and their inability to influence their careers (McGinnis, 1985). The time for changing careers is long past. The compensation and job security that were once a draw are now a trap. Officers feel uncomfortable interacting with civilians in a nonenforcement capacity and have difficulty imagining themselves working at anything but a job in public safety (Kirschman, 2007).

Officers who have earned promotions or won desired specialty assignments are better buffered against chronic negativity. Upper-level managers usually have robust self-esteem and are socially skillful and politically powerful. Still, promotion is not without problems. Middle managers walk a tightrope, balancing the needs of upper management with those of frontline officers. Their workload is increased, and it is difficult to be in charge of former peers who may resent being supervised or expect preferential treatment (Hogan, 2011). Middle managers may miss the street action and hate being at the bottom of the managerial pile. With every promotion comes more responsibility, longer working hours, and more isolation. Police chiefs are among the most isolated and underappreciated employees in a police organization. No matter what they do, someone is mad at them.

They may appear powerful to their subordinates, yet feel powerless in their dealings with mayors, city managers, city councils, police unions, and the press (Kirschman, 2007).

RESOLUTION: MOVING TOWARD RETIREMENT

The final years of an officer's career are a time of introspection (Violanti, 1983). Officers in this phase have little left to lose. Some have attained their highest level of promotion and don't want to go further. Others have accepted that they are not promotable and can stop trying. Kirschman (2007) calls it a crossroads. Officers can become bitter or they can look for opportunities to reconnect with what they once found gratifying about their work—having fun, helping people, working as part of a team, and earning community respect. There are many ways to do this, especially in moderate- to large-size agencies, for example:

- Mentor younger officers.
- Start or join an existing peer support program.
- Get involved in the police officers' association.
- Start or join a community activity for disadvantaged youth.
- Teach in the citizens' academy or mentor a neighborhood watch program.
- Start a social program for retired officers.
- Sponsor or participate in a fundraising event.

In his study of police careers, Violanti (1983) asserts that stress decreases significantly as service time extends. He finds this period of introspection and resolution to be the least stressful time of an officer's career with one exception, a spike at 25 years that suggests anxiety about retirement. Others, like Burke and Mikkelsen (2006) and Gerson (2002) have a different point of view. They find older officers to be less satisfied with work and at increased risk for stress-related health problems, especially those who habitually use maladaptive coping to combat stress.

Stress is commonly defined as a state of high demands and low control. The road to reducing stress is to increase control and lower demands or some combination of the two. Officers who become overinvested in work and underinvested at home have pinned all their hopes, wishes, and expectations on the one thing over which they have little control—the job. Home is where an officer has influence. The only things officers can control at work are their integrity, their professionalism, and their safety. They cannot control their assignments, their partners, their supervisors, their police chiefs, the media, the community, or the criminals. The challenge of this period before retirement is no different than the challenge officers have faced since day one: to minimize stress by staying connected with those aspects of life over which one has influence—family, friends, health, personal and professional interests or hobbies, and deferred dreams. The only difference is that in the run-up to retirement the emphasis may be on reconnecting and repairing relationships that were damaged or lost, including the relationship with one's prepolice self.

Ideally, departments should offer help with the transition from officer to civilian, starting 5 years from the anticipated date of separation. For most officers, this will be around the age of 50 with 20–30 years of service. Realistically, departments, rarely offer anything beyond financial advice, and sometimes not even that. Financial health is important, but it isn't the entire picture. Officers, especially those seeking employment in non–public safety fields, need assistance articulating and valuing what has become second nature to them. For example, the ability to take decisive action or to analyze problems are valuable work skills that officers rarely think to include in a résumé. Officers may also need to prepare responses to questions or hostile reactions they may get from others during their job search (see Chapter 15). Visualizations, rehearsals, and feedback on their interactive style can all be helpful.

RETIREMENT

On my last day at work I walked out the back door of the San Rafael Police Department. I had been a police officer for a total of 32 years. I was grateful that no one else was in the parking lot. I stopped halfway between the back door and my car, wondering what it was I was supposed to be feeling at that moment. Should I be happy or sad? Anxious or calm? As I stood there an image came to mind, that of a roof being supported by a single pillar. If that one pillar were removed the entire roof would collapse. But I had a lot of pillars in my life besides work. I had friends, family, volunteer work, sports, and many other interests. I could afford to lose this one pillar. At that moment I knew I was going to be OK.
—JOEL FAY (personal communication, 2012)

Rookie officers expect to retire voluntarily following a full-term career. Unfortunately, many will retire prematurely because they are injured, physically or psychologically. Some officers accept that they are no longer medically fit to work, others will feel pushed out and abandoned by the agency to whom they gave so much. Those who feel pushed out are often bitter and unwilling to let go of their grievances toward the department or the workers' compensation system. Bitterness only complicates the psychological work needed to make the transition from officer to civilian.

The authors know many officers who are enjoying retirement, living long and healthy lives. Their time is their own, and they no longer have to be perfect. They have new interests and hobbies, and are spending more time with their grandchildren than they did with their own kids. They travel, go to sports events, have regular reunions, and stay in touch via the Internet.

> Johanna is retiring after 30 years, celebrated by a room full of police officers, some working, many happily retired. There's a lot of laughter and applause, a raft of embarrassing jokes and old stories. Johanna takes obvious pride in her exceptional career. She has spent much of the last 15 years as an administrator, developing programs and mentoring subordinates. But the memories she most cherishes and the funniest stories she tells are about the bad guys she put in jail. As the evening ends, the emcee hands Johanna her retirement badge. "Once a cop, always a cop," he says.

Replacing the camaraderie of the police family takes energy, effort and planning. It is perhaps the key task of retirement along with establishing a new identity. Retirees are POWs—pictures on a wall. No longer part of the everyday mission of their agency, they are forgotten surprisingly quickly. They may still carry a weapon and a badge, but their uniform is gone and so is their sense of belonging. Many are happy to hear the sirens and know that whatever misery is occurring on the street or back at headquarters no longer concerns them. Others feel sad and mourn the loss of the power and influence they once had. It is a time to reevaluate earlier goals and achievements as well as a time to let go of anger and resentment.

Because officers retire at a relatively young age, many will have spouses or significant others who are still working, maybe even just hitting their stride. There may be issues of role reversal, feelings of loneliness, and loss of purpose. Families who have played second fiddle to the job for years may resent having their officer at home giving orders and rearranging things that have worked well without his or her input.

In the quiet of retirement, long-repressed emotions can rise to the surface. This is both good and bad. On the positive side, access to the totality of one's feelings can be like meeting an old, cherished friend. There is the joy of recognition and relief at reconnecting with someone who once enriched your life.

> It was Thanksgiving and Ed had been retired for 6 months. He was on his way to the supermarket when he passed three "bums" sitting against the supermarket wall, panhandling. At first, he walked by them, and then he thought to himself "no one should be without turkey on Thanksgiving." He walked back to where they were sitting and

Growing Old in a Young Person's Profession

asked to speak to the "Chief Bum." One man instantly held out his hand. Ed gave him a $20 bill and told him to buy turkey sandwiches for himself and his friends. Ed had dealt with street people for years and was certain that the minute he turned his back the three men would head for the nearest bar or the nearest dealer. But he didn't care. He felt a sense of joy and satisfaction at his generosity. "I'm not a cop anymore," he thought. "I'm a person."

On the downside, some newly arising emotions are related to disturbing memories set aside in the name of expedience (see Chapter 15). As one officer put it, these old memories are "like dancing with ghosts." Some researchers indicate that the suicide rate for retirees is higher than that of active officers (*www.badgeoflife.org*, "Police Retirement: The Final Trauma"). They attribute this to isolation, loss of companionship, and a duffel bag of unresolved and unprocessed traumatic incidents.

We sometimes ask cops to list their first, worst, and last critical incidents. Other times we ask them to simply make a chronological list of every incident they remember. It is amazing to watch how surprised they are at the number of events they have forgotten. It doesn't take much for them to connect the dots between these incidents and their current emotional struggles (see Chapter 5). Not every officer will have had major exposure to trauma. So much depends on the community, the crime rate, and the assignments an officer has had.

While we make a point to ask about these remarkable incidents, we also ask about positive outcomes. With time, many terrible events ultimately lead to a sense of self-efficacy, pride, relief, renewed enthusiasm, and psychological and spiritual growth (Klinger, 2006). Although we emphasize resilience and posttraumatic growth at all stages in an officer's career, we find it especially useful in the years leading up to retirement and in retirement itself (see Chapter 9).

KEY POINTS

- Never tell an officer that he should quit. He will resist the suggestion. Being a police officer is an identity, not just a job. If it seems inevitable or imperative for reasons of mental health for an officer to think of resigning, proceed slowly and be tentative when raising the issue.

- Educate yourself about career counseling and life-span development. Know the career counseling resources in your community.

- Include the family in decisions regarding promotions, transfers, retirement planning, and so on. Their lives will be affected as much as, if not more than, the officer's.

- Encourage families to develop independent extended support systems, learn to go places on their own, and know how to get help when their spouses are at work.

- Ideally, officers should start planning for retirement and saving money from day one. This rarely happens.

- Financial health is part of career planning. Cops are notoriously fond of "toys"—cars, trucks, motorcycles, boats, and so on. Some get in trouble through gambling (see Chapter 11) or by living on their overtime pay. Know the financial counseling resources in your community.

Part II

LINE-OF-DUTY ISSUES

This section explores the unavoidable challenges that come with the job. Taken separately, the issues of trauma, risk, betrayal, and shift work are not unique to law enforcement. But we believe the police culture amplifies their influence. As a result, officers can become isolated from their friends and family, even from the community at large. Consider what you as a clinician can do to mitigate what you cannot change. Think about how these issues shape an officer's behavior at work and at home. Imagine the ways in which you can make a difference in a cop's life.

5

Death by 1,000 Cuts

Critical Incidents, Trauma, and Posttraumatic Stress Injuries

I remember the moment I figured it out.
Other people's tragedies are not my trauma.
—POLICE OFFICER

Mickey's symptoms were exacerbated when he was given a medal for killing an armed suspect who was wearing body armor and shooting at the police and at people on the street. Mickey felt like a fraud. "My beat-buddies don't know what to say, so they joke around, saying 'way to go, killer.' The brass and the politicians are using this as a photo-op. I feel like crap for having to take a life. Where was everyone when I was actually helping somebody?"

Most cops will never shoot their guns in the line of duty except when training and practicing at the range. Police work doesn't even rank among the top 10 most lethal jobs in America. Of nearly 700,000 LEOs in the United States, about 150 will be killed on the job every year (*www.fbi.gov/about-us/cjis/ucr/leoka/2011*). Half will die in accidents, and the other half will be murdered while on duty. Loggers, pilots, commercial fishermen, iron and steel workers, garbage collectors, farmers and ranchers, roofers, power line installers and repairers, truck drivers, taxi drivers, and chauffeurs are more likely to die on the job (U.S. Bureau of Labor Statistics, 2012). The difference is they won't be intentionally murdered for their choice of profession.

The psychological hazards of police work are less obvious and more ubiquitous than the physical ones. Police officers and many first responders see more misery and despair in the first few years of their jobs than the rest of us do in a lifetime. The list is long: exposure to people in pain, exposure to unthinkable cruelty, exposure to innocent victims, and exposure to the infinite ways, many quite grotesque, that humans die—all of this amplified by concern for one's safety, frustration with the judicial system, the weight of responsibility, negative media coverage, organizational stress, betrayal, and wear and tear on family life.

In this chapter we investigate the kinds of remarkable incidents and assignments that are emotionally hazardous for officers, discuss the risk factors that set them up for trouble, and present two therapeutic interventions. We use the term *posttraumatic stress injuries* throughout, because we want to communicate to our clients that they can recover from traumatic stress just as they have recovered from physical injuries. The term *posttraumatic stress disorder* invokes stigma and implies a pathological state that is the equivalent of a lifetime sentence.

Keep in mind that the majority of officers involved in critical incidents do not develop long-term debilitating problems. Most experience physical, emotional, or cognitive symptoms during or shortly after such an event but are able to resolve them quickly, usually after a few days to a few weeks. This information is useful to cops who are suffering from posttraumatic stress injuries because it normalizes their symptoms, reduces stigma, and provides hope. We endorse working collaboratively with our law enforcement clients by sharing with them the latest research about the causes and cures for posttraumatic stress injuries.

Our goal, whether or not the officer meets the current diagnostic criteria for PTSD, is symptom reduction, helping the officer return to his or her previous level of functioning, and relapse prevention. Whether or not the officer returns to work is a personal and administrative decision in which we have no investment and over which we have little control. All we can do is help the officer make a skillful decision about his or her future. With the client's written permission, we may attempt to mitigate conflicts between the officer and his or her agency by educating administrators about clinical issues. But we do so with caution. More will be said about this in the following pages.

CRITICAL INCIDENTS

What makes an incident critical as opposed to routine? It is not what happens to the individual that makes a difference, but what the individual thinks about what has happened. Trauma is in the eye of the beholder (Kirschman, 2007). Being assigned to the front desk or as a school resource officer may be more hazardous to one officer's well-being than chasing a bad guy down a dark alley. For others, the reverse may be true. Urban police officers are challenged by poverty, high crime volume, gang activity, and other stressors, whereas rural officers can be challenged by illicit drug manufacture, insufficient personnel available for backup, and personal knowledge of both perpetrators and victims. There is wide variation among departments and among circumstances.

While any given event will be perceived differently by those involved, there are several contextual and personal reactions that up the ante and can jeopardize an officer's ability to stabilize following an event:

1. The officer perceives that his or her safety is threatened.
2. The officer has significant physiological reactions during the incident (e.g., a resting heart rate in excess of 90 beats per minute) and is unable to calm down physically after the event.
3. The officer is confronting multiple stressors in other parts of his or her life.
4. Negative self-appraisals. In the police culture, the effort to make meaning out of a random universe sometimes results in cops thinking less of themselves. This may sound odd, but in the world of policing, the thought "I'm a bad cop" can be more acceptable than the thought "I'm not in control."

The continuum of critical incident stress ranges from a flight-fight-freeze response that lasts a few seconds to long-term symptoms that are resistant to change. In our work with first responders we have seen that it is not the incident per se that determines whether an officer develops persistent symptoms; rather, it is the degree to which the officer personalizes responsibility for the outcome of the incident.

Categorizing Critical Incidents

Working with cops we have observed that critical incidents seem to fall into three general categories. Some officers have incidents that fall into all three; some of these events are easier than others for clients to talk about.

Index Incident

This is a major critical incident that opens a psychological wound. It may be the presenting problem talked about at intake because the officer considers it culturally appropriate to discuss. For many, it is only the tip of the iceberg.

Subcritical Incidents

These are the micro or smaller events that slowly erode a person's self-concept. These incidents tend not to engender intense feelings of fear or anger. But the officer may hesitate to discuss them because they seem unimportant or irrelevant. Only after being encouraged to talk about them does the LEO realize how much they are bothering him or her.

Incidents That Reactivate Childhood Trauma

These are incidents that connect to the officer's own childhood trauma on a conscious or unconscious level. Don't go here until you have the officer's trust because you will meet with resistance and disbelief before acknowledgment. Officers expect you to "muck about" in their childhoods and have their defenses up.

Special Categories of High Clinical Risk

The following experiences carry special risks for the officers involved in them, each has its own meaning and calls for careful assessment and intervention on the therapist's part. Two of the most clinically challenging, line-of-duty deaths (LODDs) and officer-involved shootings (OISs), are discussed in separate sections.

• Serious line-of-duty injury. When an officer is seriously injured on the job, the event is likely to have intense psychological consequences. Denial is shattered. The officer now knows he or she is vulnerable and wonders what will happen next. As with an LODD, cops and their families who don't even know the injured coworker are so closely identified that they too can feel vulnerable.

• Suicide of a coworker. The suicide of a fellow officer, while not considered an LODD and often not accorded an official funeral, is very traumatic because of the close bond between first responders (O'Hara & Violanti, 2009). If the suicide is a total surprise, as it often is, it can damage officers' confidence in their ability to read others (see Chapter 12 for more on law enforcement suicide).

• Injury or death to a child. Calls involving children can be particularly tough, especially when the victim resembles the officer's own child in any way: age, body type, hair color, clothing, and so on. An irrational self-expectation to rescue may develop as a result. Blaming the victim doesn't work because the officer cannot hold a child to blame for the actions and misdeeds of adults. Defusing emotion with gallows humor, another usually effective coping skill, doesn't work either because there's nothing funny about a child who has been kidnapped, raped, murdered, or run over by a car. Or, as mentioned earlier, the situation may be similar to the officer's own childhood experiences. Right or wrong, many deaths can be rationalized—the driver was drunk, the victim was a known criminal—but it is almost impossible to rationalize the death of a child who drowns in the backyard pool or is a victim of sudden infant death syndrome.

• Prolonged exposure to the dead or dying. Exposure can last hours or only a few seconds. Trouble comes when the officer loses his or her ability to remain emotionally detached. It's particularly painful to stay with someone who is dying, to look into his eyes, hear his dying words and be helpless as his life drains away.

• Mass casualty incidents such as 9/11 or an airplane crash.

• Victim is known to the responder. This happens frequently in rural areas and small towns where the LEO knows everyone and has a personal relationship with many.

• Any incident in which the officer's personal safety is jeopardized or the officer is injured. Cops tend to savor the adrenaline rush they get from taking risks. But every now and then, a close call forces LEOs to realize they are lucky to be alive and it had nothing to do with their response to danger. The feeling of vulnerability that follows can be unsettling.

• Exposure to infectious diseases. The advent of AIDS, antibiotic-resistant bacterial infections, SARS, E. coli, anthrax, and other blood-borne or airborne infections affects not only officers but their loved ones as well. The psychological effects of a needlestick can last for months as the officer waits to find out if he has been infected.

• Organizational or personal betrayal. Betrayal comes in many forms: personal, organizational, and social. Whenever it occurs, it makes everything else worse. The dynamics of betrayal are described in the next chapter.

• Slanted media attention. It is common for agencies to take a self-protective stance after a high-profile incident and offer limited responses to the media. The officer involved may want the chance to tell her side of the story but is not allowed to talk to anyone outside the department. Being skewered in public is a painful experience for the officer and the officer's family and has the potential to destroy that officer's career, rob her of her dedication, and take all the joy out of her work. In general, cops are skeptical about journalists' ability to be objective in their reporting and cynical about the public's appetite for sensationalism.

• Psychologically hazardous assignments. Although there is variation among departments and circumstances, certain assignments are commonly regarded as highly stressful and psychologically hazardous. It is critical to learn about your client's current and past assignments with specific details about the pluses and minuses of each. Police work is more nuanced than portrayed on television. Getting a detailed work history can turn up those subcritical incidents we described above.

• Internet child pornography. Calls involving children are horrible, and investigating child predators can be particularly gruesome. Watching videos in which children are being exploited or sexually abused wears on a cop's soul and can contaminate his or her intimate relationships. It is frequently recommended that officers have limited time in this assignment, ongoing psychological support, and a psychological exit interview.

• Undercover work. This assignment is dangerous on various levels (Delaney & Scheiber, 2008). Officers left on these assignments too long run the risk of identifying with the very persons they were assigned to catch. Vice assignments may require dealing with gangsters, pimps, prostitutes, runaways, and drug addicts, as well as conducting undercover stings to reduce the prevalence of these crimes. The amount of violence and carnage can become overwhelming.

• Death notifications. Police officers are often called upon to contact family members when a death has occurred, sometimes accompanied by a chaplain. One of our clients said that he was so used to informing family members of the death of a loved one that he could tell the difference between the screams and wails of mothers, siblings, and spouses.

• Corrections. Sheriff's deputies are assigned to detention facilities for some portion of their careers while a corrections officer's main assignment is guarding prisoners. Corrections work is dangerous, and the work environment can be toxic. We will say more about corrections in Chapter 19.

• Dispatch. Dispatchers, also known as communicators, are likely the most overlooked personnel in a police department and are equally at risk for ERES (Fay, Kamena, Benner, Buscho, & Nagle, 2006; see Chapter 19). The sedentary nature of their work combined with occasional high levels of stress can lead to health problems as well as emotional concerns.

• Gang units. Officers in gang units are repeatedly exposed to senseless violence and youthful death. One officer said, "It feels like I'm trying to hold back a tidal wave."

• Traffic enforcement. Highway Patrol officers, in particular, have a steady diet of mayhem and mutilated bodies. They minister to the dying and endure the agony of the survivors. Some of what they see is unthinkably grotesque.

• Serving felony warrants. This is likely one of the most dangerous jobs in police work. Felons are often heavily armed and dangerous. The assignments are carried out by highly trained teams. A lot of planning goes into every warrant service. Still, the outcome can be disastrous.

Line-of-Duty Death

LEOs are affected any time a fellow officer is killed on the job in a murder, an accident, or, the worst, friendly fire. Whether the slain officer is near or far, working in corrections or on the street, a deputy sheriff or a member of the highway patrol, reactions may vary, but the impact is the same. There is grief for the officer's death and a fearful reminder to officers and their families of the dangers of the job. If the officer's death was accidental rather than felonious, the impact is still great, but there may less fear and anger attached.

LODDs are among the most shattering events in an officer's career. Grief, sadness, anger, and a sense of vulnerability hang over a department for a long time, affecting everyone. Even cops who do not personally know the dead officer are affected because they have walked in his or her shoes and are thus closely identified. Many departments will have in-house debriefings and chaplain services for the surviving officers. The grieving process takes a long time and is extended by protracted investigations, trials, media coverage, and yearly memorial events on a local and national scale. We have found that most responders do not seek treatment soon after the event but instead use a variety of coping strategies. Maladaptive strategies (alcohol, sex, and risky behavior) become problematic and can cost officers their jobs or families, or both. The shame of being caught engaging in these behaviors can lead to serious depression and suicidal ideation.

Officer-Involved Shootings

What are the psychological consequences of shooting at or killing someone and later discovering that the person you shot had a toy gun, or was a mentally handicapped citizen, or a child? What is it like to try to save the life of a person you have just tried to kill because he has just tried to kill you? The variations of police shootings are endless (Klinger, 2004), and we are going to explore some of them now in depth.

What is universal about an OIS is that most officers have to make life-and-death decisions in a split second, with little or no information, often in the dark. They have to control their responses and think clearly while under an avalanche of stress hormones involuntarily activated by the human response to threats against survival. A result of this storm of hormones is that officers experience a range of cognitive and perceptual changes or distortions as well as a degradation of memory. Without proper understanding, these involuntary changes to the brain and body can be misinterpreted by others as deception on the part of the officer. The officer herself may feel as though she is going crazy.

> Winifred was involved in a situation where a coworker was killed. She secretly blamed herself and developed PTSD symptoms. At a training, years later, she learned about PTSD. After the class was over, she approached the instructor and said, "So all I have is PTSD, and I'm not going nuts?"

It would be unusual for a community therapist to be called upon in the immediate aftermath of an OIS; most of these incidents will be covered by a police psychologist. Still, it is important to have a working knowledge of how severe stress can distort vision, perception, memory, and other mental and neurological functions (Kirschman, 2007).

Because the context of an OIS can be quite complex, an officer can be both perpetrator and victim. We recognize that not all OISs are justified or skillful. But in our experience, so-called "bad," meaning unjustified or criminal, shootings are the exception, not the rule.

> Len was involved in a victim-precipitated shooting (also known as suicide by cop). The dead man was mentally ill and high on drugs. He charged at Len with a long sword, forcing Len to shoot him. The dead man was African American and Len was Caucasian. The whole event was caught on tape by a bystander and went viral. There were community protests accusing Len and the entire police force of racism, some of which became violent. Posters of Len with the caption "cold blooded killer" were placed all over town. Newspaper reporters began knocking on his front door and calling his wife for interviews. His children were mocked at school. The deceased man's family filed a civil suit claiming wrongful death. Ultimately, he was exonerated by an independent investigation, which provoked another series of public protests.

Traumatic reactions to OIS events are shaped by a number of factors, including the following:

- The media, and how they cover an event.
- The community response—especially when there are accusations of racism or brutality.
- The status of the individual who was shot—was this a child or an adult, a parolee, a returning combat veteran, a celebrity, or a mentally ill person?
- The condition of the person who was shot—was he killed, injured, or disabled for life?

- The distance between the officer and the victim—eye contact between the two creates a heavy emotional load (Kirschman, 2007).
- Individual factors such as the officer's level of experience, pileup of stressors, administrative support, family support, and coping skills.

Therapists are likely to be part of the community where a shooting has occurred. Be forewarned, the controversy surrounding these events can penetrate your consulting room, burdening the therapeutic alliance and affecting the outcome of therapy. Therapy with LEOs can seem more exciting than therapy with, for example, an office worker. It's tempting to ask questions to satisfy your own curiosity, especially when your client has been involved in a high-profile incident or knows people who were. Tread lightly. When an EAP therapist pronounced her client "fine" following a shooting, but worried aloud about the "poor shooting victims" and how tragic it must be for them the officer went back to his department and insisted that this therapist be dropped from his department's approved referral list. Mistakes like these will not only break therapeutic trust with your client but will likely make him or her believe that therapists don't understand and there is no point talking to them.

This may seem contradictory or paradoxical, but there are times when officers are victims and deserve to be acknowledged as such. An officer who is forced to use deadly force against another person is the victim of a crime—attempted murder, assault with a deadly weapon, and so on. The person who compelled the officer to use deadly force is the suspect. This is an important distinction. Failing to use the correct language tells your officer client that you don't know much about police work and haven't a clue that you've just said something that is offensive and hurtful.

Sometimes officers are reluctant to talk about a shooting incident because there is an ongoing investigation or legal suit and they are forbidden to talk about what happened. Perhaps they have discussed the incident so often with coworkers and family that they cannot tolerate going over it again. They will be assessing your motivation: are you a "lookey loo," a person who wants to satisfy his or her own prurient interests without considering the officer's feelings or the consequences of retelling the same story over and over? On the other hand, some officers will be grateful for the opportunity to tell their story from beginning to end without interruptions or questions. It is enough to acknowledge the event, inquire after the officer's well-being, and say you are willing to discuss it, when and if the officer brings the subject up. Providing psychoeducation about reactions and symptoms is important in early post-OIS sessions. Never presume or insist that you know what an officer is feeling. Don't overpraise or overreact. Simply tell your client you are glad he is safe and to inquire about how the publicity is affecting his life and family.

The quickest way to make a cop uncomfortable is to call him or her a hero. The affirmation comes at a huge cost, especially when the incident at hand was a team effort and one officer was singled out for praise. We are aware of several anecdotal incidents in which first responders who were at the center of a high-profile event felt so exploited or so let down afterwards that they committed suicide. The label of hero is a lot harder to wear than to earn.

There is little satisfaction in killing or wounding someone. Afterwards, officers can oscillate between remorse for actions not taken and guilt for acts committed. Praise from coworkers can wound more than it heals. Cop humor cuts both ways. LEOs may laugh in public but wince inwardly at being called "killer" or "dead eye" by their fellow officers.

WHO IS AT RISK FOR DEVELOPING POSTTRAUMATIC STRESS INJURIES?

Some events, and some officers' lives, have features that heighten the chances an officer will suffer symptoms afterward. We will investigate some of these features below with the caveat that posttraumatic stress injuries frequently involve a cluster of attributes such as the intensity of the event, whether it was a preventable event caused by human negligence or malevolent intention (versus a natural disaster), or involved personal knowledge of the victim.

Surprise

There is an increased risk for developing severe symptoms if an officer was blind-sided. Swat teams and snipers rarely experience severe post-incident distress because their actions are carefully planned beforehand. Things can go wrong, of course, but by and large events play out as expected. But for regular cops, unpredictability is a daily challenge for which the only antidote—short of mind reading—is practicing exceptional officer safety. And even that doesn't work all the time.

Helplessness

The risk of psychological injury is heightened if, during the event, the officer experiences intense feelings of helplessness. Helplessness may occur when a LEO loses control of a situation or never had it to start with, found himself without options, was overpowered by his opponents, or unable to help a victim. Because cops are trained to be in control, these moments of helplessness stand out, even when they are only seconds long and often lead to negative self beliefs such as "I'm not safe or I made a mistake."

Cumulative Stress

Critical incidents are like Mack trucks: big, catastrophic events . . . cumulative [stress] is like one bee sting after another. . . . These are the incidents that are missed by everyone, even the officer: . . . the shame, the mistakes, the "routine" horrors, the betrayals, abuses, and the dark fears. . . . We call them "soul woundings."

—THE BADGE OF LIFE POLICE MENTAL HEALTH
ORGANIZATION (*www.badgeoflife.com*)

Cumulative stress from consecutive traumas is another risk factor. An officer may have been able to cope with similar incidents in the past, but the accumulation of incidents makes the most recent event intolerable, like the proverbial straw that broke the camel's back. In our experience, two childhood stressors in particular potentially exacerbate an officer's symptoms and complicate recovery: having had a narcissistic, absent, or alcoholic parent and having been a victim of childhood sexual or physical abuse. John Briere stated that "...the most common factor seen in people who have been diagnosed with PTSD is neglect, specifically being neglected as a child by parents or guardians." It is rare to find a person who has been diagnosed with PTSD who has not had at least one other traumatic experience in his or her life (Briere, 2012 personal communication). Lifetime co-occurring psychiatric disorders are found in approximately 80% of people who have been diagnosed with PTSD (Foa, Keane, Friedman, & Cohen, 2009). Research on stress disorders (Briere, 1992; Ford, 1999; Herman, 1992; Yehuda & McFarlane, 1995) validates the impact of childhood trauma on the severity of symptoms following a traumatic incident. We have personally and repeatedly observed how unresolved historical traumas contribute to an officer's current level of distress.

Genetics

Genetic research has found that persons who possess specific variants of two genes, *TPH1* and *TPH2*, are more likely to develop PTSD than those who do not (Goenjian et al., 2012). These genes control the production of serotonin, a neurotransmitter that regulates mood, sleep, and alertness (all of which are disrupted in PTSD). Other biological research on trauma suggests that possessing a genetic variation in the *FKBP5* gene, which involves glucocorticoids, places individuals who have had significant childhood trauma at risk for later development of PTSD by permanently altering their hypothalamic–pituitary–adrenal (HPA) axis sensitivity (Binder et al., 2008). Mercer and colleagues (2012) found that the gene variant *5-HTTLPR* was implicated in differentiating those who develop PTSD symptoms. Our genetic makeup may account for as much as 40% of the variance associated with the development of PTSD (Medina, 2008). This information can be shared with LEOs to help normalize their symptoms and help them to see that there may be factors over which they had no control. Or as we ask colloquially, "What part of this did you get to vote on?"

CORE BELIEFS

As we said earlier, helping cops reveal and discuss early traumatic experiences allows connections to be made with their current reactions (Cunningham, 2003; Keenan & Royle, 2008; McCann & Pearlman, 1990) and gets to the heart of their deeply held, but perhaps unexpressed or unacknowledged, core beliefs about themselves or the world. We get at this by posing the following questions:

1. "Where and when have you felt this way before?" (An officer who complains of pain in his abdomen may have been punched in the gut as a child by an abusive parent.)
2. "As a result of that early experience, what do you believe about yourself?"
   a. "I believe that I . . . "
   b. "I continue to feel like I . . . "
   c. "I am afraid that I . . . "

The second set of questions directs the client away from the past, toward a positive present.

1. "What beliefs, skills, and traits do you possess that would challenge these earlier beliefs?" Figure 5.1 is a good prompt if your client is stuck. The list was created from statements made by first responder clients.
2. "How would your life be different if you were able to reject these old beliefs?"

We spend a lot of time talking to clients about their core beliefs because a traumatic experience is interpreted in the context of a person's preexisting core beliefs. Thus, if the officer's preexisting beliefs are positive (e.g., the world is a safe place), then the officer must reconcile the traumatic event with that positive belief. If the preexisting core beliefs are negative (e.g.,

Skills	Traits	Beliefs
I can accept help and caring from others. I can ask for help when needed. I'm a good communicator. I'm empathic. I give myself permission to show emotion. I'm good with boundaries—able to set limits and create a comfort zone. I'm grounded/centered. I'm honest. I let go of secrets. I'm a good listener. I was able to not just reflect but confront myself. I live with others in tight quarters. I'm nonjudgmental. I use the four P's: perseverance, persistence, positive thinking, problem solving. I resisted the urge to resist change. I took my own advice. I write things down.	I overcome obstacles (like substance abuse). I'm affable, especially with new people. I'm brave. I'm compassionate. I'm curious. I'm decisive. I want to improve. I have faith. I'm forgiving of myself and others. I'm intelligent. I'm kind. I'm logical. I'm nurturing. I'm open-minded. I'm patient. I never give up on myself. I'm protective. I'm reliable. I'm respectful. I'm responsible. I have a sense of humor. I treat people with respect and dignity. I trust. I understand through compassion, sympathy, and tolerance. I'm warm. I'm willing to take risks.	Being here, right now, is where I need to be. I have hope that the process will work. I am able to bounce back. I am not alone. I am not the worst. I can do this. I can learn from my experience. I have made a difference. I'm a good person. I'm a strong person, and it takes strength to ask for help. Knowing my weaknesses makes me stronger. My higher power, God, religion, or spiritual beliefs will carry me through. Other people are there for me and will protect me. People value what I have to say. Sometimes talking can make things better. Things will get better. This too shall pass.

FIGURE 5.1. Skills, traits, and beliefs.

people will always take advantage of you), then the traumatic experience reinforces the negative beliefs about the world. In both cases, the client is stuck with beliefs that can interfere with the recovery process and need to be placed in proper perspective, such as "sometimes the world is unsafe" or "some people will always take advantage."

Another common core belief, used as a recruiting tool and reinforced over and over in the academy, is that an officer's department and/or the officer's coworkers will have her back and protect her when problems occur. How and if departments back their officers in times of trouble is complicated (see Chapter 6). We mention it here because officers frequently feel their departments have let them down in times of crisis, activating previously unresolved abandonment issues. The result is crippling.

THERAPEUTIC INTERVENTIONS

The following two therapeutic interventions are specifically geared toward dealing with trauma. Additional strategies for treating trauma and other psychological conditions are described in Chapter 9.

• Ask your client to complete the List of Stressful Life Events and Critical Incidents form (Figure 5.2). This form asks how stressful the event was when it occurred and how much it is bothering your client now, using the subjective units of distress (SUDS) scale that ranges from 1 to 5. You and your client can then create a treatment plan based on that hierarchy of events. Don't be surprised if officers begin remembering incidents they haven't thought about in years. It may be useful to have your client provide you with a synopsis of particularly stressful events, obtain scores from his or her peritraumatic experience, and compare them to current levels of distress.

• The following exercise was developed by a psychiatrist colleague, Emily Keram, MD. It can be done with a group or an individual in the office or as a homework assignment. Draw three columns and label them "mind," "body," and "spirit/soul," representing the categories of posttraumatic stress symptoms. Ask your clients to call out symptoms they are experiencing and put them into the appropriate columns. Once the first chart is filled, repeat the exercise, this time asking for activities that would address these symptoms. See the examples in Figure 5.3. This exercise demonstrates two crucial points: (1) traumatic stress injuries affect the whole person and (2) recovery requires a multidimensional approach (E. Keram, personal communication, March 9, 2013; Sapolsky, 1998). As indicated, some items will fall into more than one column.

KEY POINTS

• Learn about your client's department and the community where your client works, including any recent LODDs, critical incidents, or scandals. These events will influence how your client handles his or her issues

• We suggest that our clients not read blogs or newspapers or watch TV news after a highly publicized event. They rarely follow our advice.

• Some officers feel exhilarated following a shooting but later feel doubt and guilt for having such feelings. Experiencing great relief at having survived a deadly encounter can and should be normalized by a clinician or a peer.

FIGURE 5.2. List of stressful life events and critical incidents.

If you answer "yes" to any of these incidents, please rate how stressful the incident felt then and how stressful it feels now using the following scale:

1 = not at all   2 = a little   3 = somewhat   4 = very   5 = extremely

Event	Yes	No	Stressfulness level then	Stressfulness level now
1. I have witnessed or experienced a natural disaster like a flood or earthquake.				
2. I have witnessed or experienced an explosion, fire, or other disaster when I thought I would be seriously hurt or was afraid I would be hurt or killed.				
3. I have witnessed, responded to, or experienced a serious accident or injury.				
4. I have witnessed or experienced the death of my spouse, significant other, or child.				
5. I have witnessed or experienced the death of a coworker, close friend, or family member (other than spouse, significant other, or child).				
6. I or a close friend or family member has been kidnapped or taken hostage.				
7. I have been involved in combat or a war.				
8. I have seen or handled dead bodies other than at a funeral.				
9. I have felt responsible for the serious injury or death of another person.				
10. I have witnessed or been in an officer-involved shooting, or been attacked with a weapon (other than in military combat) and thought I would be seriously hurt or killed.				
11. As a child/teen I was hit, spanked, choked, or pushed hard enough to cause injury.				
12. As an adult I was hit, choked, or pushed hard enough to cause injury or was afraid I would be seriously hurt or killed.				

(continued)

FIGURE 5.2. (*continued*)

Event	Yes	No	Stressfulness level then	Stressfulness level now
13. As an adult or child I have witnessed someone else being choked, hit, spanked, or pushed hard enough to cause injury.				
14. As a child/teen (under 17) I was forced to have unwanted sexual contact.				
15. I have witnessed or experienced an event that caused me to be seriously hurt or fear that I might be hurt or killed.				
16. I have felt betrayed by a parent, partner, or organization.				
17. I had to take someone's life.				
18. I have experienced sexual harassment or a hostile work environment.				
19. I have experienced the suicide of a coworker.				
20. I have been involved in a prolonged or failed rescue.				
21. I have seen or handled an incident involving the death or serious injury of a child.				
22. I have been involved in or witnessed an incident of mass casualty.				
23. I have been involved in an incident that was publicized with negative media influence.				
24. I have been involved in an incident where the victim was known to me.				
25. I have experienced an on-duty incident when I believed my safety was in peril.				

- The following is a useful question to ask officers who may be denying the extent of the abuse they suffered in childhood: "If what happened to you as a child occurred on your watch today, what would you do as a police officer?"

- Tragedies involving children often create a crisis in spirituality as officers ask "How could God could let this happen?" If this is your client, consider working in tandem with a police chaplain or the officer's spiritual adviser.

- Officers who were not on scene because they were on vacation or sick leave can suffer from survivor's guilt and magical thinking, imagining that if they were present no one would have been hurt or killed.

- DSM-5 (American Psychiatric Association, 2013) expands the definition of PTSD to include actual or threatened death, serious injury, or sexual violation; being a witness to these events; learning that such events happened to a close relative or friend; and experiencing repeated or extreme exposure to aversive details of these events. Examples given of the latter are responders collecting body parts, or taking repeated child abuse reports. We believe this expanded definition will be helpful to the first responder population.

FIGURE 5.3. Symptoms and solutions.

Ask your clients to call out symptoms they are experiencing and put them into the appropriate columns. Once the chart is filled, repeat the exercise, this time asking for activities that would address these symptoms. Some items belong in more than one column.

Mind	Body	Spirit/soul
Irritable	Headaches	Push family away
Nightmares	Nightmares	Nightmares
Can't concentrate	G.I. problems	Stop going to church
Obsessing over my incident	Sexual problems	Don't enjoy things I used to
Angry all the time	Startle response	Don't answer phone calls

Mind	Body	Spirit/soul
Get counseling	Medication consult	Listen to music
Talk to my family	Sleep hygiene	Get out in nature
Exercise	Exercise	Exercise
Stop watching TV/read more	Go to my MD for a checkup	Spend more time with my kids
Meditate	Cut down on my drinking	Go back to church

6

BETRAYAL

The Hidden Critical Incident

The only time you need a vest is in the station
because that's where they stab you in the back.
—POLICE OFFICER

Hatred is like drinking poison and hoping the other
person dies.
—POLICE CHAPLAIN

It's cheaper to bury a cop than train one; cheaper
still to throw a cop to the wolves than defend one.
—POLICE OFFICER

For cops, organizational stress exceeds line-of-duty stress in
every study we know. The rigors of police work, from the daily grind to
the headline-making incidents, are all made worse when there is no support from the administration, fellow officers, and the community. For some
LEOs, nonsupport feels like betrayal when it connects to old, unresolved
childhood traumas. Officers get mired in a morass of anger or depression,
unable get past the incident that precipitated this storm of emotion. This
chapter speaks to those acts of betrayal, blatant and subtle, and describes
several therapeutic interventions we have found helpful for clients who are
clinging to past betrayals and cannot move ahead. These include forgiving

self and others, cognitive-behavioral therapy (CBT), and managing triggers.

Police officers will tell you that what first attracted them to police work was the allure of family, the promise that no matter what, the police family will back you up. As we asserted earlier, in our experience many officers come from dysfunctional and emotionally detached families. While we never actually say this to our clients, we joke among ourselves that if our clients would tell us up front about their absent, narcissistic, alcoholic fathers we could shorten therapy by several months. The idea of a loyal and loving police family is a point of pride and a part of an officer's identity. Cops expect the bad guys to try to hurt them. When their work family turns on them, in either blatant or subtle ways, three things can happen that will make it difficult for the officer to return to work:

1. The officer loses faith that his or her agency, friends, and community can be counted on for support when the next crisis comes, as it will.
2. Old childhood issues and emotions are reactivated, causing emotional and behavioral problems.
3. The dream of an idealized family is shattered, leaving the officer depressed, angry, and lacking in morale.

THROWN TO THE WOLVES

There are four types of betrayal: administrative, organizational, personal, and community. The following examples, blatant and subtle, are drawn from our case histories and those of our colleagues.

Administrative Betrayal

This kind of betrayal emanates from the LEO's superior officers, especially the chief, and constitutes both "sins" of omission and commission.

> Perry responded to a violent confrontation, during which both he and the suspect were injured. Perry's uniform was covered with blood, hair, and tissue—necessary for forensic evidence. Rather than carefully transporting him back to the station to change, his supervisor ordered Perry to change into a paper jumpsuit that is reserved for transporting arrestees who are covered in their own filth. The supervisor's order showed complete disregard for Perry's self-image and self-respect.

Rick shot and killed a suspect who was walking around his neighborhood randomly shooting at people, including Rick. After the incident, the chief asked Rick to write a letter of apology to the dead suspect's family in hopes the letter would help avoid a lawsuit.

Lynne killed a suspect. She was feeling competent and confident about her actions until the supervisor who was handling the postshooting investigation approached her and said, "Just so you know, from here on out it is nothing personal." Lynne had just risked her life to protect the community and was in essence told, "We don't care about you and if we can get you, we will."

Ted was on disability leave after a work-related injury. He never received a call from his chief or any other administrator until a lieutenant called to ask when Ted was coming back to work because his absence was costing the department too much overtime.

Greg finished first on the promotional exam but was not promoted. When he asked why he had been passed over, the chief told him they needed more diversity. The officer believed he had played by the rules and done everything the department asked.

After a shooting incident during which Frank killed a hostage taker, the chief released his name and photo to the media. Community activists printed posters with Frank's picture on them and the words "sadistic killer" underneath. Frank was unable to leave his home because of the notoriety.

Organizational Betrayal

A variation on administrative betrayal, this type is bureaucratic rather than personal.

Tony was injured on the job and filed a workers' compensation claim. The workers' compensation company had 90 days to accept or reject his claim. At the end of the 90 days they rejected it. Tony asked his agency for help but was told there was nothing anyone could do.

Mick worked for his department for many years. After a lengthy leave stemming from a work-related injury, he ran out of compensable time off and was unable to pay his bills. His department made no effort to help him with his retirement claim, and no one tried to get him on a catastrophic insurance plan. He had no medical insurance for his children and was in danger of losing his home.

A drug cartel discovered Lee's true identity as an undercover officer and put a contract out on his life. He and his family went into hiding. It took months until his agency was able to relocate the family and get him some money. In the interim Lee's family was on welfare, living in a hotel.

Personal Betrayal

This occurs when people within the organization, or in his or her personal life, let an officer down.

Max was injured and unable to work. Only one or two people he considered friends called to check on him. No one offered to help with the tasks he needed done around his house.

Bryan was confronted by a man with a gun. As his partner moved to take a protected position, Bryan was shot by the suspect. The partner believed he had used proper officer safety procedure. Bryan felt he had abandoned his post.

Petra discovered that her husband and her partner were having an affair.

Michael came home covered with bruises following a fight with three suspects. His wife didn't have time to talk or examine his injuries because she was on her way to the gym and didn't want to miss her workout.

Community Betrayal

This occurs when the community turns against the agency or the officer.

Grant shot and killed a man who attacked him with a baseball bat without provocation or warning. He was criticized by the local chapter of the NAACP, who called him a racist even though he is African American and a member of the National Organization of Black Law Enforcement (NOBLE). Other members of the community called him an "Uncle Tom."

HOW CHILDHOOD INJURIES COMPLICATE THE EXPERIENCE OF BETRAYAL

Betrayal of any sort complicates traumatic reactions by creating huge doubts about the future. How can officers return to work knowing that the agency, their friends, or the community may not support them in a future crisis? When the betrayal mirrors the officer's childhood abandonment, neglect, or abuse, the emotions it brings forth are especially powerful.

John grew up in an abusive, sometimes violent home. As the oldest child he developed a belief that it was his role to protect his younger sisters. His attempts at protection often failed and he felt defeated. As he grew older and stronger, John took on his father in a violent confrontation after which neither he nor his sisters were ever abused again.

As a young man John excelled at sports, where he could establish control and be aggressive. He went on to play sports in college and eventually put himself through a police academy. Upon graduation, he was warmly greeted by his new agency. Over and over he heard the words "Welcome to our police family." Finally, John had found what he was looking for, a family he could trust, a family that wouldn't let him down. Right from the start, he excelled at police work. His aggressive nature and his desire to win were assets. Field training officers and supervisors complimented his work ethic and productivity.

One day John responded to a call by a suicidal teenager. John spoke with the young man, who convinced him that the call was a prank and that he was not suicidal. Minutes after John left for another call, the teenager killed himself. John didn't find out about the suicide until he returned to work the following day and a coworker greeted him in the locker room, saying, "Good job on that call. I guess you convinced the kid to off himself."

John was devastated but couldn't show his emotions. He covered his shock with humor, making jokes about "resolving the case" and "making sure no one gets repeat calls from that house." Soon after, he started having nightmares and panic attacks. He began drinking, hoping alcohol would help him sleep. He heard the teenager's voice in his sleep and believed the boy was calling to him because he had failed to save him.

At work John was withdrawn and terrified of making another "mistake" that might cause the death of a citizen, or worse, a fellow officer. He received a complaint for being too aggressive on a mental health call, and his supervisor gave him a written warning about his behavior. The family that promised to be there for him didn't recognize his distress and, consequently, didn't offer any help. He finally sought therapy after his wife told him that if he didn't get help she would leave.

In therapy John talked about how he had "killed" the teenager and admitted to being suicidal himself. He had a plan but no current intent, because he couldn't bear to harm his children. It took several meetings before his therapist was able to develop sufficient rapport and explore John's childhood history. Together they unearthed the terrible burden John carried protecting his sisters, and how this connected to the shame and failure he felt for not preventing the teenager from killing himself. They identified John's feeling of helplessness to control things as an echo of the helplessness he felt as a child.

Clinically, this is a complicated situation. It involved John's forgiving others and forgiving himself. It forced him to face his own fallibility and vulnerability. While John felt betrayed by the teenager for lying to him, he also believed that he betrayed the teenager by not recognizing his suicidal ideation and stopping him from killing himself. He struggled with feeling that, once again, it was his responsibility to protect children, and that he had failed.

TREATING BETRAYAL

There are two important steps in treating betrayal. The first is acknowledging the betrayal with the goal of gradually moving the responder toward forgiveness. The second is helping the officer see the connection between the current event and his or her personal history, which is what makes the feeling of betrayal so powerful.

Moving toward Forgiveness

Much has been written about forgiveness over the centuries, but it was Fred Luskin of Stanford University (Luskin, 2002) who found a way to bring the concept into the popular culture. While the concept may seem simple, engaging cops in a discussion of forgiveness can be difficult. Most responders reject the concept and prefer to see issues in black and white. They say things like: "If I forgive him that would mean what he did was right" and "How can I forgive him for what he did?"

The term "letting go of a grudge" is a far more acceptable concept to law enforcement personnel than "forgiveness." We understand that police officers don't like to think of themselves as victims. In working with cops, we point out the paradox that allowing someone else to determine how you feel about your life and yourself is the trait of a victim. Forgiving someone for an act of betrayal doesn't condone the act but states that you choose to take back your power. The person may have ruined your past, but you can refuse to give them the power to ruin one more day.

Many years ago Smitty's good friend and fellow officer was shot and killed. Smitty was so angry that he put the suspect's picture on his refrigerator, so he could wake up and see him every day. He was so focused on hating the suspect that one day he woke up and could not remember what his friend looked like. When he told us this story, he was sobbing.

Several studies support the benefits of forgiveness. Harris and colleagues (2006) conducted a randomized study using a 6-week forgiveness intervention model that significantly reduced negative thoughts and increased positive ones. Lawler and colleagues (2005) found that having a forgiving personality significantly reduced tension, anger, depression, and stress, leading to better health, fewer somatic complaints, reduced medication use, increased sleep quality, and less fatigue. Everett, Worthington, Van Oyen Witvliet, Pietrini, and Miller (2008) also found a connection between sleep quality and forgiveness.

Enright (1996) developed the concept of a forgiveness triad: forgiving others, receiving forgiveness from others, and self-forgiveness. Once clients learned the forgiveness model, he found they could generalize it to new events. We begin our work with clients in a similar fashion, starting with an educational discussion of forgiveness followed by the concept of the "unenforceable rule" (Luskin, 2007).

An unenforceable rule is a rule for the behavior of others that cannot possibly be enforced such as wives should be faithful, parents shouldn't hurt their children, people shouldn't steal, and so on. The same holds true for creating unenforceable rules for oneself: I must be perfect, I can't make mistakes. We go on to explain to clients that trying to enforce something over which you have no control often leads to despair, frustration, bitterness, and helplessness.

When our clients understand the concept of the unenforceable rule we help them identify the specific rules that are currently causing problems in their lives and the lives of people who love and care about them. The following questions provide a good framework to focus the conversation:

- "What is your unenforceable rule?"
- "How have your efforts to enforce this rule affected your life?"
- "How have your efforts to enforce this rule affected other people?"
- "How much of your life has been consumed by the rule?"
- "How much time do you want to devote to it?"

Once these questions are resolved, we move toward challenging the client's rules and predicting improved outcomes by asking the officer to complete the following two statements:

- "Accepting that I will not get what I want allows me to . . . "
- "Accepting that I will not get what I want will allow the people I care about to . . . "

Remember John, the officer who failed to prevent the teenage boy from killing himself? Here's how John answered questions about unenforceable rules:

- "What is your unenforceable rule?"
  - *"I should be able to keep children from killing themselves."*

- "How have your efforts to enforce this rule affected your life?"
  - *"I can't sleep, I live in dread of another call, and I hate work."*

- "How have your efforts to enforce this rule affected other people?"
  - *"My wife is angry with me, and my kids seem afraid to be around me."*

- "How much of your life has been consumed by the rule?"
  - *"All of it."*

- "How much time do you want to devote to it?"
  - *"I am not sure."*

- "What happens if you challenge the rule?"
  - *"Accepting that I will not get what I want allows me to let go of the teenager."*

- What do you think would happen if you were able to let go of the situation?
  - *"Accepting that I will not get what I want will allow the people I care about to connect with me again."*

Connecting the Event to Personal History

To engage an officer in conversation about early childhood issues, it is critical first to review the facts, as well as the officer's reaction to the critical incident and his or her thoughts and beliefs about it. While family-of-origin issues may seem obvious to you, and you may have a strong desire to pursue those dynamics, we advise you to hold back. Going for those connections before you develop a deep understanding of the presenting incident will cause an officer to withdraw.

Many responders find it hard to understand how growing up in an abusive or otherwise dysfunctional home may have some connection to the way they are reacting to current incidents. When we suggest a possible connection, what we most often hear is "I dealt with that already." Cops have a stereotypical view that all we "shrinks" want to know about is their potty training. There is some truth to this stereotype because we know that many issues can be traced back to early developmental experiences. But if you want an officer to consider the possibility that his or her current reactions are related to the distant past, you must be patient and wait until you have established a strong relationship and demonstrated a thorough understanding of the event. For example, at our 6-day trauma retreat for first responders, we do not formally bring up family issues until the 5th day. By that time, officers are ready to make the connection.

Once you have established a therapeutic connection, the next step is to obtain a family-of-origin history. There are a couple of issues and strategies that we have found helpful. As we said earlier, cops do better in therapy when the therapy is interactive and directive. We direct our history taking by asking officers to finish the following statements, which ultimately form the basis for additional illuminating conversations.[1]

- "When I was growing up I knew . . . "
- "When I was growing up I could never . . . "
- "I learned early on that . . . "
- "The primary unspoken rule on my family was . . . "

Here's how John finished those statements:

- "When I was growing up I knew if I didn't protect my sisters no one would."
- "When I was growing up I could never express my feelings."
- "I learned early on that some people never take responsibility for their actions."
- "The primary unspoken rule in my family was 'you are on your own.' "

One of the ways John's therapist helped him make a connection between his current incident and his childhood was by asking him to identify the worst moment of the call. John said it was when he was told that the teenager had killed himself. When asked what negative belief he had about himself as a result of the call, he replied, "I failed again." When his

---

[1]Therapists trained in eye movement desensitization and reprocessing (EMDR) will recognize some of these questions as part of the EMDR protocol.

therapist asked about other times that he had felt like a failure, John was able to see the connection to his earlier history.

While John's therapist guided him along, John made this connection for himself. The therapist did not offer an interpretation. This is the kind of collaborative work we believe is best suited to treating first responders, because information gathering and teamwork are second nature to them.

KEY POINTS

- When dealing with administrative betrayal, be wary of either advocating for the officer or siding with the administration. We have, on occasion, advocated for officers, but it is a political minefield. In some instances we were labeled as "cop lovers," and the agency looked for another clinician.

- Understand that cops and their administrators are often at odds. Administrators take a long-term view of the organization's health, and line-level officers are more interested in the welfare and immediate concerns of individuals.

- Police chiefs report to many masters: the city manager, the board of supervisors, and the local community. A police officer reports up the chain of command.

- We generally empathize with officers' feelings of betrayal and do not explore the officer's potential contribution to the situation until and unless we have a firm alliance and a lot of trust.

7

SHIFT WORK
AND SLEEP DEPRIVATION

> I sleep with my wife, but I live with my partner.
> —POLICE OFFICER

Shift work is a given of law enforcement (see Chapter 15 for other givens). It won't change, not until society decides it no longer needs police officers on the job 24/7. Shift work, while not unique to law enforcement, exerts a major influence on individual officers and their family life. Families need to adjust to spending holidays alone, to celebrating birthdays the day before or the day after, to making up for missed recitals and ball games, and to keeping children quiet while one parent sleeps during the day. Lovers sleep alone and have to schedule time for intimacy. When each partner works different hours or different shifts, making time to be together is a major challenge. Some shifts give parents more time with children, but less time with spouses, than people who work a traditional 9-to-5 job. Shift work affects sleep. The rigors of adjusting to various shifts or to rapidly changing shifts can affect an officer's alcohol intake, cognitive abilities, and mood. Sleepy cops have accidents, make poor decisions, and are grumpy at home. Some studies associate shift work with a higher incidence of cardiovascular, gastrointestinal and metabolic disease, chronic insomnia, sleep apnea, depression, and even suicidal ideation (Violanti et al., 2008).

Given that we know this, why isn't the problem fixed? Because society expects that law enforcement, not parents or communities, is entirely responsible for stopping crime. Sometimes police officers accept this mandate, proclaiming that they alone hold back chaos and societal decay. This mindset can lead to self-inflation and unrealistic expectations of their abilities to fend off fatigue. Police declare that unlike most other occupations, law enforcement is not a 9 to 5 job. They are right. Trouble comes at all hours, and bad guys tend to work under cover of darkness. Police managers who ignore the potential costs created by a tired, sleep-deprived officer do so at their own peril. It may be cheaper to pay an officer 1½ times his or her salary for overtime than to hire a new officer, but it's only a matter of time before there is a costly mistake.

Community therapists are in a good position to spot problems related to shift work and sleep deprivation. You can help officers and their families cope with shift work and improve sleep hygiene. Once you are familiar with the subject, teaching sleep hygiene is a useful workshop to offer to your local police department (see Chapter 20), although it is not recommended as a stand-alone intervention (Loomis, 2011).

THE THREE SHIFTS

While there is variety from department to department, generally speaking, there are three shifts for officers working in the patrol division (sometimes called the field services division): day shift (dawn to mid-afternoon); swing shift (mid-afternoon to late night); and midnights or dogwatch (midnight to morning). Frequent switching ("rotation") from a day to a night schedule is the most difficult for the body to accommodate, especially when that rotation goes counterclockwise, midnights to swings to days. People who work rotating schedules never get used to any one schedule and tend to have more complaints than other workers about their physical health and psychological well-being. Administrators and other nonuniformed, nonpatrol personnel generally work during the day. Investigators' (or detectives') schedules tend to conform to the needs of the cases they are following.

Shift lengths vary considerably. The three most common work schedules are 8 hours a day, 5 days a week; 10 hours a day, 4 days a week; and 12 hours a day, 3 days a week. The longer the shift, the greater the risk for fatigue-related problems, especially for LEOs working double shifts. Experts in the field recommend a 10-hour shift as the best option for patrol officers (Amendola et al., 2011; Vila, 2009). Some departments have rotating days off, and others have fixed days off. In a crisis, all shifts are changeable and extendable at a moment's notice. Crises, mandatory overtime, filling in for an injured coworker, off-duty court appearances (frequently involving hours of waiting and never being called to testify), arrests made late in the shift, and protracted investigations often wreak havoc with an officer's schedule, his or her sleep habits, and planned family activities.

Shifts are assigned according to seniority or department need. Some agencies allow officers to bid for their shifts. How long an officer stays on one shift depends on department policy. Some departments have mandatory shift rotation, others do not. Officers tend to have preferences for different shifts. Some prefer to work nights because there is more criminal activity, commute traffic is at a minimum, they get nighttime differential pay, and the "brass" isn't usually around. Others like working days because they have child care responsibilities or are enrolled in school.

Financial need or want may be a factor in voluntary overtime and moonlighting—working a second job. Officers can become dependent on overtime. With overtime, many officers make salaries equivalent to or surpassing those of physicians. At some point early on in your assessment, be sure to ask about your client's financial health and how money is managed. Is the officer working so much overtime to support the family that he or she rarely gets to spend quality time with them?

SLEEP DEPRIVATION

Human beings are meant to work during the day and sleep at night. Our internal clocks cycle around approximately every 24 hours, and we work best when we have regular routines and adequate exposure to daylight, something night workers rarely get. The sleep we get during the day is often shorter and less restorative than sleeping during the night. Our brain and body functions slow down at night and during the early-morning hours. Loss of good sleep combined with working when the body is at its low point can lead to fatigue, sleepiness, poor job performance, and increased risk for mistakes and accidents. This holds true for day-shift officers as well, who may sacrifice sleep in order to get to work on time (especially officers with long commutes).

Because nighttime officers are separated from the normal schedules their families and friends keep, they may try to stay up on their days off. This is not an easy task. The attempt to stay awake during the day results in even more sleep deprivation. It is difficult, if not impossible, to bank sleep in advance; what's lost apparently stays lost.

In a study of 2,566 American and Canadian police officers (Rajaratnam et al., 2011), more than half reported that they got less than 6.5 hours of sleep daily, compared to 30% of the population. More than 90 percent of the respondents reported being routinely fatigued, 85% reported driving while drowsy, and 39% reported falling asleep at the wheel. A study of nearly 5,000 North American police officers found that 40% screened positive for at least one sleep disorder, and 33% screened positive for obstructive sleep apnea. In addition, 26% reported falling asleep while driving at least once a month. Respondents with sleep apnea or other sleep disorders reported more physical and mental health conditions. A 2-year follow-up comparing respondents who screened positive for a sleep disorder with those who did not found that the subjects with sleep disorders reported higher rates of errors, safety violations, and other adverse work-related outcomes, including uncontrolled anger toward suspects.

Sleep deprivation is dangerous. When people who lack sleep are tested on a driving simulator, they perform as badly as those who are drunk. Being awake for 19 hours produces impairments comparable to having a blood alcohol concentration of .05%. Being awake for 24 hours is comparable to having a blood alcohol concentration of roughly 0.1%. This is a remarkable finding, given that in all 50 states and the District of Columbia, it is a crime to drive with a blood alcohol concentration of .08% or above. An officer who has worked a 10-hour shift, then goes to court, picks up her kids from the babysitter's house, and drives home to catch a couple of hours of sleep before going back to work, may, after 1 week, be just as impaired driving her patrol car as the last person she arrested for driving under the influence.

More police officers die on the job as a result of accidents than as a result of criminal assaults. Research shows that the risk for accidents increases after a person has been on duty 9 or more hours and keeps on increasing with each additional hour of work. Accidents are almost three times more likely to occur during a night shift than during the day (Vila, 2000).

It's astonishing that societal norms that restrict the work hours of truck drivers, pilots, and nuclear power plant operators in order to avoid fatigue-related accidents and injuries do not apply to police officers—despite the fact that police officers are armed, drive cars that weigh two tons, go from boredom to emotionally and physically challenging crises in a matter of seconds, and are responsible for making decisions with critical, sometimes life-and-death, consequences for themselves and for the citizenry. Short-term sleep loss is associated with the kind of on-duty events that most frequently kill or injure officers. Fatigue almost certainly interferes with rational thinking, attentiveness, and the ability to make sound judgments while simultaneously increasing irritability, anxiety, and stress levels—all of which raises the likelihood that an officer will make poor decisions in the field and at home.

SHIFT WORK AND THE FAMILY

Lucy longed for her husband to have more normal hours. Brad had no seniority, plus he liked working midnights because he enjoyed the excitement and felt he was learning more about police work than he would on the day shift, when most of his duties involved traffic enforcement and trivial complaints. They argued about it frequently. Lucy was lonely and frightened being home alone at night with total responsibility for their young children. She didn't like going to social events alone and thought her friends and family felt sorry for her. Most of all she hated having to keep their young children quiet in their small apartment during the day while Brad tried to sleep. Some days Lucy's only option was to take the kids out and fill the time until Brad woke up. She looked forward to Brad's days off and was often disappointed that he was still tired, grumpy, and uninterested in going out. Their sex life had dwindled to almost never. Brad, on the other hand, complained that Lucy hit him with problems the minute he woke up. He resented the fact that Lucy didn't understand how much he missed kissing his kids good night and reading them bedtime stories. He had occasional bursts of activity on midnights, but he wished she understood that many of his shifts were long, cold, and boring. He hated coming back to a dark apartment and began stopping for a beer with his shift mates before driving home in the morning.

Managing shifts and sleep deprivation is a family affair (see Chapter 16). Everyone in the family is affected in unique ways. Strategizing with a client and not including the family is counterproductive and likely to increase conflict. Sleep management is not just about physiology, it's about getting everyone's needs met, and about helping family members stay connected and healthy. There are many straightforward ways to improve your client's sleep hygiene, some of which may require further sacrifice or imposition on the family. This is why it is crucial to involve the family. One way to do this is to use problem solving, an approach that works well with LEOs—because it fixes the problem, not the blame. There is no point in arguing about something that won't change (Kirschman, 2007).

Coping with shift work, unpredictable schedules, and long hours is a challenge to which many families adapt. The following suggestions have been collected from veteran families who have been our clients and colleagues.

- Minimize fear and maximize safety. No one should be fearful about being home alone at night. Secure your house with alarms, motion-detector lights, and working locks. Consider getting a dog.
- Avoid isolation. Police families need their own support systems. Encourage your clients' non-law-enforcement spouses to get together with other LEO families on the same shift to share child care and to celebrate special occasions and holidays. Recommend starting a phone tree, a list serve, or an online chat room that functions 24/7.

- Stay positive. Shift work doesn't last forever. Think of ways shift work is an advantage.
- Use alone time to develop hobbies and interests apart from your spouse or intimate partner.
- Use a calendar to make dates with your spouse or intimate partner.
- Manage money wisely to avoid working a second job or voluntary overtime.
- Be self-sufficient. Learn how to deal with emergencies and basic home repairs.
- Be tech savvy. Use cell phones and other devices to stay in touch.
- Consider shift work an opportunity to creatively use the time you have.

SELF-MEDICATION

It's a paradox that cops who are resistant to taking medication (see Chapter 10) have little concern about using so-called energy drinks to stay awake. The first thing to ask an officer who is experiencing sleep problems is how much caffeine he or she consumes in a day. (This is also an important question for an officer diagnosed with anxiety, because the symptoms can be similar to those of taking excessive caffeine.) Caffeine is a stimulant that can be effectively used to help maintain alertness for a period of 3 to 5 hours, longer in some sensitive people. Drinking two to three cups of coffee or other caffeinated beverage during the first half of a night shift can counter drowsiness. Drinking caffeinated drinks during the last half of the shift will interfere with an officer's ability to fall asleep at home. Caffeine has a long half-life, about 6–8 hours for males, longer for females, which can be potentiated by prescribed and over-the-counter medications. The dose of caffeine needed to improve alertness is approximately 250 mg (two cups of average-strength brewed coffee). Higher doses are not more beneficial and can increase side effects. The relative strength of various caffeinated products is as follows:

- Monster Energy (24 oz) – 240 mg
- Maximum Strength No-Doz – 200 mg
- Brewed coffee – 135 mg
- Instant coffee – 100 mg
- Espresso (2 oz) – 100 mg
- Red Bull (8.2 oz) – 80 mg
- Mountain Dew – 55 mg
- Brewed tea – 50 mg
- Coke Classic – 35 mg

It is not uncommon for cops to use caffeine and over-the-counter stimulants to stay alert and then drink alcohol to fall asleep. This mix can be injurious to the officer's health, quality of sleep, and relationships (see Chapter 11).

WHAT IS SLEEP?

There are five phases of sleep:

- Phase 1: falling asleep.
- Phase 2: brain slowdown.
- Phase 3 and 4: deep restorative sleep.
- Phase 5: rapid eye movement (REM) sleep.

Dreaming can occur during any sleep phase. We randomly cycle among these stages approximately every 100 minutes. Alcohol has a paradoxical effect on sleep; it knocks you out quickly but then it wakes you up, robbing you of the deep, restorative sleep needed to feel refreshed and alert. Rather than using self-medication, steer your client toward more effective means to get good sleep. CBT for insomnia has been shown to be as effective as pharmacotherapy for treatment of sleep disorders (Loomis, 2011). In 2006, the American Academy of Sleep Medicine gave CBT their highest rating as an intervention.

While the research is inconclusive, there are two other approaches to getting better sleep and promoting wakefulness. Some sleep experts suggest that melatonin, a hormone naturally produced by the body and available as an over-the-counter supplement, helps promote sleep. Since light provides the cues that tell our bodies when to sleep, some nighttime shift workers may profit from bright-light therapy that is used to treat seasonal affective disorder. Exposure to the light mechanism must be properly timed (the recommended length of exposure is 30–90 minutes) and carried out consistently in accordance with the sleeper's circadian clock. Once it has been reset, the sleeper is advised to maintain a fixed sleep schedule even on weekends and vacations. Workers returning home from the night shift are advised to wear dark glasses to avoid morning sunlight. (Go to the Resources for information about where to go to learn more about these therapies.)

SLEEP HYGIENE

How much sleep does a person need? Most of us require 8 to 10 hours of sleep, although there are variations between people depending on age, gender, and health. Some people are night owls and do their best work in the evening. Others are early birds, alert and ready to go at dawn. The important question is, does your client get enough sleep to feel rested and function effectively? Some people find it helpful to use a sleep debt calculator to determine if they are sleep deficient. (See the Resources for references to free sleepiness scales and a free sleep debt calculator.) Some cops claim that they can get by on 4 hours of sleep. This is not possible over the long haul. We will question what is keeping them from sleeping longer and ask them to define what they mean by "getting by." We then ask what the LEO's loved ones or coworkers would say if asked how well the officer is functioning on 4 hours of sleep. The answer we get is closer to the truth.

Sleep hygiene is related to overall health. The first order of business in assessing a sleep-deprived client is her overall fitness. Does she smoke? Does she drink and how much? Does she get enough exercise? Is she at a healthy weight? Does she eat properly? Working cops rarely have time to enjoy a relaxed, nutritious meal on duty. Instead, they patronize fast-food restaurants and vending machines, eating in a hurry in anticipation of, or response to, being dispatched to the field.

Routine is an important factor in getting good sleep. It helps to go to sleep at the same time, in the same place, as often as possible, which can be difficult for cops who catch a call late in their shift or are held over for a variety of reasons. When necessary, clients should make every effort to improve their sleep environments. Their bedrooms should be dark, quiet, cool, and pleasant places dedicated to sleep and sex. They need to work or watch TV in another room and avoid getting in the habit of falling asleep on the sofa. Television tends to stimulate the brain (although, for some people, the noise interferes with anxious thoughts). Day sleepers should consider investing in room-darkening curtains, white noise machines, ear-plugs, and eye masks.

A 20-minute power nap has been shown to improve performance, elevate mood, and increase creativity. Some departments are allowing their midnight shift officers to nap on duty and be deployed as needed, like fire fighters. Naps longer than 30 minutes can cause grogginess and slow an officer's ability to regain a safe level of alertness. Some experts recommend trying to get a catnap before going on shift. Resting in a comfortable position for 20 to 30 minutes with closed eyes can be beneficial, although the only definite solution for fatigue is sleep (Vila, 2009).

Exercise is an essential component of good health as well as a necessary part of almost every police officer's ability to do the job safely. However, exercise before sleeping energizes rather than enervates, and can interfere with a person's ability to fall asleep. A heavy meal before sleep also is not a good idea. It's far better to eat a light snack like toast or cereal.

KEY POINTS

- Sleep deprivation has many causes. In your initial assessment of your client's sleep issues, be sure to ask about nightmares and other symptoms of PTSD.

- If your client is frequently tired, drowsy, snores (ask his or her partner), or has a large build, consider the possibility of sleep apnea and refer your client to a sleep specialist for assessment. Police officers are estimated to have 44% more obstructive sleep apnea than the general public (Vila, 2009).

- Identify sleep specialists in your area. Insomnia rarely resolves using traditional psychotherapy. A sleep study, often done in a laboratory setting, can identify any organic or functional problems associated with sleep disorders.

- It is rare for sleep hygiene to be taught in police academies or advanced officer training. Don't assume clients know anything about shift work or sleep deprivation. Officers may not realize that shift work is affecting their performance, their moods, or their family life.

- Use problem solving and education in treating sleep deprivation and shift work. Have handouts available on sleep hygiene, imagery and relaxation exercises, and self-assessment tools.

- If all else fails, advise a sleepless client to get out of bed and do some boring task in a low-light situation rather than toss and turn while staring at the clock.

- Whenever possible include the family in discussions or training about shift work.

Part III

TREATMENT TACTICS

Part III is, as our clients like to say, where the rubber meets the road. Our primary, but not exclusive, focus in this section is the assessment and treatment of posttraumatic stress injuries including therapy and medication. (See Part IV for other common presenting problems.) As we said earlier, we use the term *injuries* rather than *PTSD* because being diagnosed with a disorder sounds like a life sentence to a cop, whereas being injured implies the possibility of recovery. We recognize that no one clinician will be proficient in all these strategies. As you read ahead, consider your current practice. Do you feel confident that the modalities you now use will work well with traumatized cops? Are there additional strategies that might enhance what you already can offer to this special population?

8

READING YOUR CLIENT

Assessment Strategies

I used to feel like a freak in a sideshow.
It's good to know I'm just a face in the crowd.
—POLICE OFFICER

Cops are suspicious of psychometrics, perhaps remember-
ing the endless battery of tests they had to complete in their preemployment psychological evaluations. Testing is a tool they associate with their
employers and with fitness-for-duty (FFD) evaluations. FFD evaluations
are generated by behavioral problems on the job and almost always feel
punitive to the officer. In 2003, over 90% of law enforcement agencies used
assessment tools, and that percentage is likely even higher now (Cochrane,
Tett, & Vandecreek, 2003).

This chapter introduces the reader to some specific assessment tools
we find helpful. (Tools for assessing substance abuse and alcoholism can
be found in Chapter 11.) Our presumption is that most broadband testing, such as the Minnesota Multiphasic Personality Inventory (MMPI), is
beyond the expertise of the community clinician, who will need to refer
complex diagnostic cases to a qualified psychologist.

INTRODUCTION TO ASSESSMENT

Most LEOs have undergone extensive preemployment psychological screening and have been found to be psychologically healthy at the start of their careers (Brewster, Wickline, & Stoloff, 2010; see also Chapter 4). Officers will generally resist seeking mental health services. By the time an LEO seeks counseling he is likely to have been exposed to significant stress, both on the job and off and has been suffering for a long time. He and his family may even feel they are near a breaking point.

Formulating your initial diagnostic impression of a police officer is substantively no different than with any other client, with one caveat. In many cases, officers will first present with a culturally appropriate problem, such as critical incident trauma, when in fact they have serious underlying issues like depression, suicidality, substance abuse, relationship conflicts, and so on. In other instances, the issue underlying a variety of symptoms, like chronic pain or insomnia, is actually one or more untreated traumatic incidents or significant cumulative stress. As you identify and address comorbid conditions such as substance abuse or health issues (diabetes, obesity, hypertension), you will need to refer to appropriate health care providers. As we said earlier, trauma, in particular, is a whole-person injury that requires collaborative and comprehensive interdisciplinary teamwork to optimize recovery.

INTRODUCING ASSESSMENT TO YOUR CLIENT

Cops use codes for everything and understand the need for codes. We have found it useful to describe the *Diagnostic and Statistical Manual of Mental Disorders* (DSM) as the vehicle code of mental health. Cops get the analogy and appreciate the joke. Because they are professional problem solvers, when you frame assessment as a way to identify and measure problems to be solved by you and your client together, you reduce anxiety, minimize resistance, and maximize your working relationship. What you are sharing is information that can be used to demystify diagnostic categories and psychological concepts. Cops don't like mystery. Mystery equals danger, while information equals safety. With rare exceptions, only TV cops break down doors by themselves without knowing what or who is on the other side.

Help your client to think of assessment as a therapeutic "ops [operations] plan" that identifies current symptoms, shapes the treatment strategy, and establishes goals. Most cops like sports. They understand that it is impossible to make a touchdown until you and they know where the goal lines are. When officers understand that assessment can work for them, not against them, and is confidential, some are actually more apt to self-disclose by putting pen to paper than when they are being interviewed (Ghahramanlou-Holloway, Cox, Fritz, & George, 2011).

Before we begin the discussion of specific assessment instruments, we need to state loudly and clearly that you must establish a therapeutic alliance with your client before you begin testing or ask for releases of information. If you don't, you'll never see that officer again. Educate your client before doing any formal assessment. For example, if you plan to assess for trauma, first teach your client about trauma. You not only provide new information, but you also provide hope. The kinds of teaching points to cover would include: the fact that symptoms commonly occur in all people who experience trauma and most will abate over time; retelling the critical incident in detail, without interruption or interrogation, promotes healing (Foa, Keane, & Friedman, 2000); and progress occurs when triggers (sights, smells, places, tactile sensations, and so on) once associated with the incident no longer produce distress (Horowitz, 2011).

ASSESSMENT SCALES

In the universe of assessment instruments there are several tests that we think work well with our client population. Most of these are symptom specific, rather than broadband instruments that measure multiple aspects of personality or functioning. The last instrument we describe measures posttraumatic growth and includes some of our thoughts about this phenomenon. It is beyond the scope of this chapter to do more than provide the reader with a brief summary of each. We urge readers to seek training in administration and interpretation of any psychological scale before using it with clients.

Symptom Check List—Revised

The Symptom Check List (SCL-90-R; Derogatis, 1994) contains 90 questions using a 5-point scale and requires about 20 minutes to complete. It measures nine dimensions: somatization, obsessive–compulsive, interpersonal sensitivity, depression, anxiety, hostility, phobic anxiety, paranoid ideation, and psychoticism. The psychoticism dimension includes symptoms of withdrawal, isolation, sexual concerns, guilt, and alienation. Officers may admit to several of these symptoms and can score in the clinically significant range, but this should not be interpreted to mean that the officer is psychotic. That would be extremely unusual. Rather, these symptoms are probably indicative of posttraumatic stress injury and require further inquiry. Cops who are hypervigilant can also score high on the paranoia dimension because they are cynical (Gilmartin, 2002) or have had threats made against them and their family. Other items on the SCL-90-R assess for eating disorders, insomnia, feelings of guilt, and thoughts of death or dying. Further assessment is needed if your client endorses these critical items. Three global indices indicate the severity of the endorsed symptoms. After considering the dimensions and indices, you may want to administer or refer for additional tests that focus on particular diagnostic categories.

Beck Scales

The Beck Scales focus on affective disorders and can further identify clients with depressive, anxious, or suicidal tendencies. The Beck Anxiety Inventory (BAI; Beck, 1993) contains 21 questions using a 4-point scale: It assesses the client's physiological and cognitive anxiety describing subjective, somatic, and panic-related symptoms. The Beck Depression Inventory—2nd edition (BDI-II; Beck, Steer, & Brown, 1996) contains 21 questions in a multiple-choice format. It also provides information regarding suicidal ideation and can indicate whether further suicidal assessment need be done. The Beck Hopelessness Scale (BHS; Beck, 1998) contains 20 true–false statements that are designed to assess pessimism about the future and resignation, two factors that have been correlated with suicide attempts (Beck, Brown, & Steer, 1997). Patients who scored 9 or higher were 11 times more likely to commit suicide than patients who scored 8 or lower (Beck, 1998), alerting the therapist to conduct a more thorough suicide assessment (Dahlsgaard, Beck, & Brown, 1998). The Beck Scale for Suicide Ideation (BSS; Beck & Steer, 1993) is a 21-item self-report instrument for detecting and measuring the intensity of the client's suicidal ideation, behaviors, and plans during the previous week.

These self-report inventories can be administered weekly. We frequently ask clients to complete the BDI and BAI in the waiting room so that the information is available during the psychotherapy session. Remember, cops like evidence. Tracking these scores over time and presenting them in graph form is a way to demystify treatment and present concrete evidence of your client's progress or lack of progress. This should, of course, be matched to your client's felt experience.

Detailed Assessment of Posttraumatic Stress

The Detailed Assessment of Posttraumatic Stress (DAPS; Briere, 2001) contains 104 questions regarding different types of traumatic events. Part One asks the client to pick one indexed incident that is particularly upsetting and then to answer symptom-related questions. The DAPS provides information about peritraumatic (at the time of the event) distress and dissociation for the indexed incident. Three scales pertain to the three domains of PTSD listed in DSM-IV: Criterion B—Reexperiencing; Criterion C—Avoidance; and Criterion D—Hyperarousal (American Psychiatric Association, 1994). Additional indices include the following: total PTSD score; dissociation and whether it is typically used as a defense; impairment in connection to work, friends, and family; substance abuse; and suicidality. The DAPS may be administered monthly, and interpretive reports are available. Scores on the interpretive report will reflect previous testing and prepare a graphic representation of the client's status over time.

There are a few things to be aware of when using the DAPS. Officers who have been involved in multiple incidents will not know which event caused which symptom. The dichotomous format also does not provide information about how many different events fell into each category. For example, officers involved in multiple shootings would not be differentiated from officers who had been involved in a single shooting. Take note of this. Be sure to get a complete work history. In our experience officers with repeated incidents may blame the most recent event for their troubles when, in fact, that incident may have only been the tipping point.

Multiscale Dissociation Inventory

The Multiscale Dissociation Inventory (MDI; Briere, 2002) contains 30 questions and uses a 5-point scale. It is useful for differentiating disengagement, depersonalization, derealization, emotional constriction, memory disturbance, and identity dissociation (previously known as multiple personality disorder). Dissociation is a common defense that is used when a person is faced with trauma and may occur during therapy sessions. This test is now in the public domain and may be accessed by contacting John Briere at *jbriere@usc.edu.*

Trauma Symptom Inventory–II

The Trauma Symptom Inventory–II (TSI-2; Briere, 2011) contains 136 questions to assess PTSD and related disorders. It contains two validity scales, four factors, 12 clinical scales, and 10 clinical subscales. The four factors are self-disturbance (insecure attachment, impaired self-reference, and depression); trauma; externalization (anger, tension reduction, sexual disturbance, and suicidality); and somatization (preoccupation with bodily concerns, physical disease, physical dysfunction, or pain). Clinical scales/subscales include anxious arousal, depression, anger, intrusive experiences, defensive avoidance, dissociation, somatic preoccupation, sexual disturbance, insecure attachment, impaired self-reference, and tension reduction behaviors (Briere, 2011). Both the MDI and the TSI-II may be given weekly in order to track progress.

Impact of Event Scale—Revised

The Impact of Event Scale—Revised (IES-R) may also be used weekly to assess an officer's ongoing level of distress associated with a particular incident (Weiss, 2007). It is a 22-item self-report measure that assesses subjective distress caused by critical incidents. It has items that assess for positive experiences as well.

Posttraumatic Growth Inventory

The Posttraumatic Growth Inventory (PTGI) assesses five factors that rate the degree to which positive adjustment to trauma has been experienced. The factors are relating to others, new possibilities, personal strength, spiritual change, and appreciation of life. Clients are asked to reflect on these factors and to repeat the test in 6 to 12 months to determine whether their scores have changed (Tedeschi & Calhoun, 1995). Posttraumatic growth is an integral part of our work with law enforcement. Too much has been said about the negative influence of critical incidents partly because there have been too few studies that ask if officers have, over the long haul, recognized that there may be a silver lining to an otherwise gloomy event (see more about posttraumatic growth in Chapter 9).

SHARING TEST RESULTS WITH YOUR CLIENT

Whether or not you've done the testing or referred it out, explaining test results must be done artfully, with great care, directness, a collaborative mindset, and sufficient time to allow for conversation. Invite your client to stop you at any time and ask questions. This is a psychoeducational opportunity. Cops are suspicious of what they don't understand. The more you explain, in everyday language, the lower their resistance and the higher their investment in their own treatment.

The following scenario highlights some of the guiding principles of test interpretation. It is not a script to be followed, but rather excerpts of an extended conversation exemplifying recommended tone and appropriate wording. It starts with Rick's therapist, Dr. Johnson, making sure that Rick is comfortable and has nothing pressing he needs to discuss before getting the results of the DAPS.

> *"I see that you are admitting to several things that are distressing. For example, you said that you felt hopeless. Tell me more about that."*
> This is Dr. Johnson's way of introducing Rick to the results and allowing him the opportunity to explain more about his current distress.

"In addition to the specific items that we have discussed, I want to show you a graphic representation of your scores." Dr. Johnson starts to educate Rick about symptom clusters and how they combine to help inform diagnoses. *"These three scales represent hyperarousal, reexperiencing and avoidance, the three main clusters of posttraumatic stress injury. This line represents a score of 50. That is the mean or average for all people who initially took this test. Scores above this line are deemed clinically significant because only 7% of the population scored in this range. I see that your score on this scale is 70. That means that you scored in the 98th percentile, or higher than 98% of the people who initially took this test. Obviously our goal would be to reduce the symptoms that are causing this high score."* Dr. Johnson then makes sure that Rick agrees to this goal.

"I also see that you scored high on the Suicide Index. I wonder if I could review these items with you?" He then reviews the specific items that aggregate into the suicidality scale, making certain Rick has understood each item and endorsed it in the right direction. Depending on Rick's responses, Dr. Johnson may decide to administer additional tests directly related to suicidality, such as the BHS and the BSS, for as long as Rick expresses suicidal thoughts and/or behaviors.

After additional testing, Dr. Johnson will periodically review the results with Rick using a graphic representation that shows changes over time. *"I see that your scores have come down over the past few weeks and wondered whether you too have noticed a difference."* If Rick's subjective experience does not match the objective measurements, Dr. Johnson will ask Rick what is impeding his progress.

A CAUTION ABOUT TEST INTERPRETATION AND VALIDITY QUESTIONS

Use care regarding validity questions on standardized tests. Validity questions on standardized tests are indicators of a client's test-taking attitude. Is the client "faking good" or "faking bad" for reasons of secondary gain? Is the client scrupulously overreporting problems, as do some very religious people, or underreporting problems, as job seekers do, in order to give a good impression. Scoring out of the normal range on a validity scale can invalidate the test results. Because LEOs have experiences that may not match the population on which these standardized tests were normed, they can misunderstand some items, thus skewing their validity scales.

Marty endorsed the item "Suddenly losing my ability to read." This item can be interpreted as an indication of malingering—hardly anyone suddenly loses the ability to read—and will affect the "faking bad" scale. When asked why he endorsed that item he answered that he thought it meant losing interest in reading, or reading the same paragraph over and over and not understanding what he'd just read. This was indicative of his difficulty concentrating rather than an attempt to malinger.

LEOs frequently endorse the validity item "Seeing flashing green and blue lights," because they may have intrusive thoughts or vivid recollections of incidents attended by numerous emergency response vehicles with variously colored flashing light bars. Delve deeply into your client's choice of response with open-ended questions such as "Tell me more about that."

When inquiring about responses to validity items or atypical responses to items on the clinical scales, proceed carefully. Be careful not to alert your client about the specific validity questions or identify items that may corrupt the test instrument for future use. If you are concerned about three responses, ask 10 questions to camouflage the specific items of interest. Remember, police officers are suspicious of tests, and they will likely be trying to second-guess the motives behind the test questions and behind your inquiries about their responses.

KEY POINTS

- Every country, state, and test publisher has its own policies and regulations regarding qualifications to administer, score, and interpret psychometric tests. Check your qualifications against these regulations.
- For help converting T-scores, go to *www.udel.edu/educ/gottfredson/451/Tscoreto percentile.pdf.*
- Diagnosis is an ongoing process, particularly in regards to trauma. Officers who are still working will engage in both critical and subcritical incidents every shift.
- When testing is made part of the treatment, officers quickly become used to the idea and anticipate taking these tests. They also appreciate the objective feedback and benefit from seeing the results on paper. In our opinion, using assessments for tracking should be a standard of care.

9

TREATMENT STRATEGIES

> John Wayne never cried, neither did Clint Eastwood,
> Jack Webb, or my father.
> —POLICE OFFICER

> I want to be a person, not an incident.
> —POLICE OFFICER

Cops seek counseling for a variety of reasons, just like the rest of us. And, like the rest of us, many are better off for having done so. In a survey of 1,114 police officers, those who had mental health counseling were significantly less stressed on self-report measures than those who had received no counseling, leading the researchers to suggest that departments should have mandatory periodic counseling in order to reduce the stigma around therapy and to promote stress management (Carlan & Nored, 2008). The Badge of Life (BOL), a nonprofit organization for the prevention of law enforcement suicide founded by retired and active-duty law enforcement officers, mental health professionals, and survivors of police suicide, also advocates for a voluntary program of confidential, annual mental health checkups for all officers. Their position is that self-care of mind and body is the officer's responsibility, just like getting regular dental examinations (*www.BOL.com*).

The idea of annual mental health checkups is controversial, and we can see both the advantages and disadvantages. Our emphasis (and our motivation for writing this book) is on the idea that once officers overcome their initial resistance and apprehension about counseling, they deserve to be seen by supportive, culturally competent therapists who know what they're doing. Our treatment goals are to restore the resilience and hardiness we assume our officer clients had when they were hired.

The focus of this chapter is on trauma and the treatments we think work best with posttraumatic stress injuries. Obviously, no single theoretical model fits everyone and every traumatic occurrence. We utilize some combination of the following models on a case-by-case basis, after considering the individual client, his or her presenting problem, and the desired outcomes. Our descriptions of these various treatment modalities are, by necessity, brief, and we urge readers to follow up by consulting the original sources and seeking formal training and supervision.

AVOIDANCE AND SECRETS

Before we begin our discussion on treatment strategies, we want to discuss two concepts—avoidance and secrets—that you will need to discuss with your clients. Avoidance is a cornerstone of the posttraumatic injury. It makes sense to avoid those people, places, and memories that cause emotional pain. Avoiding works, until it doesn't—that is, until the effort of avoiding overtakes normal life. We explain maladaptive avoidance to officers using an apocryphal story of two men named Speedy.

> Speedy #1 loved bicycle riding until the bolt that secured his seat broke and he went flying through the air and landed on his head, suffering a mild concussion. That night he lay awake, turning the incident over in his mind, asking what if the bolt had broken while he was on the highway, what if a car had run him over? As a cop, he knew what could have happened. Images of bike-versus-car accidents flashed through his mind. Speedy #1 bought a new bike and went back to riding with full knowledge that seat bolts can break. He's careful now to check the bolt. And he still gets the "willies" when he thinks about the accident.

> Speedy #2 had the same accident, but he couldn't keep himself from worrying that his seat bolt would break again. He stopped riding downhill, and then stopped riding altogether. He no longer participated in his weekly group rides. He became anxious when he saw anyone else riding a bike and forbade his kids from riding anywhere but in the backyard. He got so anxious he couldn't walk past a bicycle shop, and eventually he even stopped going downtown. At work he was offered a spot in the bike patrol because everyone knew he loved

riding. He turned it down, saying he was having knee trouble and his doctor suggested that he take a break.

Holding on to secrets is a common theme among officers. There is shame associated with talking about current or past traumas. As clinicians, we believe disclosure aids in recovery. We tell our clients that they are only as sick as their secrets—that the way to deal with problems is to go through them, not around them. We also advise them that when they're in a hole, the best thing to do is stop digging. Ours is an educational and collaborative approach. We warn our clients that their symptoms may become worse after disclosure (American Psychological Association, 2010) and that confronting rather than avoiding trauma will cause some distress before their symptoms remit. We explain that avoidance produces short-term gain, but long-term pain. We offer repeated assurance of confidentiality, adhere to a nonjudgmental stance, and promise to hang in there with them, which means being available for unscheduled appointments and phone calls.

COGNITIVE-BEHAVIORAL THERAPY

Cognitive-behavioral therapy (CBT) is especially helpful in the treatment of trauma (Benedek, Friedman, Zatzick, Robert, & Ursano, 2009; Cahill, Foa, Hembree, Marshall, & Nacash, 2006; Sharpless & Barber, 2011). In the most simplified terms, the central hypothesis of CBT is that our thoughts or cognitions cause our emotional reactions (Beck, 2011). The goal of CBT is to challenge these negative thoughts and distorted beliefs, rescript them into positive cognitions, and gradually help clients to reengage in activities that they have been avoiding. CBT requires active participation by the client, including systematic desensitization, tracking triggers and negative thoughts, journaling, relaxation, and meditation.

Cops tend to make three kinds of cognitive errors that we call the myth of perfection, cognitive dissonance, and magical thinking. Aiming for perfection is an impossible task, but it does have some benefits, such as encouraging continuous improvement in the areas of job performance, safety measures, and athletic ability. On the flip side, someone who insists on being perfect is never good enough. The report cards cops give themselves typically do not contain many A's, so perfectionism can be particularly insidious for them.

Cognitive dissonance refers to the difficulty or tension that arises from simultaneously holding two opposing or psychologically inconsistent beliefs, such as "I'm a success" and "I'm a failure" (Aronson, 1995). Cognitive dissonance results from tactical thinking errors or what we colloquially call "stinking thinking."

Rachel got into a physical confrontation trying to detain a suspected burglar. It was all she could do to hold on to her weapon. In the aftermath, she blamed herself for letting the "dirt bag" get away. She believed that good cops always win a fight, and because she lost hers, she was a bad cop. Her harsh self-judgment caused her considerable angst. She began questioning everything about herself—was she a good friend, a good daughter? She almost quit policing, a job she loved and had worked hard to get.

Rachel made three tactical thinking errors called permanence, personalization, and pervasiveness (see Figure 9.1). Rachel believed she had messed up and would always mess up (permanence); she called herself a "shit magnet" (personalization); and she assumed that messing up extended to all parts of her life, not just work (pervasiveness). Her current view of herself as a failure was dissonant with her prior, desired view of herself as competent. She couldn't reduce the dissonance she felt by minimizing her tactical errors—almost losing her gun and letting the crook escape. Nor, until she worked with a therapist, was she able to reframe her rigid thinking by saying that good cops sometimes, but not always, win fights.

Magical thinking–woulda, coulda, shoulda, and "if only" ideas that bend reality—is another common thinking error. Cops are very hard on themselves and often rigidly adhere to the notion that they should be able to predict the future and save victims through miraculous or heroic deeds.

Chris responded on a call involving a young boy who had been found unresponsive in a backyard pool. He had responded to other emergency medical calls and, to his credit, the outcomes were good. But on this call a lot went wrong. The child had been missing and probably drowned for nearly 20 minutes before his body was found. None of this was Chris's fault, of course, and he did the best he could to revive the child until the paramedics arrived. At this point, Chris had a choice. He could decide that good officers, like himself, sometimes get bad calls. This would have forced him to acknowledge that there were more bad calls and more dead children in his future. He could also decide that he was a bad cop, because if he was a good cop, that child would still be alive. As irrational as this seems, it has a kind of distorted logic. By deciding that he was at fault, he established control over his future. All he had to do was be good all the time and no one else would die, which, quite naturally, was an impossible task that caused Chris a lot of anxiety.

We could argue that Chris's choice wasn't deliberate or even conscious. The point is that Chris, like Rachel, was having trouble reconciling two opposing thoughts: that he could be a good cop and have a failed outcome.

Regardless of the type of thinking error the client is making, the clinician's job is to challenge distorted paradigms of perfection, point out magical thinking, and resolve cognitive dissonance by helping the client take a both/and rather than an either/or view. You can challenge a client's thinking errors in many ways. The following list is not exhaustive.

1. Challenge the distorted view of self: "Bad things don't happen to good cops. Something bad happened to you, therefore you're a bad cop. Is that correct?"
2. Challenge prior beliefs in an exaggerated, over-the-top fashion: "So, you're saying that you can never again trust your judgment and will die on the job for certain."
3. Modify the previously held beliefs of perfection in a way that incorporates the traumatic experience without abandoning a positive world view: "Some people and some places are dangerous, but the risk of danger in most situations is tolerable."
4. Soften self-criticism by asking the officer how she might judge someone else facing the same situation: "What grade would you give a friend, a coworker, a child, or a sibling who acted as you did in the same circumstances?" The response is usually more reasonable.

WORKING WITH TRIGGERS

Triggers are environmental stimuli that serve as unwanted and intrusive reminders of a negative experience. Advanced awareness of triggers can minimize their impact (Briere & Scott, 2006). Triggers include not just explicit events, but implicit feelings of anger or impending doom. The goal is for LEOs to manage their emotional dysregulation so that they can stay in the disturbing environment long enough to let the amygdala know there is nothing to fear and that fleeing or avoidance will only reinforce their symptoms (Beckner & Arden, 2008). When a client is emotional or highly reactive and doesn't know why, we teach the officer to look for the trigger that started the reaction. We become emotional detectives, looking for clues by asking the following questions:

1. "What was the event [sight, sound, smell, physical sensation, etc.] that caused you to react?"
2. "What thought followed the trigger?" This will usually be a negative or irrational belief such as "I'm a loser." It happens so quickly it is often difficult to retrieve.

FIGURE 9.1. Fighting Back Worksheet. Tactical thinking errors adapted from Resick, Monson, and Chard (2008, p. 153).

TRIGGER (Something happens)	UNHELPFUL THOUGHT (I tell myself something)	INITIAL REACTION (I do, feel, or say something)	TACTICAL THINKING ERRORS (Choose from below)	REALISTIC, RATIONAL, OR HELPFUL THOUGHT/ACTION (What I can tell myself or do in the future)
I was criticized.	I never do things right.	I get angry and withdraw.	1, 2, 3, 7, 8	It is human to make a mistake.
DA fails to prosecute.	Bad guys always win.	What's the use?	2	What is the evidence? How many cases of this type do they prosecute each year? How does that compare to similar jurisdictions?
Passing location where I was injured and lost my gun.	I am such a klutz.	I shouldn't have let that happen. I must be at fault.	6	Humor: It was like the Keystone Kops. I've heard much worse stories that have happened to well-respected coworkers.
Ordered to work overtime on daughter's birthday.	I should have known that Sgt. was out to get me.	I'm a horrible father.	2, 5, 7, 8	What would your backup/mentor do in this situation? I can make a phone call and ask for advice.

104

1) ALL-OR-NOTHING THINKING	2) OVERGENERALIZING	3) MAGICAL THINKING	4) DISQUALIFYING THE POSITIVE
Also called black-and-white thinking, exaggeration, or minimization. You believe only one thing can be true at any one time (and it's often an extreme kind of thing—like when something or someone is "all good" or "all bad"). If a situation falls short of perfect, you see it or yourself as a failure. You might say things like: • "I'm right, they are wrong."	You see a single negative event as never-ending (permanent). You conclude that something that happened to you once will occur over and over. You use terms like: • "It always, I never, you never . . ." • "I always get the shitty calls." • "They never recognize me." • "It has always been this way and will continue."	Making an unrealistic connection between two ideas. You say things like: • "If I had only been working that day . . ." • "Had I arrived 5 minutes earlier . . ."	Or only seeing the negative. You reject positive experiences by insisting they "don't count." If you do a good job, you may tell yourself that it wasn't good enough or that someone else could have done it better. You say things like: • "That was a fluke." • "It doesn't matter." • "It may have turned out OK, but . . . ."

5) SUPER POWERS	6) EMOTIONAL REASONING	7) LABELING	8) SELF-BLAME/BLAME OTHERS/GUILT
MIND READING: Believing you know what other people are thinking. • "I know he hates me." FORTUNE TELLING: Knowing how things will turn out before they happen. • "It will never work out." JUMPING TO CONCLUSIONS AND/OR CATASTROPHIZING: Seeing only the worst possible outcomes. Reaching conclusions (usually negative) from little (if any) evidence.	You take your emotions as truth. You feel it, so it must be true. You say things like: • "I feel guilty; therefore I must have done something wrong." • "I feel overwhelmed and hopeless, therefore my problems are impossible to solve." • "I feel inadequate, therefore I must be a worthless person."	You attach a negative label to yourself: • "I'm a loser." • "I am hopeless." • "I'm a fraud." • "If you really knew me (and my secrets) you wouldn't want to have anything to do with me."	You see yourself as the cause of some negative event over which you had no control: • "It happened because I was not able to prevent it from happening." Or you blame others: • "The reason my marriage is so lousy is because my spouse is totally unreasonable."

3. "What was your initial reaction or behavior after the thought?"
4. "What tactical thinking error applies to your situation?" We give an LEO the Fighting Back Worksheet (Figure 9.1), which has a list of tactical thinking errors.
5. "Knowing what you now know, what could you have done or thought that would have been more helpful?"

Remember Chris, who couldn't revive the child who drowned in the backyard pool? Here's how he answered these questions:

1. The trigger: "My son asked me to take him to the swimming pool."
2. The fleeting thought: "My son will drown, and I won't be able to save him like I couldn't save the other boy."
3. The reaction: "I got angry at my son, went into my bedroom, and slammed the door."
4. Tactical thinking errors: overgeneralizing ("Something that happened once will happen over and over"); magical thinking ("If only I had gotten there earlier I could have saved him"); labeling ("I'm a failure"); and self-blame (taking responsibility for an event over which he had no control).
5. The helpful action or thought: "I did the best I could under the circumstances. The child was dead long before I arrived—no one, not even the paramedics, could have revived him. My son is never alone in the swimming pool, there are lifeguards and parents all around."

PROLONGED EXPOSURE THERAPY

Prolonged exposure (PE) is based on the principle that anxiety will diminish in the absence of current danger (Benedek et al., 2009). PE occurs as the officer retells the narrative of his or her incident in as much detail as possible. It is a manualized treatment consisting of 8–15 sessions of 90 minutes each, plus homework, journaling, psychoeducation, and breathing exercises (Foa, Hembree, & Rothbaum, 2007). Exposure is both imaginal (in the mind's eye) and *in vivo* (such as at the actual scene of an incident).

Peter's shooting took place in the dark. It was a high-profile event with a great deal of community outrage. After determining that Peter could tolerate *in vivo* exposure, Peter's therapist suggested that they go back to the scene. Peter was extremely worried that someone in the neighborhood would recognize him. Because *in vivo* exposure only works in an atmosphere of safety, his therapist suggested Peter bring an armed friend along. Both men dressed in plain clothes. Peter also agreed, as a first step, to revisit the scene during the day and at a later date return at night. He was amazed by how different everything looked in the light of day, and how the punitive second-guessing he'd been doing was based on distorted memories of time and distance.

PE often creates intense emotional arousal for the client. Both therapist and client need to be prepared and equipped to tolerate such intensity. Having said this, we've never known an officer who couldn't, with preparation, revisit the scene of his or her critical incident.

EYE MOVEMENT DESENSITIZATION AND REPROCESSING (EMDR)

We like to think of eye movement desensitization and reprocessing (EMDR) as prolonged exposure without the homework. It was designed to help traumatized clients learn from their trauma history, disconfirm negative beliefs about themselves, and develop a template to apply what they have learned to future incidents.

Critical incidents leave lasting negative effects (Beckner & Arden, 2008; Briere & Scott, 2006; Brown & Campbell, 1994; Kirschman, 1997; Maxfield, 2002; Toch, 2002). The primary assumption of EMDR is that recalling critical incidents will lead to new neural connections that allow traumatic memories to be processed with normal, nontraumatic memories, resulting in a positive cognitive and emotional experience and a reduction in anxiety and other symptoms (Shapiro, 2001, 2007). It involves an integration of reason and emotion, or what may be thought of as left–right hemispheric integration of the brain. It combines CBT and PE with a unique attention to bilateral stimulation (Benedek, Friedman, Zatzick, & Ursano, 2009).

The adaptive information processing model (Shapiro & Maxfield, 2002) theorizes that normal images, thoughts, and reactions are processed so that experience can be used as a predictive guide for future behaviors. Traumatic memories, however, can remain unprocessed, and apparently not stored like regular memories but blocked from making new neural connections. EMDR is thought to remove this blockage and allow natural healing to occur by linking traumatic memories to more adaptive memories. The technique does not remove the memories but reduces the emotional charge associated with them. This allows the traumatic memories to be understood in the context of what happened, along with a corresponding feeling of no longer being powerless.

The American Psychological Association (2010) asserts that

> EMDR belongs within a continuum of exposure-related and cognitive behavior treatments. Because it is less reliant on a verbal account, EMDR gives the client more control over the exposure experience and provides techniques to regulate anxiety during treatment. Consequently, it may prove advantageous for clients who cannot tolerate prolonged exposure as well as for people who have difficulty verbalizing their traumatic experiences. (p. 59)

This endorsement makes EMDR a good match for LEOs, who are frequently reluctant to reveal the details of their past and present traumas.

The theory underlying EMDR is too technical to explain to a layperson. In our experience, when EMDR is suggested in the context of a trusting and safe relationship between client and therapist, officers are satisfied with a brief description. We tend to say something along the lines of the following:

> "EMDR has been around for about 20 years. What we hope to do is use EMDR to change the way you think of an event. We can't change what occurred, or even your memory of what occurred, but we can work to reduce the distressing impact of that memory. While the idea must seem a bit odd, it has been studied repeatedly, is recognized as an effective treatment for PTSD, and used by the Department of Veterans Affairs."

A review of the literature on the efficacy of EMDR as a treatment for PTSD concluded that eye movements were not essential in obtaining positive outcomes (Chemtob, Tolin, van der Kolk, & Pitman, 2000) and that bilateral stimulation appeared to be more important (Devilly & Spence, 1999; McNally, 1999). Therefore, clients should be given the opportunity to try many types of stimulation before choosing the one with which they are most comfortable. These can range from hand tappers that buzz in the palm to alternating ear tones, light bars, or even following the therapist's hand as it moves from left to right.

RESOURCING

Part of the preparation for EMDR bilateral stimulation is the installation of resources such as a "calm place" that clients can visualize (Parnell, 2008). Resource installation is a required part of the EMDR protocol, but we also think it is useful as a stand-alone technique.

The objective of resource installation is to remind officers of their inner resources and to give them self-soothing tools they can use during stressful times, including difficult therapy sessions. We introduce the concept by pointing out how humans are hard-wired so that when we think of difficult memories the emotions attached to those memories are revived, and our bodies "rev up" as if the whole incident were happening all over again. We point out that when we think of something soothing our bodies will calm down.

We ask officers for three resources: a calm place; a skill, trait, or belief that serves them well; and a backup figure. These resources can be real or imagined, but the more specific and detailed they are, the better they work. It is helpful to anchor each resource with a cue word or a body sensation.

1. *A calm place.* This can be anywhere your client feels calm or safe—a favorite fishing hole or Grandmother's kitchen. If an officer chooses a room in his or her home, be sure to inquire about family life. If it is currently tumultuous, ask your client to choose another place. Occasionally, cops will say that no place feels safe to them. In this case, ask them to focus on a calm place. Alternatively, ask them to use their imaginations and consider magical or fanciful places, or switch time frames to the past or the future.

2. *Inner resources.* We ask LEOs to identify the strengths, qualities, skills, traits, and beliefs they use in life that may be helpful in accomplishing their therapeutic goals. Once these are identified, we ask them to give us a detailed example of a time they used a specific trait and any accompanying physical sensations they may have had at the time. If your client is unable to think of a skill, trait, or belief, we have generated a list you can share (see Figure 5.1). An additional question—"Who in your life would be least surprised to find that you have this resource?"—also produces valuable information.

Bill identified determination as a helpful trait and his grandfather as the person who would be least surprised because his grandfather had taught him to ride a bike. Bill's grandfather now becomes a helpful therapeutic ally, or in more formal terms, a positive introject, someone Bill's therapist can call upon, as in "What would your grandfather say to you in this circumstance?"

3. *Backup:* We next ask the client to pick a backup figure, someone they can rely on who has been supportive in the past. This usually turns out to be a coworker, mentor, trainer, or friend. Backup

figures can be real or imagined, living or dead, human or animal, such as a K-9.

Once the resourcing exercise is complete, ask your client to imagine times during therapy or in the general future when invoking these resources will be helpful.

NARRATIVE THERAPY

Police officers love stories, particularly war stories. Stories are teaching tools, vehicles for communicating cultural norms and connecting with each other. This may be why narrative therapy is such a good fit with LEOs.

Be careful not to confuse narrative therapy with narrative exposure therapy (NET; Schauer, Neuner, & Elbert, 2011). In reality they are quite different. Narrative therapy, developed by Michael White and David Epston (1990), approaches counseling by focusing on the stories people tell themselves about their lives, the meaning they derive from these stories, and the social, cultural, and political contexts in which these stories arise. NET is used in the treatment of torture victims and refugees. It involves telling the details of one's life experiences to a counselor who records it and reads it back. It is generally not used in the treatment of LEOs. A basic tenet of narrative therapy is that there is no one objective truth, but rather there are many ways to interpret any given event. Stories are constructed from subjectively selected elements that, over time, become thematic, shaping the teller's identity. The themes and the identities can become "problem saturated" and "oppressive."

> Mitch's father told him repeatedly that he would amount to nothing in life. Mitch worked hard to prove his father wrong. He excelled in sports, got excellent grades in high school, and graduated from the police academy at the top of his class. In his fourth year as a cop, he made a traffic stop on a speeding car. There was something about the driver and his passenger that made Mitch uncomfortable. With their permission, he "tossed" the car, meaning he searched it thoroughly, but found nothing. With no probable cause to detain the driver, he wrote a ticket and let the driver go. Days later he learned that the driver and the passenger robbed a convenience store and killed the teenage clerk. Mitch blamed himself. He was convinced that the murder weapon was in the vehicle and he had missed it.

In talking with his therapist, Mitch selected elements from this and other incidents that conformed to his dominant self-story—that his father was right, he didn't amount to anything. He overlooked or minimized any details that didn't fit, such as his many achievements or the possibility that there was no weapon in the car at the time of the traffic stop.

Mitch struggled to understand how much his oppressive self-story contributed to his reading of the situation. The idea that there is no essential truth or that there are many truths and interpretations of a given event was difficult for him to accept. Police work deals with black-and-white issues. Cops make quick decisions, determining right from wrong and safe from unsafe, in situations that are at best ambiguous (Hays, 1994).

PROBLEM SOLVING

You would think cops, who are professional problem solvers, would be experts in problem solving. Indeed they are, but, just like clinicians, they are better at solving other people's problems than they are at solving their own. This is understandable. Our own problems are compounded by a variety of emotions, a crisis of objectivity, and the conflicting needs of our friends and family.

Problem solving is a way to organize complex information and emotions. It works with individuals, couples, families, and work groups.

1. Ask each person to define the problem from his or her perspective.
2. Ask each to define the goal from his or her perspective.
3. Together, brainstorm three potential solutions. For each potential solution, list the pros—why is this solution a good idea? Then list the cons in terms of effort, time, money, emotions, and other issues. Rate the cons as slightly, moderately, or very important.
4. Choose a solution from the list of potential solutions.
5. Develop an action plan with precisely defined specific steps.
6. Set a timeline: who is responsible for completing what steps by what date?
7. Follow up: Evaluate what is working and for whom? What is not working and for whom? What needs modification? If necessary, return to a previous step.

DEBRIEFINGS

Critical incident stress debriefings (CISD) are early postincident interventions that are conducted individually or in a group format (Adler et al., 2008; Devilly, Gist, & Cotton, 2006). Debriefings, especially group debriefings facilitated by a team of mental health professionals and peers, have become increasingly popular and widespread. But they are not without critics.

For example, there has been controversy over the use of the Mitchell model, a highly popularized group format (Carlier, van Uchelen, Lamberts, & Gersons, 1998; Carlier, Voerman, & Gersons, 2000; Gist & Devilly, 2002; Harris, Baloglu, & Stacks, 2002; Mitchell, 2003). One concern is the possibility of secondary traumatization via overconsolidation of traumatic memories. A second concern is that debriefings have been oversold as preventing PTSD. The development of PTSD, as we have asserted, is complicated (J. Briere, personal communication, 2012). A third concern is that the popularization of the trauma industry has created a volunteer force of "trauma junkies" who, with minimal training, can do more harm than good (Kirschman, 2007). We have all mopped up after unskilled and culturally incompetent debriefers who have insulted or angered a group of cops. Finally, a fourth concern relates to whether or not attendance at CISDs should be voluntary or mandatory. We tend to come down on the mandatory side, thinking that (1) LEOs who most need the information would opt out if given the chance and (2) because no one is ever forced to talk, even the most resistant officer can learn something through listening. Honig and Sultan (2004), in their study of 982 Los Angeles deputy sheriffs, reported that 60% admitted they would not have attended an individual debriefing if given the option although 100% said they found the debriefing valuable.

Debriefing technology is hard to research because of the variability of the circumstances and the people involved. Comparing LEOs to burn victims or people involved in motor vehicle accidents is not really useful. Our experience and that of our colleagues is that properly conducted debriefings are helpful in a number of ways and are most efficacious when used as part of a comprehensive treatment program. In the study just described, Honig and Sultan (2004) found no evidence to suggest that participants in individual critical incident stress debriefings were harmed. Nearly all of the 982 Los Angeles deputies surveyed found the intervention valuable.

CISDs are a form of psychoeducation that lets LEOs know what to expect of themselves, psychologically and physically, over the next few days or weeks (Bisson, McFarlane, Rose, Ruzek, & Watson, 2009). They allow for the reconstruction of events to fill in memory gaps, normalize symptoms, and provide self-care and referral information for those whose symptoms don't remit over time. Team members have the opportunity to reconnect and demonstrate solidarity and support for one another (Best, Artwohl, & Kirschman, 2011; Sharpless & Barber, 2011). Although debriefings should never be used to critique the operation, they do provide an opportunity to understand what has just occurred from several different points of view, often starting with the dispatcher who took the original 911 call.

PEER SUPPORT

We consider ourselves fortunate to have a wide network of trained peer supporters who work with us, side by side, at the West Coast Post-Trauma Retreat (WCPR). Our peer supporters assist us during debriefings and are willing to do whatever it takes to help a fellow first responder and his or her family.

The mission of a peer support team is to provide confidential emotional, social, and practical support to other officers during times of personal or professional crisis (Kamena, Gentz, Hays, Bohl-Penrod, & Greene, 2011). Peer supporters are taught how to make referrals to local therapists (Roland, 2010) and can provide education about critical incident stress, thus increasing the likelihood that officers and their families will seek treatment when needed.

Peer support has been an important part of the law enforcement culture for a long time (Benner, 1982; Graff, 1986). Peers can normalize both emotional reactions and tactical decisions that family members and mental health professionals cannot. Peers often work the same shifts and can provide support 24/7. They are credible resources because they've walked in one another's shoes and are often perceived as being more empathic than mental health professionals (Finn & Tomz, 1997; Linden & Klein, 1988; Roland, 2011). Their calming presence is precisely what a troubled LEO needs (Kamena et al., 2011).

Peers can also be assigned to stay in contact with officers who are on administrative leave or off duty because of injury. LEOs on leave are sometimes isolated due to legal issues or administrative actions that prohibit contact with other officers. Properly trained peers may be the only people who are permitted to stay in contact and help the isolated officer cope with feelings of disgrace, abandonment, shame, embarrassment, and rejection (Roland, 2011).

VIRTUAL ENVIRONMENT

New technology has not only improved virtual reality treatment but has also made it more affordable. The Department of Veterans Affairs has used this treatment to provide convincing experiences of revisiting a traumatic incident (Wilson, Onorati, Mishkind, Reger, & Gahm, 2008) by creating visual, auditory, and olfactory reproductions of the event using lifelike avatars (Rizzo, Reger, Gahm, Difede, & Rothbaum, 2009). This type of treatment may be particularly useful for LEOs who have difficulty imagining or talking about their events in therapy. It is not indicated for clients who become overengaged when recalling traumatic events (Cukor, Spitalnick, Difede, Rizzo, & Rothbaum, 2009).

RESILIENCE AND POSTTRAUMATIC GROWTH

The ability to bounce back from adversity and play a bad hand well is the hallmark of resilience. Following a critical incident, officers can come to have an increased appreciation of life and recognize that their family and friends stood by them, or that they themselves showed courage and competence (Kirschman, 2004, 2007). This doesn't happen overnight, of course. Sometimes it takes months or years for officers to realize that had it not been for their critical incidents, they would not have made lifestyle changes leading to positive experiences, changes that they never imagined possible and for which they are grateful. This is not just wishful thinking or spin. Evidence of growth has been corroborated by those significant others who knew the officer before his or her traumatic incident (Shakespeare-Finch & Enders, 2008).

Posttraumatic growth is paradoxical in that it not only comes from an individual's experience of great distress but is maintained through continuing distress (Tedeschi & Kilmer, 2005), as the officer's newfound sense of continuing vulnerability is part of his or her growth (Janoff-Bullman, 1992). Officers who are forced to take a life often question their morality and raise issues about death and the purpose of life. Facing these difficult questions can lead to a more meaningful life. The process of recovery from trauma involves an often painful reexamination of what the LEO has previously taken for granted: worldviews, personal strengths, relationships with others, appreciation of life, spirituality, and openness to new possibilities (Tedeschi & Calhoun, 1995). The greater the struggle, the greater the possibility of experiencing growth (Calhoun et al., 2010; Cann et al., 2010).

We and many of our colleagues think there is far too much emphasis placed on psychopathology and not enough emphasis on strengths (Hitchcock, Weiss, Weiss, Rostow, & Davis, 2010). Excessive negative rumination may interfere with the deliberate, intentional, and constructive rumination that is necessary for posttraumatic growth. Timing, of course, is everything. The following suggestions must be carefully timed.

- Ask your client the following: "Some people benefit from their struggle following a critical incident. They may have a different view of the world or they may feel differently about their relationships or themselves. Sometimes they've learned something worth knowing. Do you think that is possible given your recent experience?"

- Ask your client to create and display a list of things for which he or she is grateful; start with small things, like access to clean water or good schools for his or her children.
- Ask your client to, once a day, think of something inspiring, moving, or just plain good that has happened (Beckner & Arden, 2008). Again, we are talking about learning to appreciate the small things in life, like playing with a dog, because they are readily available. Winning the lottery or getting an award for bravery, a promotion, or a new car happen too rarely to be sustaining.
- Ask your client to first write about how he or she would like to be remembered, and then create an action plan to be that person.
- Ask your client to look back and remember how he was doing 6 months or a year ago. Is he doing better today? If so, what changes has he made in his life that have helped him? When possible, attach this conversation to a triggering event or a reclaimed skill.

Bill was on sick leave and in therapy following a diagnosis of PTSD. He showed up for a counseling session feeling like a failure. He had gone grocery shopping at the supermarket and felt so overwhelmed that he could only stay for 10 minutes before fleeing for home. His therapist asked him if he would have been able to go to the supermarket at all 6 months ago. Bill thought about it and answered "no." This realization reframed his sense of failure. Now his 10-minute shopping trip seemed like a success and he was eager to try for 12. When asked what changes contributed to his success he cited therapy, medication, exercising, and forcing himself to get out of the house. He allowed himself to see that change is a slow process and difficult to see from day to day.

RESCRIPTING NIGHTMARES

As we've described earlier, it is common for cops to have nightmares on a routine basis, not just following a critical incident. The general theme is one of fear: bullets bouncing off the bad guy or dribbling helplessly out of barrel of their gun. We find that psychoanalytic interpretations of such dreams are generally useless for cops and often insulting. What does help is medication and rescripting. Rescripting involves writing out the nightmare, reading the narrative aloud, and then changing it in a constructive, yet realistic, manner. If your client is having one of those common nightmares, an alternate ending might be that the suspect was tasered and taken into custody. Your client would then rewrite the dream with the new ending and read it aloud (Davis & Wright, 2007).

SPIRITUALITY

Police chaplains are wonderful resources. Many of the tragedies that LEOs see on a too-regular basis weigh heavily, causing them to question their former beliefs and doubt that there is goodness in the world. These questions are spiritual, not psychological, in nature. While cautioning against pushing religion or proselytizing for any specific religion, we recognize that many of our clients have spiritual needs that we cannot fill. Instead, we urge clinicians to develop relationships with police chaplains. If there are no police chaplains in your area, consult the International Association of Police Chaplains for assistance (*www.icpc4cops.org*).

SOCRATIC DIALOGUE

Socratic dialogue (Miller & Rollnick, 2002) is an active, yet nondirective style of interaction between client and therapist. The key clinical skill is to help clients discover their maladaptive thoughts and logical fallacies by asking thoughtful, yet challenging questions. This style works well with cops, who prefer interaction to sitting with a therapist who listens well but rarely says anything. There are six main types of Socratic questions:

1. Clarification questions help patients examine beliefs or assumptions more deeply by requesting more information.
2. Probing the patient's assumptions challenges the unquestioned beliefs that underlie his or her stuck points.
3. Probing reasons and evidence helps patients examine the actual evidence supporting their beliefs, which is usually not very strong.
4. Questioning viewpoints and perspectives encourages patients to come up with alternative perspectives.
5. Analyzing implications helps patients examine the unpleasant outcomes that logically flow from holding maladaptive beliefs.
6. Questions about questions place the focus back on the patient when potentially inappropriate questions get asked of the psychotherapist. While we advocate transparency (see Chapter 1), we also feel free to respond to an inappropriate question in the following way:

"I'm willing to answer your question, but I would first like to know how this information will be useful to you."

RESIDENTIAL TREATMENT

To the best of our knowledge, in the United States there are only two residential treatment programs for LEOs suffering with symptoms of posttraumatic stress injuries: the On-Site Academy in Westminster, Massachusetts, and the First Responder Support Network (FRSN), a nonprofit organization that supports the West Coast Post Trauma Retreat (WCPR), in California. Two of us (Fay and Kamena) are founding members of WCPR and Kirschman is a longtime volunteer. FRSN has two main treatment programs: one for first responders (WCPR) and one for spouses and significant others (SOS). The WCPR program began in 2001, meets monthly or semimonthly, and, as of May 2013, has graduated over 600 first responder clients. The semiannual SOS program, which started later, has graduated 60. All staff members, clinicians, peers, and chaplains participate on a pro-bono basis. The following is a summary. More detail about WCPR can be found in the Appendix.

WCPR is an eclectic, peer-based, clinically guided 6-day intensive program that utilizes all of the above-described strategies. The presence of peers is essential for the level of trust and safety our clients need to disclose things they have resisted discussing. Sometimes staff are the first people with whom our clients have ever shared a long-held secret.

The goal of WCPR is symptom reduction. The core of the program is a PE debriefing during which clients review their incident three times in three phases:

1. The fact phase: a frame-by-frame narrative.
2. The thought phase: deconstructing negative thoughts and cognitive dissonance.
3. The reaction phase: addressing the client's physical and emotional reactions during and after the incident.

In addition, our program includes a segment about family. Officers are first educated about how they are affected by their past experiences. They are then asked to choose a person with whom they have had a significant negative relationship, usually a parent, and to discuss how that relationship affected their past and current reactions to their incidents.

A large component of the WCPR program is psychoeducation on the following topics: the emergency responder's exhaustion syndrome (ERES), the physiology of stress, the emergency responders' personality, forgiveness, family, medication, tactical thinking errors, and alcohol use (including a first responders' AA meeting).

KEY POINTS

- EMDR requires special training and certification. See the Resources for training information.
- Well worth mentioning is psychological first aid (PFA), a form of immediate postincident intervention that is usually provided by law enforcement chaplains and/or members of a peer support team. The goal of PFA is to reduce initial stress, foster safety and comfort, and provide for immediate needs such as food, shelter, and getting in touch with family (see the Resources).

10

WHEN YOUR CLIENT
NEEDS MEDICATION

> If I take a pill, does that make the other guy
> less of an asshole?
>
> —POLICE OFFICER

Cops will drink coffee and caffeine drinks until their hands shake, but have a hard time accepting that they may benefit from the same medications they associate with drug addicts and psychotic street people. They also have concerns about confidentiality, legal issues, and the impact of medications on their response time. This chapter offers ideas about how best to talk to cops about taking medications and includes the latest information on appropriate drugs for law enforcement personnel. It is important to point out that none of us is licensed to prescribe medication, so we are basing our comments on our experience and collaborative work with prescribing professionals. We strongly encourage any officer considering taking a psychiatric medication to meet with an appropriate medical professional who understands what police officers do for a living.

The American Academy of Family Physicians (2011) reports that most psychiatric medications are prescribed by primary care physicians. Few people seek or get appointments with psychiatrists. Many people don't understand the difference between a psychologist and a psychiatrist and don't know where to turn to get appropriate information regarding medication.

Primary care physicians have limited time to sufficiently explain to patients the use of psychiatric medications. Moreover, in our experience most primary care physicians have little experience with PTSD.

> Sandy had been prescribed a selective serotonin reuptake inhibitor (SSRI) for depression at a very low starting dose. He received no instructions regarding increasing the dosage and did not have a follow-up appointment with the primary care doctor. This is, unfortunately, all too common in the busy world of managed health care, where most primary care doctors get 15 minutes to meet with their patients.

In recent years studies that examined the number of psychiatrists accepting insurance concluded that many clients will have a difficult time finding a psychiatrist who will accept their private insurance or deal with workers' compensation (Wilk, West, Narrow, Rae, & Regier, 2005). Primary care physicians need to stay on top of a broad range of medication issues and may not have the time to update themselves on the latest psychiatric advances (Lieberman, 2003).

As a clinician working with a population that is reluctant to take medication, it is important to be conversant and knowledgeable about medications—how they're used, their possible side effects, and potential benefits. In addition there are a number of concerns specific to law enforcement that need to be addressed. Our job is to make officers better-educated consumers of medication and encourage communication with their prescribing professionals.

RESISTANCE

If you ask a group of police officers about their concerns regarding psychiatric medications they will come up with long list of reasons they don't want to take them. Some are based on stigma, some on real concerns, and some on a lack of knowledge. It takes education and reassurance to help cops move past their apprehensions. This chapter addresses the most commonly cited concerns and what you might say to overcome them. We have also included a brief review of some commonly used medications, as well as guidelines developed specifically for LEOs by the American College of Occupational and Environmental Medicine (ACOEM).

"Only crazy people take medication."

A police officer's view of the psychiatric world and psychiatric patients is skewed. While police officers meet many people with psychiatric illnesses, the ones they most remember are the people who are seriously mentally ill, in acute distress, violent, or barely functioning. It is helpful to provide information that will normalize taking psychotropic medications. For example, your client may not know that more than one in five adults in the United States are now taking at least one psychotropic medication to treat a psychological or behavioral disorder (Smith, 2012). When appropriate, we are transparent about our own medication histories.

"If I was involved in a shooting or a motor vehicle accident, someone would find out about the medication through blood or urine tests, and I would be in trouble."

LEOs are very concerned about what would happen after a shooting if it was discovered that they were taking psychotropic medications. This isn't baseless paranoia but reflects real-life concerns. After a shooting, an officer's actions will be reviewed by many different groups, including the investigating unit or department, the district attorney's office, an attorney for the family of the deceased, the media, the Department of Justice, and other investigatory agencies. Officers worry that if they are taking any kind of medication it will be used against them in the investigation, as well as in civil or criminal court proceedings. It is your responsibility to know your local agencies' policies. These policies can vary widely. It is beyond the scope of this book to list policies for each state, but as an example, we will describe California's policies.

In California, after an officer-involved shooting (OIS), the officer in question is automatically assigned an attorney as part of the Police Officers Bill of Rights. The attorneys we have worked with all state that they would object to any request for a blood or urine sample, citing the fact that it is within a police officer's rights to refuse to provide such a sample. If a police officer does provide a sample, the drugs that are routinely screened for are benzodiazepines (antianxiety medications), illicit drugs, and alcohol. The screenings do not typically look for other prescribed medications.

After interviewing hundreds of officers post shooting, we have seen very few incidents where a blood or urine sample was provided by the officer, and no incidents where the sample was checked for antidepressant medications. If this is an issue that is keeping your client from considering needed medication, the best course of action for you is to encourage your client to speak with a local attorney who represents police officers to get a clearer understanding of the local laws and regulations.

"I don't want to tell my department."

Every agency has policies governing if and when a police officer must inform the administration about the use of medication. Most of those policies limit the reporting of medications to those that prevent or limit the officer from safely and effectively performing his or her assigned duties. But there are variations. One agency had a policy that required the officers to report any medication that "affected your mind." Under rules that vague, an officer would have to report taking aspirin or allergy medications, or even being in love.

"I don't want something controlling my mind."

Control is a big issue for cops. Policing is all about control—control of situations and control of one's emotions. Cops get paid to restore lost order. As they do so, they must control their own emotions or risk acting inappropriately. The thought of taking medication that has the power to control one's mind is understandably frightening, even though that concern is based on stigma and inaccurate information.

Former police officer and psychologist Al Benner used to tell treatment reluctant police officers, "Misery is optional." We endorse this statement. Our job is to tell officers what we believe is the most effective and fastest route for recovery. They get to decide what they are willing to do and how long or how slow their recovery will be. Our experience is that when provided with specific treatment recommendations from a person they trust, most officers will follow through.

"I don't want to take anything that is addicting."

It is always amusing to listen to police officers refuse to take nonaddictive medications at the same time they are getting drunk every night to cope with their psychological symptoms. One officer declared that he used alcohol to combat his PTSD symptoms because it occurs "naturally in the environment." In law enforcement it is socially acceptable to drink, and in fact, it is often encouraged. As any experienced clinician will know, there is no magic pill or technique for getting around addiction and denial. It sometimes helps to challenge the officer's thinking by pointing out that if he were taking proper medications, his symptoms might be reduced without the need to turn to alcohol—which, as everyone knows, creates its own inevitable problems.

"How would I know which medication to take?"

This is a reasonable question requiring some education. We tell officers that there is no sure way to prescribe the correct medication on the first try. Antidepressants are particularly difficult to match to an individual. Some people have to try a number of different medications until they find one with few side effects and sufficient positive benefits. This trial-and-error process could take a number of months.

We ask an officer if he or she has a first-degree blood relative who is achieving good results taking a specific antidepressant medication. If so, that medication may be a good place to start, and we recommend the officer share that information with the prescribing professional. We explain that doctors sometimes prescribe medications by matching medication side effects with obvious symptoms. So if an officer is having difficulty sleeping, a doctor might prescribe a medication with sedative effects. This doesn't always work well. Given the number of possible medications and the fact that some health plans will only pay for generic medications, we recommend that the officer see someone who is specifically trained to prescribe psychiatric medication.

"I don't want to take medication for the rest of my life."

Many officers believe that if you start taking a medication you will need to take it forever. In the vast majority of cases that is not true. Most officers take medication for about 9 months to 1 year. We ask officers to make a commitment to take the medication for at least 1 year from the time they are on a therapeutic dose.

It is also important to advise officers not to stop the medication once they start feeling better. Many officers who complain about a resurgence of their depression admit that they stopped taking their medications because they were feeling fine. Educate your client about how to taper off medication, and tell him or her to do so only under a doctor's care. Most doctors suggest a slow tapering with pauses to see if symptoms reemerge.

While it may seem obvious, officers should be encouraged to take medication as prescribed, most likely on a daily basis. Or, in the case of benzodiazepines, on an as-needed basis.

"I hear there are horrible side effects."

The most common side effects discussed among officers are sexual side effects. This includes an inability to obtain an erection, delayed orgasm, or decreased libido in both men and women. Officers should understand that not all medications have the same side effects. If they are taking one medication that is causing undesirable side effects they should speak to their doctor about switching to a different medication or supplementing one medication with another to alleviate the side effect.

ACOEM GUIDELINES

The ACOEM has created guidelines regarding medication use for law enforcement. Some ACOEM members are also members of the Physician

Services Section of the International Association of Chiefs of Police (IACP) and guide IACP members (law enforcement executives) on medical issues. The guidelines can be purchased from their website (*www.acoem.org*). One of their basic principles (4.18.15) regards the prescribing of medication:

> The effect of psychoactive medications should be evaluated in the same manner as any other medication. LEOs should not be restricted simply because they are being treated with psychoactive medication(s). They need appropriate evaluation regarding the effect of these medications, as well as the underlying condition(s). Many LEOs may work without restrictions when taking psychoactive medications with ongoing monitoring.

The guidelines also caution that although medications may be appropriate for on-duty use, there are times when officers need time away from the job in order for a medication to have its full effect. For example, depressed officers can take antidepressants without any adverse job-related affects. But if their depression is severe, then officers should not work until the depression abates.

ACEOM Medication Categories

A (Acceptable)

These medications are unlikely to adversely impact performance of job functions. Therefore, they are generally acceptable for use while on duty. Police physicians should continue to assess an LEO individually for issues related to the medication or the condition for which it is being taken.

T (Temporary)

These medications *may* have an impairing effect at the beginning of treatment. Appropriate restrictions should be applied on a temporary basis at the beginning of treatment, until it can be ascertained that the effects of the medication are unlikely to cause sudden incapacitation or inability to safely perform certain job functions. Some effects may only be present while the LEO adjusts to the medication. If they persist, use of an alternative medication should be considered, or the LEO may need continued restrictions. Depending on the medication, the police physician may need to evaluate on-the-job performance in a restricted-duty setting or perform ancillary examinations to determine the effect on the individual LEO.

S (Shift)

These medications are known to have effects of short duration that may adversely impact performance of job functions. These medications may be taken while the LEO is off duty with adequate time before returning to duty for the resolution of any negative effects. There may be two recommended dosing periods, depending on the duration of action of the medication. The duration of the restriction assumes that the medication will be taken according to recommended dosing.

R (Restricted)

These medications are likely to have an adverse impact on an officer's safety or job performance. Appropriate restrictions should be provided for LEOs taking these medications.

Some Brief Examples of the ACEOM Medication Categories

Category T: Antidepressants

These include the SSRIs Celexa (citalopram), Prozac (fluoxetine), and Zoloft (sertraline), which are approved for on-duty use. This group of drugs is both acceptable and temporary because the side effects are short-lasting. If the LEO starts using them on his or her days off, the side effects can be expected to abate before the officer returns to work. Other antidepressants, such as Wellbutrin (bupropion) and Cymbalta (duloxetine), should have a temporary restriction at the beginning of treatment to monitor for side effects.

Category S: Antianxiety Medications

These are typically classified as anxiolytics/hypnotics and benzodiazepines. Most of these medications are considered safe for short-term use if taken off duty and there is a delay prior to returning to work. When talking to your client about Category S drugs, use the analogy of drinking a beer, something LEOs understand because they are familiar with how much alcohol affects the body and for how long. They know it's OK to have a beer off duty as long as they have enough time for the alcohol to filter out of their systems. Commonly prescribed medications in this category are Ativan (lorazepam), Valium (diazepam), and Xanax (alprazolam).

Categories A and T: Sleep Medications

The commonly prescribed medications under this category are Lunesta (eszopiclone), Sonata (zaleplon), and Ambien (zolpidem). Some of these medications are safe to use at any point while the officer is off duty; While these medications are safe to use, LEOs should understand that everyone reacts differently to drugs. It is advisable that cops first try sleep medication on a night when they don't have to work the next day in case they feel groggy or feel like they have a hangover. With other medications, it is recommended that the officer allow a specific number of hours between use of the medication and return to work.

Some officers take Desyrel (trazodone) to help them sleep. Trazodone is in a class of medications called serotonin modulators and works by increasing the amount of serotonin in the brain. Trazodone was originally marketed as an antidepressant, but was found to be so sedating that it was not practical for most people. At lower doses it still has a sedating effect and can help with sleep. It also has the benefit of being nonaddicting. Other common sleep medications are over-the-counter drugs like Tylenol or Excedrin PM. These medications contain diphenhydramine and can be effective with insomnia.

AREAS OF SPECIAL CONCERN

Nightmares

In our experience officers with PTSD will frequently have nightmares. These nightmares differ from the "gun dreams" described in Chapter 2 and can vary from mildly upsetting to incredibly debilitating. There are medications that can help reduce or eliminate such nightmares.

> After a violent confrontation during which he was nearly killed, Stanley dreamed that he was walking in his house and could hear scratching inside a wall. As he looked at the wall a crack appeared, and the suspect, gun in hand, started coming at him through the crack. His wife told us that he runs in his sleep and has ruined several sets of expensive linens. "No more Egyptian cotton," she swore. "Not until his PTSD is under control."

Other officers have told us about waking up after hearing people calling out, convinced that the voices they heard were in the room with them. One LEO believed that these were the voices of people he had failed to rescue. Many report waking up with pounding hearts, soaked in sweat, but unable to remember what they were dreaming.

It is critically important to successful therapy to stop these nightmares and help your client improve her quality of sleep. Sleep deprivation makes everything worse, and so does self-medicating with alcohol and over-the-counter drugs. We have seen major improvements in clients who take prazosin. Prazosin is a beta blocker that blocks some of the effects of adrenaline. It also appears to be effective at stopping nightmares or reducing their frequency (Raskind et al., 2003; van Liempt, Vermetten, Geuze, & Westenberg, 2006).

> Jonathon was involved in a shooting and suffered from nightmares for over 20 years before being placed on prazosin. He called his therapist 3 days later, crying because he had just had his first night's sleep without a nightmare.

Intrusive and Severe PTSD Symptoms

A number of officers we have worked with report seeing dead people they once encountered on a call for service standing in line at the supermarket or on the sidewalk. These people seem absolutely real and appear during waking hours. Other officers hear voices or feel the presence of people. These terrifying symptoms are so debilitating that they often render officers unable to work.

Medications that come under a class of drugs called atypical antipsychotics can make a big difference to these men and women. These medications are usually prescribed to people with schizophrenia and other serious mental illnesses, but they can be prescribed at much lower doses to officers experiencing some of the hallucinatory symptoms described above. Understandably, officers recoil at being given medication that is meant for psychotic patients. You may need to explain to officers that medications labeled as antipsychotic are so labeled because that was the first category they were approved to treat. They were subsequently discovered to be effective in varying dosages for a variety of symptoms but still retain their original labels. Medications that fall under this category are Abilify (aripiprazole), Seroquel (quetiapine), Risperdal (risperidone), and Zyprexa (olanzapine). These drugs have a temporary restriction at the start of use. Seroquel has also been prescribed for insomnia and has been effective for some people.

Medication for Alcoholism and Other Addictions

People get sober and refrain from maladaptive behaviors through many avenues. Some recover without any intervention (Robins, 1993; Smart, 1988). For those who do not, we have found psychopharmacological interventions to be beneficial, especially medications that focus on increasing the bioavailability of serotonin and norepinephrine. For example, Suboxone has been found useful in the treatment of opioid addiction, as have medications used to treat obsessive–compulsive disorders, such as fluvoxamine (Luvox). For addictions that arise in the context of atypical bipolar or personality disorders involving emotional instability, medications such as divalproex (Depakote) or similar mood stabilizers are helpful. Research has recently revealed that mifepristone, a drug approved by the U.S. Food and Drug Administration for the termination of early pregnancy, shows some promise in helping recovering male alcoholics from relapsing (Simms, Haas-Koffler, Bito-Onon, Li, & Bartlett, 2012). (For more information on substance abuse, see Chapter 11.)

KEY POINTS

- Approach the discussion of medication from a psychoeducational perspective. Explain the difference between an antidepressant and a benzodiazepine or discuss the effect of alcohol on depression or PTSD. Information is often what is needed to overcome the stigma associated with psychotropic drugs. It's highly likely that your client's primary care physician won't have the time.

- Ask your client if she is making "perimeter checks"—waking up at night after hearing a sound, grabbing a weapon, and walking around the house to make sure nobody is breaking in. When we describe this, officers smile in recognition. Often a cop will say half-jokingly, "If you only do it once a night, that's not bad, is it?" Perimeter checks are frequently associated with posttraumatic stress injuries.

Part IV

COMMON
PRESENTING PROBLEMS

Part IV explores a range of common problems—addiction, depression and suicide, and somatization. These concerns are not unique to cops, but they are both augmented and camouflaged by the culture of law enforcement. Their prevalence is hard to establish. When these concerns come up, cultural norms will play a role in your therapeutic strategies.

11

ALCOHOLISM, SUBSTANCE ABUSE, AND OTHER ADDICTIONS

I never saw a problem that couldn't be
made worse by alcohol.
—POLICE PEER SUPPORTER

I slept like a baby:
cried, took a bottle, and pissed myself.
—POLICE OFFICER

Calls for service fall on a continuum, from horrific at one end
to routine or irritating at the other end. Oddly, it may be the ones in the
middle that bother LEOs the most. The horrific incidents are recognized
for what they are, and officers can usually expect support from their peers
and their superiors. But the minor or "subcritical" incidents attract little
attention. Officers are expected to just "suck it up" and go on to the next
call. The way some LEOs cope with the pileup of everyday misery is to
drown it in alcohol.

CHOIR PRACTICE: A BRIEF HISTORY OF DRINKING AND LAW ENFORCEMENT

The ritual of cops drinking together after work is known as choir practice, a term introduced by veteran LAPD officer Joseph Wambaugh in his 1975 book *The Choirboys*. The practice continues and is not just for boys anymore. Women officers are not immune to its dangers.

Drinking is acceptable, and sometimes encouraged, in the law enforcement culture. The same departments that have a zero tolerance policy for illegal drug use turn a blind eye to alcohol abuse. This has been going on for a long time—since at least the mid-19th century. When cops walked a beat, it was not unusual for officers to carry flasks to combat freezing temperatures, or to warm up with a quick shot in the local tavern. Alcohol was traditionally consumed at all types of celebrations, from funerals to birthday parties. Officers drank when they got a promotion and drank when they didn't. Booze accentuated accomplishments and drowned disappointments. Going out for a drink after work became routine.

In the 1950s, the Boston Police Department Stress Program pioneered an alcohol-abuse counseling program. Other departments followed: the Chicago Police Officers' Fellowship (cops' code name for AA) in 1955, the NYPD in 1966, LAPD in 1975, and San Francisco PD in 1983. Over the years, these and countless other departments have expanded their programs to include services for a broad spectrum of behavioral and psychological problems.

THE CURRENT SITUATION

Alcohol is still regarded as a social lubricant that allows LEOs to escape from the realities of their work and to compartmentalize and hermetically seal away intrusive thoughts. It is the glue than cements friendships. LEOs cite "fitting in with others" as the number one reason they drink (Lindsay & Shelley, 2009) and go to social gatherings where alcohol is consumed (Davy, Obst, & Sheehan, 2000).

Alcohol is legal, but driving under the influence (DUI), public intoxication, and alcohol-related domestic abuse are not. No longer does a police badge operate like a "get out of jail free" card. We know many officers who have been arrested for DUI, public intoxication, and domestic violence. We also know officers who overlook problem drinking and go to great lengths to cover for each other, thus setting the drinker up for bigger problems in the future (Kirschman, 1997). This avoidance is misguided because cops who abuse alcohol but do not engage in criminal activity are often considered for rehabilitation (Stone, 1995) rather than fired.

Prevalence Rates

Acording to Hackett and Violanti (2003), anecdotal evidence suggests that rates of alcohol abuse are higher among police officers than in the general public. Research on fire fighters suggests that their rates of problem drinking are high as well (Boxer & Wild, 1993; Corneil, 1995; McFarlane, 1998). But other studies of law enforcement and emergency responders suggest the opposite. A study done by the U.S. Department of Health and Human Services (Larson, Eyerman, Foster, & Gfroerer, 2007) for the years 2002–2004 showed prevalence of alcohol dependence or abuse in protective service occupations to be 7.3%, compared to 9.2% for persons age 18 to 64. Nine other professions showed significantly higher rates of alcoholism. Ballenger and colleagues (2011) sampled 747 urban police officers. Adverse consequences from alcohol use were reported by 18% of the males and 16% of the females, and 7.8% met the criteria for lifetime alcohol abuse or dependence. Another national study of drug use and health found that first responders did not have a higher rate of alcohol abuse or dependency than other professions but did report a higher rate of binge drinking (Weir, Stewart, & Morris, 2012). Honig and Samo's (2007) study of Los Angeles County sheriff's deputies showed their incidence of alcohol abuse to be lower than that of the general public. While no one knows for sure, we suspect these lower rates of alcohol use may be related to improvements in preemployment screening.

Dual Diagnosis: Alcoholism and PTSD

Epidemiological studies support the comorbidity of two disorders: PTSD and substance abuse, particularly alcohol abuse (Brown, Read, & Kahler, 2003; Kulka et al., 1990; Wedding, 1987). Kosten and Krystal (1988) suggest that the neurochemical properties of alcohol reduce the symptoms associated with PTSD. For example, alcohol acts on the locus coeruleus, which modulates the alarm reaction (Brick & Poohereckky, 1983; Lynch et al., 1983). Likewise, norepinephrine dysregulation is believed to be a central feature of PTSD, and alcohol decreases noradrenergic neuronal function (Southwick et al., 1993). (See Chapter 5 for more about trauma and posttraumatic stress injuries.)

When clients self-medicate to alleviate their symptoms, it complicates their clinical presentation and makes diagnosis more complex (Keane, Buckley, & Miller, 2003). Paradoxically, the use of alcohol or marijuana over time tends to increase the symptoms of depression and anxiety, especially for those who suffer from PTSD (Beckner & Arden, 2008). For alcoholics, in general, the risk of committing suicide is 50 to 70% higher than it is for those who do not abuse alcohol (Honig & Samo, 2007).

Alcohol use is contraindicated in conjunction with the use of medications for PTSD or depression because it neutralizes the effects of the medication. It is our experience that cops who have symptoms of PTSD do not recover if they continue to drink and abuse alcohol. We are not recommending total abstinence for all of these officers, although for some that may indeed be the proper recommendation. Rather, LEOs need to understand that the choice they are making to drink may slow or impede their ability to recover.

ASSESSING FOR ALCOHOL ABUSE

There are several tools available to assess for substance abuse. Brief screenings that include reporting of current usage have greater validity for treatment than those that look at lifetime histories of abuse. Those brief screening tools include the AUDIT, BMAST, CAGE, Quantity/Frequency Questionnaire, and the TWEAK.

The AUDIT has 10 questions and was developed by the World Health Organization for use in primary care settings (Saunders, Aasland, Babor, de la Fuente, & Grant, 1993). The BMAST is a brief version of the Michigan Alcoholism Screening Test that has been found to be useful in both clinical and nonclinical settings (Pokorny, Miller, & Kaplan, 1972). The CAGE consists of four questions:

1. Have you ever felt you should CUT down on your drinking?
2. Have people ANNOYED you by criticizing your drinking?
3. Have you ever felt bad or GUILTY about your drinking?
4. Have you ever had a drink first thing in the morning to steady your nerves or to get rid of a hangover (EYE-OPENER)?

The Quantity/Frequency Questions were developed by the National Institute on Alcohol Abuse and Alcoholism (2003) and are broadly used by physicians; this screening tool asks about frequency, and both the typical and the greatest number of drinks consumed in the past month. The TWEAK is a screen for women and consists of five items assessing tolerance, complaints from others about their drinking, use of alcohol as an eye-opener, blackouts, and attempts to cut down on alcohol intake (Russell et al., 1994). The Rapid Alcohol Problems Screen (RAPS) is effective across various ethnic groups and for use with women (Cherpitel, 1997). It consists of five items:

1. Do you sometimes take a drink in the morning when you first get up?
2. During the past year, has a friend or family member ever told you about things you said or did while you were drinking that you could not remember?
3. During the past year, have you had a feeling of guilt or remorse after drinking?
4. During the past year, have you failed to do what was normally expected of you because of drinking?
5. During the past year, have you lost friends or girlfriends or boyfriends because of drinking?

OTHER ADDICTIONS

The template for any addictive behavior, including pornography, would include clinically significant impairment or distress, tolerance preceding increased quantity or intensity, withdrawal symptoms, failed attempts to cut down or control the behavior, time spent seeking out the behavior, relinquishing enjoyable activities, and continuing the behavior despite knowing the harm it causes.

Marijuana Addiction

Many LEOs use marijuana to help them cope with job stress. Marijuana use has become more acceptable in society and especially in those states that have legalized it. In California, for example, marijuana is legal for medicinal use, although virtually anyone can get a prescription. Police officers must weigh the benefits of using marijuana for relaxation off duty against departmental regulations that may prohibit its use. Clinicians can be particularly useful in helping officers weigh the pros and cons. In addition, teaching LEOs self-soothing skills, such as hypnosis and progressive relaxation, may give them the stress reduction they seek without the risks inherent in using pot (see Chapters 9 and 13 for more information).

Sexual Addiction

Some clients attempt to satisfy their cravings through the use of pornography, compulsive masturbation, voyeurism, exhibitionism, casual sex, illicit affairs, and/or patronizing paid sex workers. Sex is big business. At the turn of the millennium, over 25 million Americans visited porn sites between 1 and 10 hours per week, and sex was the number one topic searched on the Internet (*Washington Times*, January 26, 2000). In 2010 *The Week* magazine reported that 25% of Internet searches related to pornography, 28,000 people viewed porn sites every second, and 75 million people visited adult websites every month between 2005 and 2008. In the United States during 2006, revenue from pornography was $13 billion ("The Internet Porn 'Epidemic'," 2010).

> Tommy was involved in a highly publicized incident that resulted in his having to testify against one of his best friends on the force, resulting in his friend's termination. Everything that could go wrong went wrong. There was community outrage, threats against officers, and relentless coverage by the media. Tommy and his wife, Lynda, had three children, including a newborn. His wife was overwhelmed with child care responsibilities, sleep deprived from breast-feeding, and suffering with undiagnosed postpartum depression. She barely had time to get everything done, let alone pay attention to Tommy, who was consumed with guilt and so wracked with PTSD that he couldn't go back to work. Sex was out of the question.
>
> Whenever Tommy made a bid for Lynda's attention she had no time or energy to respond. When she turned to Tommy for help, he was irritable and so caught up in his own difficulties that he had nothing to give. She got more and more depressed, and he began spending more and more time sequestered in his den looking at porn on his computer and masturbating. They both justified Tommy's behavior by saying it was better than his having affairs or drinking. Their vicious cycle was only broken when Tommy got help for his PTSD and he and Lynda started couple counseling.

Problem Gambling

Most people gamble in one form or another (Whelan, Steenbergh, & Meyers, 2007). They do so by buying lottery tickets, participating in raffles or office sports pools, dabbling in the stock market, and patronizing gambling resorts and card clubs. They don't even need to leave home because they can gamble on their computers.

But for some people, including some cops, gambling evolves from an occasional pastime into a compulsion. Compulsive gambling is characterized by clusters of symptoms classified into three groups: loss of control, disruption in the gambler's life, and dependence. It involves preoccupation with gambling in order to achieve desired excitement, restlessness or irritability when attempting to stop, betting to make up for past gambling losses, problems controlling engagement in gambling, and continuation of the gambling behavior in spite of mounting serious and negative consequences.

Inspector Conners enjoyed his vacations in Atlantic City. However, he never wanted to go on vacation anywhere else, and his wife refused to go with him because all he did was gamble while he was there. In fact, during his time in Atlantic City, he rarely slept, and he felt a need to make up his losses. People at work thought he had a problem but dared not mention anything because he was the boss. He felt entitled to a little entertainment now and then and protested that he wasn't hurting anyone. After all, he wasn't engaging in affairs or drinking alcohol. He supported his habit by taking out a second mortgage to pay the bills. He and his wife were arguing constantly. She insisted that he see a therapist or engage in couple counseling. He decided instead to retire and move to Atlantic City.

CBT has been used effectively for problem gambling. Petry and colleagues (2006) found that some gamblers can decrease their gambling with short-term interventions, although complete abstinence is rare. They found that psychotherapy using CBT decreased gambling more than referral to Gamblers Anonymous (GA) alone or GA plus the use of a CBT workbook (Petry et al., 2006). A meta-analysis of 22 treatment studies of problem gambling showed significant results both immediately posttreatment and at follow-up (Palleson, Mitsem, Kvale, Johnsen, & Molde, 2005).

Addiction to Pain Medication

Officers get injured a lot. There is little that is ergonomically correct about a patrol car. They are uncomfortable and can cause back problems. The 10-plus pounds of gear a cop wears on his or her belt adds to the risk of skeletal and muscular disabilities. In 2010, 53,469 officers were assaulted in the line of duty (Federal Bureau of Investigation, 2011), many suffering injuries. Ironically, a subset of officers get injured while trying to stay in shape.

Injured officers are often prescribed addictive analgesics such as opioids. In addition to their pain-killing effects, opioids produce enjoyable feelings of euphoria that can be addictive, leading to dependence and withdrawal symptoms if they are abruptly discontinued. There are also negative side effects such as constipation, depression of the respiratory system, and sedation.

We've already pointed out that LEOs typically do not like to lose control, and many don't like taking medications. They take their medication only as prescribed, reduce the dose when directed by their physician, and are happy to be off the pills. The LEOs who get in trouble are those who relish the momentary escape and have no other healthful means of achieving it. Once they are hooked, they doctor shop in search of prescriptions, use more than directed, and panic when their supply gets low before the next prescription. These behaviors are not unique to law enforcement, with one exception. Insurance adjusters, restaurant employees, gardeners, and other workers probably won't lose their jobs if they are discovered abusing prescription medication. For cops, it is likely the end of their careers.

TREATMENT FOR ADDICTION

For many years it was thought that for addiction treatment to be effective a client had to participate on a voluntary basis after first hitting rock bottom (Mueser, Noordsy, Drake, & Fox, 2003). Subsequent research indicates that (1) the sooner an addict is admitted to treatment, the better the prognosis is for recovery and (2) mandatory treatment can be effective (Waters, Roberts, & Morgen, 1997). Described below are various treatment modalities we have found effective when working with LEOs.

Education

As we have said repeatedly, psychoeducation is an important component of all our treatment strategies, regardless of the presenting problem. Rather than feeling judged or pathologized, cops do better with information and the opportunity to engage in collaborative problem solving. An explanation isn't the same as a cure, but providing an overview of the addiction cycle, for example, helps LEOs better understand what they are up against. Here's a sample of how we might talk to a cop about addiction:

> "A bad day at work can trigger emotional pain. If you don't have access to adaptive coping skills, then you may believe that the alcohol will relieve your pain. It is absolutely necessary to have a list of other things that you could do instead of going out to a bar or home for a drink. Exercise is a good example, but we will explore more about what other coping strategies you could use. If you continue to drink to relieve your pain, then it will likely lead to increased preoccupation with your drinking such as looking at your watch, hoping that your shift will end on time, or waiting for the kids to go to bed so you can drink. Your preoccupation with drinking might lead to isolating from others or keep you from participating in activities that you used to enjoy. If you do take a drink, you'll probably feel shame, guilt, or remorse and vow to not do it again—until the next trigger that causes you emotional pain. Then the cycle starts all over again."

Harm Reduction

Cops often believe themselves to be different from ordinary citizens. In many ways, they are. Most of us couldn't or wouldn't do what they do; we may fall apart in crises and avoid dangerous situations whenever possible. As the saying goes, cops and fire fighters run toward what the rest of us are fleeing. This prideful stance is necessary to do a dangerous job, but it can get in the way of recovering from addictions. It's foolish to believe you can drink relentlessly and not become a drunk. It's denial to protest that you are not an alcoholic because you binge on your days off but are sober during the week.

> Buck worked undercover for years. He had a knack for fitting in and was really good at his job as a "buy monkey," arresting any number of drug dealers. He was able to avoid using drugs to prove to his new "friends" that he wasn't a cop by swearing that he was on parole and had to report to his parole officer for drug testing. But he wasn't able to avoid drinking with them. He had been a heavy drinker most of his life; still he thought he was tough enough not to let his drinking get out of control. He was also abusing pain medication in an effort to keep up with the physical demands of his job. At 48, he was almost twice as old as the cops and the criminals he hung out with.

Buck's relentless pursuit of self-destruction was obvious as was his ambivalence about changing. On the verge of losing both his job and his marriage, Buck reluctantly reached out to his employee assistance program (EAP), who referred him to Mr. Torres, a substance abuse counselor. Their first appointment focused on harm reduction. Harm reduction is a nonjudgmental, philosophical stance that does not set abstinence as a goal but rather seeks to reduce the harmful effects that such use generates. The client determines his or her level of use. In essence, it promotes the idea that it is possible to turn substance abusers into social users. It works best for cops who are polysubstance abusers by concentrating on one substance at a time.

> Because Buck was abusing both alcohol and pain medication, he decided to work on limiting his use of pain medications, primarily because his doctor was refusing to prescribe more. He and Mr. Torres set a specific goal aiming to reduce Buck's use of pain pills to a level acceptable to his physician. Buck's therapy pinpointed only those specific behaviors and thoughts that supported his goal. Once he achieved that, relapse prevention became the target for therapy, after which Mr.

Torres offered him the opportunity to terminate treatment or continue with another treatment goal.

Harm reduction is valuable for officers who are in the precontemplation stage of addiction, the stage at which they are not yet convinced that they have a problem. However, there are several caveats. If your client also suffers from an anxiety or mood disorder, treatment of these disorders with co-occurring substance abuse will prove difficult, if not impossible. Additionally, there is no empirical evidence that an alcoholic police officer can be successfully turned into a social drinker. Most programs that make that claim have not demonstrated long-term success.

Motivational Interviewing

There are many treatment modalities that effectively treat alcohol dependence, including CBT, 12-step groups, rational emotive therapy (RET), and short-term dynamic therapy. But, in our experience, motivational interviewing (MI) is most useful for LEOs who are in the precontemplative stage, trying to decide if they have a drinking problem and what they want to do about it.

MI is a client-centered approach to assist conscious decision making. It involves collaboration with the therapist to create a supportive, safe, and nonjudgmental alliance from which change can be explored. It is based on the work of Carl Rogers, who believed that the way therapists communicate and interact with their clients is as important as their specific approaches and theoretical orientations.

MI theorists state that three conditions are necessary for change: (1) reflective listening that clarifies and reinforces the client's personal experience; (2) nonpossessive warmth; and (3) genuineness. Motivation for change occurs when it is safe for the client to explore his or her present pain in relation to what is wanted and valued. MI involves selectively responding to material presented by the client in a way that resolves ambivalence and moves the client toward the direction of change (Miller & Rolnick, 2002).

Buck was ambivalent about drinking. He couldn't imagine his life without alcohol and hoped he could cut down without stopping entirely. He oscillated back and forth between his desire to drink and his desire to stop: the more he leaned toward one option, the more attractive the other option seemed. He and Dr. Torres constructed a list of the benefits and costs of continuing to drink or abstaining. Dr. Torres never came down on one side or the other of Buck's dilemma or opted strongly for abstinence, but rather swung back and forth with him. Here's a sample from Buck's list:

Benefits of drinking	Costs
Helps me relax	Could lose my family
I like getting high	Wrecking my health

Benefits of abstaining	Costs
Less family conflict	I'll lose touch with peers
Good example for my kids	Don't know how to unwind

Creating this list allowed Buck and Mr. Torres to identify key challenges for Buck. He needed to develop alternate ways to relax and figure out how he was going to maintain treasured friendships without alcohol. One of Buck's claims to fame was his reputation as a heavy drinker and "party animal." Abstaining from drinking uncovered some deep-seated insecurities about his ability to "smoke and joke" with his friends if he got sober.

MI also involves analyzing the factors working toward and against sobriety, such as the peer pressure to drink, as well as serious consideration of client's confidence in his or her ability to handle specific aspects of change. For instance, Buck had so alienated his family that he wasn't sure he knew how to make amends and get things back on track. Going through this process together gave both Buck and Mr. Torres a map for treatment.

The following questions are merely samples of MI. The interested reader is encouraged to consult the Resources for recommended books.

- "Is that a fair summary of what you said? Have I missed anything?"
- "What do you think will happen if you don't change anything?"
- "What would you like your life to be like 5 years from now?"
- "When else in your life have you made a significant change like this? How did you do it?"
- "Never mind the "how" for right now—*what* do you want to happen?"
- "If you were completely successful in making the changes you want, how would things be different?"

Self-Help Groups

Having an established support system is crucial to recovery. There are well over 20 12-step groups for various addictions, including those that support friends and family members and those that include recovery without using the concept of a higher power (aka AA without God).

Various studies endorse the effectiveness of self-help groups. Winzelberg and Humphreys (1999) studied the effects of 12-step group attendance on 3,018 male abusers of alcohol and other substances at 15 Department of Veterans Affairs hospitals. They found that attendance significantly increased abstinence and reduced substance abuse problems, even for patients who did not believe in God. Vaillant (2005) concluded that "Alcoholics Anonymous appears equal to or superior to conventional treatments for alcoholism, and the skepticism of some professionals regarding AA as a first rank treatment for alcoholism would appear to be unwarranted" (p. 431). Our experience is that self-help groups are effective for those who are ready to do the work. For those who are not, therapy may be the most useful option. For those who are actively engaged in self-help work but struggling to complete the steps, therapy can be the difference that makes a difference between staying the course and dropping out.

> Mary Lou was on step nine, making amends to people she had harmed, including her children, her ex-husband, her mother, and her squad mates. This is a high-risk step with potentially serious consequences for everyone involved. Mary Lou's sponsor was encouraging but not very helpful (and the AA literature provided no specific guidance). Using techniques from MI, her therapist was able to help Mary Lou overcome her ambivalence about completing step nine. She and Mary Lou talked about forgiveness (see below) and the psychological and physical effects of holding on to resentment and hostility. She deconstructed the step into three component parts: (1) admission of wrong-doing; (2) sincere expression of a resolve to not continue the specific behavior; and (3) asking the person to whom the amends are directed, "What can I do to make it right?" This third component is often missing and is important because it returns control to the person who was harmed.

Peace Officer Fellowships: AA for Cops

Cops usually balk at attending AA meetings, fearing that they won't fit in or that they will wind up sitting next to someone they have arrested and to whom they may have "given some love" at the end of a foot chase. The Peace Officer Fellowship meetings are open to any first responder but are not listed in local AA directories. People usually find out about them through word of mouth or by seeing a flier that was sent to their department. These meetings allow the responders to discuss their work and talk about critical incidents without having to censor themselves. They are a safe place to unload. The concept is not unlike "The Other Bar" (AA for lawyers) or similar recovery groups for professionals. Some meetings are open to working and retired first responders with no alcohol abuse problem, who refer to themselves as JFU, meaning "just fucked up" or "just finding understanding." They come to these specialized groups because they realize that there is always something over which they are powerless.

Residential Treatment

In-patient or residential treatment is typically the highest level of care and is often sought when other methods have failed. The advantage of such programs is to alter the environment significantly and to build trust. Education is a major component of residential treatment, as is relapse prevention.

It is crucial that the clinician identify safe treatment programs for police officers. Treatment facilities that are cop-friendly have residents from similar socioeconomic backgrounds, are located in safe neighborhoods, have outside meetings that resemble those officers will attend after discharge, and have culturally competent staff who have experience working with LEOs (White, 2007). Such programs will have the following specific attributes:

- LEOs are unlikely to encounter criminals with whom they have had previous contact.
- LEOs are comfortable talking about their work and don't have to hide what they do.
- Residents are not housed with severely mentally ill patients.
- The facility does not have beds funded by parole, probation, or the courts.
- The facility does not take jail-like precautions such as bars on the windows, counting the silverware, locking the perimeter, or doing bed counts.

KEY POINTS

- Some LEOs believe that alcohol will help them sleep. The opposite is true. Alcohol will temporarily help them fall asleep but wake them about 90 minutes later and prevent them from entering slow-wave, restorative sleep (see Chapter 7).

- Changes introduced in DSM-5 include a revision of the category title itself from "Substance-Related Disorders" to "Substance Use and Addictive Disorders." Pending further research, Internet use disorder will be included as a new condition.

- Psychopharmacology represents an important treatment component for many alcoholics and addicts, especially when used in conjunction with psychotherapy (see Chapter 10 for additional information).

- Treating addiction is difficult. Only a small percentage of addicts and alcoholics ever achieve abstinence (Dawson et al., 2006), and problem drinkers die at a rate 1.6 times higher than non–problem drinkers (Schutte, Nichols, Brennan, & Moos, 2003).

- If there are no AA meetings for cops or police fellowship meetings in your area, consider starting one. It has been said that all you need is "a resentment and a coffee pot."

- See the Resources for residential treatment facilities that have programs for uniformed personnel.

12

DEPRESSION AND SUICIDE

> I grew up in the church. Suicide was never an option.
> But after a while, I got tired. Tired of fighting, tired of the
> symptoms, tired of trying. The unthinkable began to be
> thinkable. Suicide began to make sense.
> —POLICE OFFICER

How do officers who persisted through a demanding application process, rigorous psychological screening, and an arduous and lengthy period of training get so low that suicide appears to be their best and only option? How do professional problem solvers become so overwhelmed by their own problems that they are reduced to a state of suicidal hopelessness? There are probably as many answers as there are officers who kill themselves. This chapter addresses the controversy around frequency and prevalence rates of law enforcement suicide, cites some risk factors that may be unique to LEOs, briefly discusses the police-specific consequences of mandatory hospitalization, looks at the debate around recognizing police suicide as a legitimate line-of-duty death (LODD), offers some ideas about helping coworkers after a suicide, and concludes with some ideas for prevention.

STATISTICS AND PREVALENCE RATES

Any discussion of police suicide is bound to be controversial. Few people agree on the suicide rate for police officers, and research on the topic has produced confusing statistical contradictions. For example, studies that focused on retired as well as active police officers, rather than only those on active duty, have much higher suicide rates per 100,000, suggesting, as we will discuss later, that retirement is a risk factor for suicide. One often-quoted paper written by Gaska (1980) looked at the suicide rate among retired police officers. Gaska reported that police retirees commit suicide at a rate of 334/100,000 and disabled retirees at a rate of 2,616/100,000. Heiman (1975) found that police suicides in London were as low as 5.8 per 100,000, and Nelson and Smith (1970) found a suicide rate among Wyoming police officers of 203.7 per 100,000. Hem, Berg, and Ekeberg (2001) reviewed numerous studies on police suicides and found many to have methodological flaws. Research on police suicide is hard to do; there are problems gathering data, a general lack of reliable empirical evidence, and problems with agencies covering up suicides (Violanti, Vena, Marshall, & Petralia, 1996). Why would a police department cover up a suicide or make it look like an LODD? In an LODD, an officer's family may be entitled to a package of entitlements such as the officer's salary, free tuition at state colleges, and medical benefits. If the officer commits suicide, the family receives far less. In some instances, the officer's suicide is covered up to protect the family emotionally and preserve the dead officer's reputation.

After reviewing 30 published studies conducted since 1950, Aamodt and Stalnaker (2006) arrived at a police suicide rate of about 18/100,000, considerably higher than that of the general public, but matching a sample of white males between the ages of 25 and 54, which is the dominant police demographic. The most common identifiable reasons for suicide were relationship issues, psychological problems, and work-related stress. According to the Centers for Disease Control and Prevention (*www.cdc. gov/ncipc/wisqars*), the overall rate for suicide in the general population is 11.3 suicide deaths per 100,000 people. John Violanti is a retired police officer, psychologist, and associate professor in the Department of Social and Preventive Medicine, State University of New York at Buffalo. He has been working in conjunction with the Badge of Life (*www. badgeoflife.com*), an organization dedicated to the prevention of police suicide, using the Internet and newspapers to gather data. They reviewed FBI reports on LODDs, both felonious and accidental, and compared them to the number of officers who committed suicide. This is what they found:

- 2008: 140 LODDs; 54 killed feloniously; 142 suicides
- 2009: 114 LODDs; 48 killed feloniously; 143 suicides
- 2010: 160 LODDs; 59 killed feloniously; 145 suicides
- 2011: 177 LODDs; 63 killed feloniously; 147 suicides

The number of officers who committed suicide is two to three times the number of officers killed by suspects. We consider this to be the most relevant and disheartening finding of all, considering that LEOs are psychologically screened before they are hired and are by definition employed and insured. The average LEO who completes suicide is male, 38.7 years old with 12.2 years in the field (Clark, White, & Violanti, 2012).

WHY DO OFFICERS COMMIT SUICIDE?

This is as complicated a question as it would be for the general population. The list of risk factors for a suicidal depression is extensive. Some overlap with the general patient population, others may be unique to law enforcement: alcoholism and substance abuse, relationship problems or loss, constant exposure to people in pain, disciplinary problems, unwanted retirement, depression, poor coping skills, financial difficulties, job stress, scandal, shame, failure, a distorted but culturally consistent rugged individualism, age, gender, and the ubiquitous presence of guns (Kirschman, 2007; Tuohy et al., 2005). The following case examples, drawn from our files, are illustrative of what can lead a cop to take his or her own life.

Retirement

Many careers offer the potential for a gradual transition to retirement. If you retire as a mental health professional, you can still volunteer your services or see a few clients a week. As one of our clients said when he contemplated retirement, "You are either on top of the cliff with the police team or you are at the bottom of the cliff by yourself. There are no soft landings." (More information about the joys and stresses of police retirement can be found in Chapter 4.)

Impending Job Loss and Shame

For some officers, the thought of losing the job is worse than losing one's life. This is hard to understand and, as illustrated in the following case examples, shame and sometimes scandal play a big part. Our clients have repeatedly told us, "All I know how to do is be a police officer. What other job could I find that would allow me to have the same lifestyle and benefits?" We know they're not only concerned about money. As we stated earlier, being a cop is not just a job, it's an identity, and losing it before you're ready, for whatever reason, can cause depression. Fear of losing the job is also the reason that cops will sometimes fail to report a suicidal colleague. They're afraid that doing so will cost their colleague his or her job.

Jason was involved in a public argument with his spouse. They were in a restaurant, and Jason believed that other diners overheard the shameful and damaging things he and his wife said to each other. Jason was convinced that this information, if revealed to his department, could cost him his job. That evening he committed suicide. As it turned out, the information, if it had been shared with his agency, would not have resulted in his termination.

Billy was on probation for drinking on the job. He was told that he could not drink again. If he did and was caught, he would be fired. About a year later he relapsed, and when the department found out, he killed himself. What is poignant is that Billy had many skills and wasn't even sure he wanted to stay in law enforcement. But he couldn't take the shame of being kicked out of the profession.

In September 2008, Lt. Michael Piggott, assigned to the Emergency Services Unit of the New York City Police Department, ordered a member of his unit to taser a mentally ill man who was striking out at the officer with an 8-foot-long section of a fluorescent light. As a result of being tasered, the emotionally disturbed individual fell from a balcony to the sidewalk, striking his head and dying. One month later, on his 46th birthday, Officer Piggott committed suicide. He wrote a suicide note to his family saying, "I love you all. I'm sorry for the mess!! I was trying to protect my guys that day! I ordered Nick to fire the Taser. I can't bear to lose my family and go to jail." His widow sued the department, claiming their statements to the press and actions toward her husband constituted negligent infliction of emotional distress. She lost her case (*Piggott v. City of New York*, 2011).

Perceived Failure

Police officers are responsibility absorbers. As mentioned in Chapter 3, cops often blame themselves for their perceived failure to save a victim, particularly a child. For one thing, you can't blame a child; for another, blaming yourself is apparently an easier pill to swallow than thinking you had no control over an event in the first place. Most of us have little tolerance for the notion that the world operates randomly and that we are limited operatives (Kirschman, 2007). Cops, especially, abhor feeling helpless. Blaming oneself is a way to restore the illusion of control: "All I need to do is not screw up and that—fill in the blank—won't happen again."

Ken was describing an incident when a hostage taker killed two hostages before taking his own life. "I killed those hostages," he told the therapist who was there to debrief the call. The therapist pressed the point, asking what Ken meant. As she expanded the narrative and made Ken go through the incident frame by frame, it turned out that the officers arrived too late to save the hostages, who were both probably dead before they hit the ground.

This is not Ken's individual pathology but a pattern we see repeatedly in our dealings with law enforcement. Dig hard enough and you'll discover that statements like "I killed him" or "It's my fault she died," actually mean something like "I didn't put it out on the radio soon enough" or "We drove down the wrong street." Tread carefully: when LEOs understand they weren't at fault, they have to live with the reality that it could happen again.

> Janice pursued a suspect through a wooded area. As she approached him, he pulled out a gun. Janice fired several rounds, some of which struck the suspect and incapacitated him. She was lauded as a hero, but she couldn't accept the praise. She believed that she had failed because the suspect was alive and a continuing risk to the other officers during the event. She blamed herself for failing to hit him with all six rounds.
>
> Janice carried so much guilt over this shooting that she fell into a deep depression. She was obsessed with the notion that she was a failure and decided to return to the scene and shoot herself in the head. The message she wanted to convey to her fellow officers was that they were wrong. She wasn't a hero. Because several of her rounds failed to hit the suspect, he could have killed another officer.

Betrayal

Betrayal, particularly administrative betrayal, was discussed in detail in Chapter 6. Administrative betrayal most likely played a part in Lt. Michael Piggott's suicide, although we are only surmising this after reading public accounts of his incident and the court ruling on his widow's lawsuit. What we do know is that any time an agency turns on an officer, the likely result is depression and anger. The gravity of the depression and the intensity of the anger will be amplified by earlier acts of betrayal, particularly those stemming from the officer's childhood.

> Fred was assaulted by a mentally ill man wielding a knife. Though the attack was a surprise, Fred handled it well, and the suspect was taken into custody without further incident. A year later, Fred's life was a mess. He was experiencing numerous PTSD symptoms and was quite depressed. During a therapy session, Fred, almost as an aside, mentioned that a friend of his had committed suicide many years ago.

His therapist almost passed over the remark with a simple statement of condolence, but something prompted him to ask a few questions and Fred went into more detail. The dead man had been Fred's best friend. On the day he killed himself, they had been hunting together, something they did all the time. Fred blamed himself for two reasons: first, he had failed to recognize that his friend was suicidal, and second, he had done nothing to protect himself. His friend could easily have killed him before taking his own life. Fred vowed never to let his guard down again. For the next 10 years he never went hunting with anyone else because he believed the risks were too great.

When he was attacked by the mentally ill man, Fred was caught by surprise. While the attack was gruesome and dangerous, the real issue eating at Fred was that he had once again betrayed his own directive never to let his guard down. He couldn't forgive himself and almost committed suicide. The therapeutic work that followed had two objectives: forgiving his friend for killing himself and forgiving himself for his perceived flaws.

GUNS AND PSYCHIATRIC HOSPITALIZATION

Officers in crisis are concerned that they may be placed on a psychiatric hold because they are a danger to themselves. Being conscripted to the "rubber gun squad" poses a unique risk to LEOs, a risk the average person doesn't face. In many states if you are placed on a psychiatric hold you could lose the right to possess a firearm for anywhere from 5 years to the rest of your life. For an officer, this means the end of his or her career.

For example, in California a person placed on a 5150 Welfare and Institutions Code (WIC) hold may not be eligible to possess a firearm for 5 years. If that person agrees to be admitted to a hospital voluntarily, there is no firearm restriction, regardless of the length of the hospital stay. An officer who is placed on a 5250 WIC hold—a 14-day extension of a 3-day hold—will lose the right to possess a firearm for the rest of his or her life. However, an officer in California who loses the right to possess a weapon can petition the court to get that right back. Courts generally will want to get an expert opinion on the matter.

We understand that sometimes clinical work necessarily shifts from saving a career to saving a life. Still, being effective almost always depends on your gaining the officer's cooperation in treatment. The takeaway is this: your knowledge of state law and your ability to explain it to an officer could mean the difference between an officer working with you and voluntarily going to a hospital versus an officer refusing to get treatment. It can also mean the difference between an officer losing his or her career and being able to return to the job. We have all worked with officers who, post-hospitalization, returned to work and had full, untroubled careers. This is a win, not just for the officers, but for their departments and the communities they serve. In some instances, these officers have started AA groups for cops, initiated peer support programs, and gone public with their stories in an attempt to get other officers to seek help in a timely way.

Guns are a real concern. Ninety percent of all police officer suicides are committed with a gun. An officer, even a suicidal officer, may be reluctant to give up his or her weapons. Think about how you might help a potentially suicidal officer turn over his or her guns to someone for safekeeping without endangering yourself. Sometimes officers will agree to have a close friend, a trusted member of the peer support team, or even a trusted therapist hold the weapons.

> Cory agreed to keep one gun at work but turn over all his other weapons to a friend. While this was an unusual arrangement, it worked. Cory felt in control on the job, and his suicidal ideation diminished.

Requesting a client make a verbal or written contract not to commit suicide or to call you when feeling suicidal is a common practice among clinicians, but not a very reliable one. The no-suicide contract builds on the notion that the strength of the client–therapist relationship will keep the client from killing himself (Kroll, 2007). There is no empirical evidence that a no-suicide contract works. On the other hand, because cops tend to stand by their word, we have found it useful to use the no-suicide contract strategy to identify an officer who is so distressed he cannot lie to his therapist about how deeply suicidal he is even if he planned to deny the depth of his depression.

In our opinion, it is just as important for the clinician to be flexible, creative, and committed to helping an officer stay safe as it is to be dedicated to helping the LEO keep his or her career. An officer's devotion to the job may be your best ally against self-destruction. There are always exceptions; some LEOs have endured too much to return to active duty, and what they need is permission, encouragement, and support to retire.

AFTERMATH: HELPING AN AGENCY AFTER A SUICIDE

If you've been asked to provide consultation to the department, your best course of action is to gather as much information as possible beforehand. The peer support team, if there is one, can provide you with some background. Ask not just about the dead officer, but the political climate in the agency. When you start to meet with people, in groups or individually, you'll no doubt encounter a varied range of emotion and multiple agendas.

Anger

In some cases peers feel that someone should have seen the suicide coming. Employees will want to know why the agency didn't do more to help the officer. Some will believe that "agency bullying" pushed the officer to suicide.

Guilt

Officers are trained to identify and manage suicidal people. So what does it mean when friends and coworkers missed the signs?

> Marty sent out an e-mail message with a photo of himself holding a bottle of alcohol. In the background, his gun lay on his coffee table. It was only after his death that his coworkers saw the gun. They were beside themselves for missing it. One officer berated himself for having coffee with Marty the day before he died but not picking up any hints that Marty was depressed.

Officers are adept at masking their feelings. They couldn't elicit a confession or avoid a fight if they didn't know how to hide their disgust or their fear. Sixty-four percent of the suicides reported in the National Study of Police Suicide (NSOPS) were a surprise (O'Hara & Violanti, 2009). Officers do a lot of magical thinking about suicides, believing that because they have been trained in suicide prevention, they should have kept their friend alive. Not only does this create a lot of guilt, it damages an officer's predictive confidence.

Blame

The idea that someone has to be at fault takes up a lot of time. Officers are action-oriented people. Beating up on someone, even oneself, can feel better than sinking into a morass of grief and helplessness (Kirschman, 2007). Common targets are surviving spouses, supervisors, and administrators, who can be regarded as uncaring, uninformed, or actively hostile. Unless handled appropriately, blame can cause long-term organizational damage.

THE POLITICS OF DEATH

When an officer is feloniously killed in the line of duty, that is an honorable death, accompanied by a huge formal police funeral with praise for the officer and a multitude of services for the grieving family. If the officer is accidently killed on the job, the response is similar, but with somewhat less outrage shown within the law enforcement community. But when an officer kills himself or herself, even if there is a good case for linking the suicide to work, the way to proceed isn't clear.

There is considerable controversy about whether an officer's suicide should be considered an LODD. One perspective on this is that some officers kill themselves as a consequence of suffering from years of unresolved job-related posttraumatic stress.

> Philip committed suicide shortly after retiring from a long career. He left a note to his family stating that he couldn't sleep and was constantly having nightmares. In the note he described many PTSD symptoms. He was clearly emotionally injured, but he had never sought help or told anyone else about these symptoms. Had he still been working, his suicide would not have qualified as an LODD, even though his injuries were sustained in the line of duty.

On the other hand, there are clinicians and law enforcement professionals who are concerned about legitimizing suicide. The question is, if suicide is considered an LODD, will that prompt more officers to kill themselves? There are no easy answers to this dilemma.

Officers are often unclear about how to proceed after a colleague's suicide. They have questions: Will there be a police funeral? Can I attend the funeral in uniform? Can I go on duty? How do LEOs pay respect to a friend and a colleague whose death doesn't fit the cultural norm? There are no perfect answers, but in our opinion a lot of goodwill can be gained if administrators choose to allow the officers to have some type of organizationally sanctioned response. The following example shows how community clinicians can be helpful in the aftermath of a suicide.

> Lenny was the last person anyone thought would kill himself. He was always so upbeat and full of life. Chief Raymond, was confused about how to announce his death to the department. Should she say Lenny committed suicide or simply omit any mention of the cause of death? Finally, out of respect for Lenny and his family, she chose the latter. By the time she called a department-wide meeting, everyone in the room knew that Lenny had committed suicide. They had already sanitized Lenny's locker—a ritual meant to save the deceased and the survivors from embarrassment should there be any evidence, for example, that the officer was having an affair.
>
> Chief Raymond arranged for a debriefing and contracted with Dr. Wheeling, a provider with the department's EAP, to facilitate. When Dr. Wheeling arrived at headquarters he found over 150 people waiting for him.

Dr. Wheeling faced an unworkable situation. First, it is impossible to successfully debrief 150 people at the same time. Second, a debriefing is reserved for people who work together and experienced the same event. For instance, you would not debrief police officers who responded to a traffic accident along with citizens who witnessed it, although both groups might be in need of debriefing services. Some of the people at the debriefing were there out of respect or curiosity. They barely knew Lenny. Others were deeply affected by his loss.

Dr. Wheeling suggested an alternative debriefing process. He quickly pulled together a lineup of speakers, starting with the chief. Chief Raymond gave a straightforward account of Lenny's death while omitting what she now knew to be the underlying cause, an impending divorce. She addressed her officers' questions about taking time off to attend the funeral: Were they allowed to wear uniforms? Could they take marked patrol vehicles? The chief expressed her support for the agency and all the people involved and offered to speak with anyone who wanted to talk with her.

The next speaker was the chaplain, who provided information about grief from a spiritual perspective. He briefly described the chaplaincy program, what chaplains could do to help officers and the grieving family, and how they could be contacted if someone needed assistance.

Dr. Wheeling himself was the third speaker. He talked about grief and how officers could support each other during these difficult times. He also mentioned the confidential EAP program and how officers could access counseling.

The final speakers were representatives of the peer support program. They provided specific information about the funeral, what people could do to support the family, and additional information about the peer support program. The meeting was over in less than an hour. Once the speakers were done, there were food and drinks for the attendees and time for people to mingle and talk. The chaplains, the peer supporters, and Dr. Wheeling stayed around making themselves available.

SUICIDE PREVENTION

Now that suicide is no longer a secret in law enforcement and in the military, departments and clinicians are dealing with the issue head on. The following are only two out of many examples of how this is being done.

Over the 4-year period between 2003 and 2007, 13 officers in the California Highway Patrol (CHP) committed suicide. As a result of this alarming statistic, the CHP, in collaboration with mental health consultants and the CHP peer support program, developed a 4-hour training block called "Not One More." The training, taught by peer support team members, was presented to every member of the department. The most powerful moment in the training is a video of CHP officers talking about their friends who committed suicide. While the suicide rate has not dropped to zero, it has been significantly reduced

In 2009, the International Association of Chiefs of Police (IACP), in collaboration with their Psychological Services Section, gathered suicide prevention training material from multiple agencies and combined it in one CD, which they provide to anyone who asks for it at no cost. The CD contains sample suicide-prevention print materials, PowerPoint presentations, videos, and a list of references (see the Resources).

In addition, the IACP wants to build a suicide prevention strategy that will amplify awareness of suicide among LEOs, combat the stigma around it, and assist large and small agencies to develop comprehensive and effective strategies for suicide prevention, intervention, and postvention. The following is a summary of IACP recommendations (Clark et al., 2012):

1. Encourage agencies to endorse and develop peer support programs.
2. Refute the stigma that accompanies attempts to get professional help and the myth that seeking help will cost officers their jobs.
3. Train officers to engage in healthy self-care rather than maladaptive coping, such as drinking to excess or "stuffing it." Include classes on resilience.
4. Raise awareness about risk factors and what steps to take when a fellow officer is contemplating suicide.
5. Develop and distribute a recommended course of action for chiefs following a completed LEO suicide.
6. Encourage agencies to investigate and report suspected LEO suicides using a psychological autopsy format.

KEY POINTS

- Most officers who kill themselves do so with guns. The first step to take with suicidal officers is to separate them from their duty weapon and any other weapons they own, including those they may keep at home. The more delay and distance you can place between the officer and his or her weapon, the less likely the LEO is to commit suicide.

- Familiarize yourself with your state's laws regarding involuntary hospitalization and the right to possess a weapon.

- The vast majority of police agencies employ fewer than 50 employees, who may be at increased risk for suicide because their workload is more intense and there is a lack of anonymity. Smaller budgets mean fewer resources (Clark et al., 2012).
- Clinicians can help local agencies by developing preretirement programs to prepare officers and their families for retirement and separation from the police identity.

13

SOMATIZATION, PANIC ATTACKS, AND STRESS REDUCTION

Body armor works both ways.
—POSTER IN A POLICE STATION

Police officers are no different from other clients when it comes to pain, although they may be less willing to talk about it with others or admit it to themselves. "Part of the territory," they might say, or "Comes with the job." Think of the professional baseball player who gets hit by a 95-mph fastball and refuses to rub the injured area. It's a "macho" thing affecting both female and male officers. The underlying ethos goes like this: Better not to let others know you are hurt or they'll think you're weak. Worse still, they'll wonder if you can do the job.

On the other hand, LEOs know that physical injuries are more easily accepted by their peers than are emotional or mental problems. Thus, having physical symptoms can be a face-saving way to express what an officer considers unspeakable. Expressing emotions via bodily pain or discomfort is a way of dealing with unpleasant feelings or memories without having to talk about them. This is not to say that all pain is psychic. Rather, there is a feedback loop—physical injuries create psychic stress, and psychic stress can create physical problems. The therapist's job is to identify, in an atmosphere of support and safety, the factors involved in the client's somatic complaint.

In this chapter we address a number of contributing factors that can lead to somatization such as health problems, physical injuries, personal history, genetics, and culture. We then go on to talk about related problems like panic attacks and hypervigilance, then close with some suggested stress reduction strategies.

HEALTH PROBLEMS

Health problems are common among LEOs (Brown & Campbell, 1994). The Buffalo Cardio-Metabolic Occupational Police Stress Study (BCOPS; Violanti, 2011) asserts that the psychological stresses police officers experience at work put them at significantly higher risk than the general population for long-term physical and mental health problems. The study of 464 officers using questionnaires, medical and laboratory tests, sleep data, and work history records dating back five decades, draws some alarming conclusions:

- The prevalence of depressive symptoms among the sample was nearly double that in the general population.
- Over 25% of the study officers had metabolic syndrome—placing them at risk for coronary artery disease, stroke, and type 2 diabetes. This compares to 18.7% of the U.S. employed population.
- Study officers were nearly four times more likely to sleep less than 6 hours per 24-hour time period than the employed population with whom they were compared.
- Officers with 30 years of police service had an increased risk of developing Hodgkin's lymphoma and brain cancer.

INJURIES

Data collected from over 10,000 law enforcement agencies employing 556,155 officers indicated that 57,268 (10.3%) were assaulted in the line of duty (U.S. Census Bureau, 2012). The California Public Employees' Retirement System (CALPERS) reported that 9.3% of all employees receiving benefits retired on disability (*www.calpers.ca.gov/eip-docs/about/pubs/employer/2012-idr.pdf*).

Cops get injured in all sorts of ways: in car chases, on slick rainy streets, jumping over fences, or in hand-to-hand combat with one or more people. It is amazing what adrenaline can do for a suspect who doesn't want to go back to jail or is high on PCP and feels no pain. An injured cop can be a liability in a crisis. Officers depend on their command presence, their stature, even their uniforms to control a situation.

> Juan hurt his hand playing baseball and was wearing a bandage. He stopped a suspicious person on the street and asked to see some identification. The man pulled out his driver's license, and Juan took it with his bandaged hand. Moments later the suspect grabbed the license and fled on foot. He was apprehended several blocks away. When asked why he ran, he said that he thought he could get away with it because the officer was injured.

Cops, in general, are action-oriented folks who are attracted by the physical nature of police work. They love the adrenaline rush they get from high-risk hobbies like hang gliding, skydiving, fast cars, and motorcycles. Some are thrill seekers at work, refusing to wear their bulletproof vests, not waiting for backup, and always first in the door on a dangerous felony warrant service. Others take chances because they are trying to conquer their fears with counterphobic behavior.

Cops are not usually patient people. They are used to making quick decisions and moving on. They eat fast because they don't know when the next call will come. Regardless of how they're injured, they are usually in a hurry to get better. At home, they are often terrible patients, irritable and difficult to console (Kirschman, 2007). Their expectations about the speed of their recovery, including their own efforts and the efforts of their treating professionals, may be unrealistic.

As we've stated before, cops, particularly young cops, protect themselves with a psychological trick—adaptive denial—that allows them to return to work, shift after shift, despite the emotional and physical risks. Denial breaks down with age, the birth of children, a close brush with death, or the death or injury of a fellow officer.

PSYCHOLOGICAL TRAUMA

The things that officers see and experience are sometimes too difficult to absorb, let alone talk about. Officers who are not psychologically minded or verbally fluent are apt to be influenced by the cultural pressure to suppress negative emotions like fear and sadness.

> Doug was assigned to patrol the Golden Gate Bridge as part of a post-911 task force formed to identify terrorists seeking another

high-visibility landmark. It was a beautiful day. The bridge was crowded with pedestrians, mostly tourists, looking at the view. There was nothing unusual about the man in his mid-30s who was walking by himself—not until he turned around, took two graceful steps, leapt onto the railing, and dropped like a stone off the side.

At first, Doug felt nothing. Many people have jumped from the bridge. He also knew there was nothing he could have done to stop it. Within a month, he started having night terrors and an annoying hand twitch. He wondered why this incident had so much more power than his other critical incidents when he had seen far worse things.

Somatization among people exposed to trauma is pervasive. Body memories of trauma are apparently stored on a somatosensory level and encoded on a sensorimotor level, without orientation to time and space. They are not easily retrieved or translated into language (Erdelyi, 1990; Horowitz, 1994; Howe, Courage, & Peterson, 1994; Terr, 1988, 1991; van der Kolk & van der Hart, 1991). Neural nets connect various traumatic events that have occurred over a lifetime. It is why Doug's therapist asked him, "When have you felt like this before?"

At first, Doug didn't understand the significance of his night terrors or the uncontrollable twitching in his hand. It was his therapist's job to help him explore these bodily sensations as a way to untangle the past. Metaphorically, physical sensations create a cover story or, in psychodynamic terms, the externalization of traumatic material (Schauer, Neuner, & Elbert, 2011). Cops know about cover stories, it just never occurs to them that they may be using one on themselves.

A word about PTSD and traumatic brain injuries (TBIs): TBIs require imaging, neuropsychological testing, and medical intervention. While the symptoms can overlap with those of PTSD, the client with a TBI and his or her family will complain of deficits in functioning that are chronologically related to the head trauma: memory lapses, difficulty completing certain tasks, and irritability. There may be noticeable language deficits and motor impairments as well. Treatment for both PTSD and TBI has much in common. The major difference is that treatment for PTSD emphasizes exposure to the past incident and treatment for TBI emphasizes cognitive rehabilitation and manipulation of the current environment (L. Parks, personal communication, September 8, 2012).

PANIC DISORDER

Robyn used a failure drill—a close-quarter technique involving two shots to an advancing target's chest, followed by one shot to the head—to stop a knife-wielding suspect who first charged her with a 9-inch blade and then tried to shoot her with a .45 caliber pistol. In the background, she could hear the dead man's parents screaming and calling her a murderer. The shooting was cleared by the district attorney's office, and Robyn received counseling for posttraumatic injury. Over the next few years she rarely thought about the incident, until she accidently passed the dead suspect's mother on the street.

Robyn froze. She felt dizzy and nauseous, her hands were sweating profusely, and she had pain in her chest that extended down her left arm. Her vision blurred. She had difficulty hearing what others were saying. She couldn't breathe, and her fingers went numb. Without saying a word, she got back in her patrol car, drove to headquarters, and called her husband. She told him she thought she was going to die. After an extensive workup, the emergency room doctor told her that he had found nothing physically wrong. The likely diagnosis was that she had had a panic attack.

A panic attack involves intense fear or discomfort coupled with physical symptoms that develop quickly and reach a peak within 10 minutes. The symptoms include nausea, numbness, chest pain, dizziness, sweating, fear of dying, palpitations, pounding heart or rapid heartbeat, trembling, shaking, shortness of breath, choking, derealization or depersonalization, fear of losing control, and chills or hot flashes. It's a terrible experience.

Panic attacks can happen to anyone; lifetime rates range from 1.6 to 3.5% (Katschnig & Amering, 1998). Attacks can last from minutes to hours, but most frequently subside within an hour. The physical symptoms are extremely difficult to fake. Over half of those diagnosed with PTSD will experience a panic attack (Falsetti & Resnick, 1997).

When a stimulus triggers the fight, flight, or freeze response, the sympathetic branch of the autonomic nervous system is activated. Whereas most of us will react with a freeze or flight response, LEOs are trained to confront danger. A panic attack when no actual danger exists, as happened to Robyn when she walked by the dead suspect's mother, is a terrible experience. Few other non-life-threatening experiences evoke such strong reactions as panic attacks. Like Robyn, many officers feel too embarrassed to tell anyone. They struggle in silence or they make up a cover story, pretending to have food poisoning or some other ailment. Some are given benzodiazepines at the ER and told to seek therapy.

In the worse-case scenario, officers refuse treatment after a panic attack and start to self-medicate in an attempt to reduce their symptoms. The untreated symptoms may increase, and the number of settings where they feel panicky may expand to the point where they have trouble working because they are compelled to avoid certain districts or streets, they're uncomfortable in crowds, can only travel in certain types of vehicles, and must avoid bridges. They're terrified of being in places or situations from which escape seems impossible. In other words, they now have full-blown agoraphobia and can't leave home.

Treatment for Panic Attacks

The treatment of panic attacks can involve a combination of medication and structured therapy. It's important to start with normalization and education about what is happening. One of the most important things for an officer to understand is that the attack cannot cause harm, will likely only last minutes, and will not kill her. Rather than fight the panic head on, which is the culturally correct way LEOs responded to fear, try teaching your client to step aside and substitute calming language for fear-provoking self-statements. Many cops are familiar with "Verbal Judo" (Thompson & Jenkins, 2004), a tactical communication skill set designed to calm and redirect or diffuse the behavior of hostile or emotionally disturbed people. This may be a good template for helping them rewrite a fear-provoking script.

Another technique that we teach panicky responders is grounding. Dissociative experiences, during which the client appears to be daydreaming or distracted, are common to people who have been exposed to traumatic incidents. Grounding techniques are useful for pulling your client back into the room, redirecting the focus away from the inner turmoil and toward the outer world (Beckner & Arden, 2008). One technique used by the military is for the client to describe something he sees, hears, and feels in the present moment. For instance, your client might respond by saying, "I see a clock, I hear the fan, and I feel my feet on the ground." Another grounding technique is to ask your client, "What is going on with you right now?" Asking simple orienting questions about day, time, and place can provide a sense of safety. Do what you can to release the buildup of tension. The goal is for the officer to stay relaxed and emotionally present in the face of exposure.

Keeping a written record of panic attacks—what triggered them, where they happened, and how long they lasted—is helpful both to the client and the clinician, although it takes a motivated client to keep this kind of journal. Other stress reduction and relaxation techniques can be found at the end of this chapter.

HYPERVIGILANCE

The potential for danger is lodged in the psyche of most officers and reinforced by all-too-frequent reports of officers who are killed or injured in the line of duty, sometimes only because they were wearing a uniform. As one officer said, "When I put on my uniform, I feel like I have a target on my back." It doesn't make any difference where or how such fatalities occur, when they hear of them, officers and their families automatically think, "What if this happened to me?" We speculate that this constant vigilance can carve deeper and deeper neurological pathways in the brain. The actual and potential dangers of their jobs can make LEOs highly reactive to the perception of danger, real and imagined. Officers who have a higher baseline of stress chemicals like cortisol in their system may be physiologically primed toward even more intense reactions (Neylan et al., 2005). One of us (Kirschman) noticed a significant uptick in her awareness of potential danger after associating with the police. This perception of danger, often acute after a critical incident, can greatly restrict officers' comfort in crowds, at sporting events, or in new places where they feel diminished in control. This can have a domino effect on the family and their ability to travel, socialize, and engage in normal recreational activities. High levels of hypervigilance, cynicism, and controlling behaviors should always prompt a clinician to ask the officer if he has experienced some kind of critical incident.

Hypervigilance also puts anger and disagreement in a different context. From day one in the academy, there is an emphasis on safety and control in the service of making certain every officer returns home at night. LEOs are constantly trained in safety behaviors—some would say overtrained—and warned that they will get hurt or get someone else hurt if they fail to practice proper safety. Because a suspect's lack of compliance is often a prelude to a physical confrontation, officers can overreact to things like normal family fights or disagreements.

Most officers will never unholster their weapons in the line of duty except on the firing range. Only about 10% of the job involves physical confrontations. Many LEOs are engaged in routine patrol work, community policing, helping the homeless, comforting the lost and frightened, and working in schools. And while it may help a frightened spouse to recognize that it is more lethal to be a commercial fisherman, drive a taxi, or work in construction, it is cold comfort, especially when he or she hears of the death or injury of an officer.

Hypervigilance affects the family in other ways as well. Police psychologist and retired sheriff's deputy Dr. Kevin Gilmartin describes hypervigilance as a "biological roller coaster" (2002, p. 247). Officers feel "alive, alert, energetic, involved and humorous" at work because their bodies are producing adrenaline. This pattern of behavior may be what is meant when cops says they have become "addicted" to the job. Off work, officers can rebound from the adrenaline and sink into a trough, where they feel "tired, detached, isolated and apathetic," unable to participate in family activities or make the simplest decisions, like where to go for dinner. Without conscious awareness of this cycle and how to stop it, officers begin spending more time at work and invest less and less time and emotional energy at home. Or they try to "re-adrenalize" through reckless off-duty pursuits like substance abuse, gambling, spending sprees, or affairs.

STRESS REDUCTION STRATEGIES

Physical Exercise

There is substantial research showing that exercise alleviates symptoms of depression (Hamer & Chida, 2009). Evidence is mounting to demonstrate its benefits for alleviating anxiety as well (Otto & Smits, 2011). In fact, people who used to exercise regularly but no longer do so are more prone to becoming depressed (Blumenthal, 2007) and anxious (Otto & Smits, 2011). Exercise is both therapeutic and preventative. It promotes increased self-efficacy and self-esteem, disconfirms negative thoughts, and decreases rumination. The ideal exercise program combines weight training with high-intensity aerobic exercise (Dowd, Vickers, & Krahn, 2004; Sidhue, Vandana, & Balon, 2009). Exercise is not just about getting in shape, it's about increased brain volume, better executive functioning, and increased vascularization (Colcombe & Kramer, 2003; Erickson & Kramer, 2009; Hamer & Chida, 2009) along with significant cognitive benefits (McMorris et al., 2009).

Exercise tends to disperse adrenaline and reenergize the tired officer in wholesome ways. Ninety minutes of exercise doubles the amount of serotonin in the brain (Deslandes et al., 2009; Stathopoulou, Powers, Berry, Smits, & Otto, 2006). The problem is that exercising regularly more than 30 minutes a day is like having a part-time job. Some departments allow officers to exercise on the job and provide on-site gyms or gym memberships. The 24-hour fitness clubs are a boon to cops, especially those whose shift schedules force them to exercise in the dark. Physical exercise can also fill an officer's social needs by involving family and friends.

Some cops have a prove-it-to-me attitude. You'll need an informed presentation emphasizing the benefits of working out to gain their compliance, especially those who are not athletically inclined. Kemeny and colleagues (2012) suggest that a person's beliefs can physically alter his or her stress response and promote health. For example, if LEOs believe they can lower their blood pressure by vigorously exercising 35 minutes per day, it is more likely that they will do so. As we've noted before, cops are action-oriented problem solvers. They prefer doing something over talking things through. The wise clinician uses this preference to advantage.

Habits are hard to change, especially if the benefits of changing are not immediately apparent. Anshel, Robertson, and Caputi (2011) suggest that five objectives need to be completed in order to build better health habits for LEOs: developing a mission statement, obtaining social support, receiving progress reports, developing routines, and sharing one's values with others. Anshel and colleagues' 10-week program, titled the Disconnected Values Model (DVM), uses motivational interviewing, described in Chapter 11, to determine if officers are ready to replace negative behaviors with healthier choices. The benefits of change are directly linked to a hierarchy of values, including tangibly better work performance, quicker reaction time, and better decision making.

Yoga and Tai Chi

Yoga has been practiced for over 5,000 years and is currently used by over 10 million Americans to reduce stress and increase health. Some police officers may already be stretching as part of their physical activity regimen.

Tai chi has been around as long as yoga. It involves a series of movements that are performed in a slow and graceful manner. When it is used for health maintenance, rather than as a martial art, the focus is on perfecting the movements. This focus allows distressing thoughts to diminish and produces a sense of relaxation and peace of mind.

Biofeedback

Biofeedback therapy uses computer-assisted equipment to measure stress and enhance relaxation by monitoring electrical activity (galvanic skin response), heart rate, brain waves, temperature, and so on. Biofeedback allows clients to see, in real time with immediate feedback, the amount of control they have over their autonomic functioning and what thoughts alleviate or exacerbate symptoms like pain and tension. This feedback can be delivered in any number of ways: graphically, visually, or aurally. There's room here for creativity. For example, it is possible to link a client's relaxation response to moving toy trains around a track—the more relaxed the client, the faster the train moves. Once symptom reduction has stabilized, the client's actions or thoughts can be practiced without the use of the equipment, although biofeedback machines are publicly available and portable. There are even biofeedback apps for smartphones. Some police officers may prefer this type of therapy because it reinforces the officer's need to be in control and inclination toward treatments with positive, measurable results.

Relaxation Techniques and Deep Breathing

Relaxation techniques seek to restore balance between the parasympathetic and sympathetic branches of the autonomic nervous systems. Autogenic training and progressive relaxation both involve body scans, deep breathing, and the progressive relaxation of various muscle groups and body parts in a systematic progression.

Officers are used to controlled or diaphragmatic breathing. They learn this technique on the firing range and in defensive tactics classes. For example, we instruct LEOs to first visualize a trapezoid and then to track their breathing around all four sides. Inhaling to the count of four on side one, pausing on side two, exhaling to the count of seven on side three, and pausing again side four. We find this works well because cops are usually good visualizers.

SELF-HYPNOSIS

Clinicians who have been trained in hypnosis can teach their clients to use self-hypnosis whenever the need arises. Typical inductions include visualizing a calm, safe place. Cops seem to like the image of lying comfortably in a hammock, protected and surrounded, yet with easy access to an escape route. The safe place does not have to be a real place, but it is important to vet it with the officer.

> Natalie chose the Hawaiian condominium she shared with her husband as her safe place. Because her therapist knew that Natalie's marriage was in trouble, she asked if, under the circumstances, Natalie felt secure enough there. On second thought, Natalie chose a different scene.

Meditation

In general, LEOs seem resistant to the concept of meditation. The officer who could most benefit from meditation is often the one who is too hypervigilant to do it. Some LEOs associate meditation with dope-smoking "earth biscuits." They don't realize that there are many familiar activities that mimic the benefits of meditation, such as fly-fishing, mowing the lawn, or staring into a fire. They are unaware of Westernized meditation programs such as mindfulness-based stress reduction (MBSR) that do not require chanting, mantras, candles, or religious beliefs (Seaward, 2012). And they probably haven't read the meta-analysis of meditation studies that concluded that meditation is as helpful as psychotherapy (Sedlmeier et al., 2012).

KEY POINTS

- Some LEOs may score high on somatic test subscales because of physical injuries sustained on the job. However, tests like the TSI-2 can separate the psychic and physical components of a somatic complaint (see Chapter 8).

- Use scaling to set intermediate goals. If the officer's current level of pain is a 10 on a scale of 1 (minimal) to 10 (unbearable), find out what level of pain he or she could live with.

- The treatment of pain is a team effort. Establish relationships with local pain clinics and university health services so that you can make a confident medical referral.

- Peripheral neuropathy, pain in the extremities, and gastrointestinal problems with no known medical etiology are difficult to diagnose and may involve malingering or secondary gain. The detection of malingering is difficult and best left to those who specialize in it.

- Pay attention to cultural differences in the perception of health, illness, disability, and paths to recovery (Hays, 2008; Waitzkin & Magana, 1997).

- Some LEOs find relaxation techniques too "woo-woo." Others are too hypervigilant to meditate or do anything with closed eyes. Frame these techniques as similar to the mental training used by martial artists and competitive athletes.

- Massage aids in stress reduction (Culpepper-Richards, 1998; Shulman & Jones, 1996). But proceed carefully—many cops associate massage with prostitution.

Part V

WORKING WITH POLICE FAMILIES

The person a clinician is first apt to see is a spouse, usually but not always a female; usually but not always from a heterosexual couple. Behind every cop is a family whose needs and experiences are all but invisible. This section addresses the challenges facing police families, from shift work to watching a once familiar person turn into a near stranger. We begin the section with a letter written by a police wife to her husband of many years after he completed a WCPR retreat. She wrote it on behalf of all first responder partners.

> *We see you. We know who we married. You're strong, you value your job, or you did. You wanted to have an impact. You wanted to protect and control the chaos in other people's lives. Some things you can't control. Some things control you. We want you to know that we see the person you want to be. We feel the pain that ensnares you—pulls you from us, even if we don't understand it. We want to make it better for you, but we can only control ourselves.*
>
> *We try to hold it in: the fear, the uncertainty, the loss, the anger. We feel thwarted. You can't let the wall down to let us in because*

then you'd have to let the wall down. We rage and we plead and we beg and cry. We can't talk to our friends, we're isolated, we're lonely. But under all this, we are strong. We married someone who goes out every day and risks their lives for others. We know who we married, even if we don't understand where you have gone, how you have changed. We believe that the person we fell in love with is still YOU. We just can't find YOU through all the pain you feel. Come back to us. We want you, not as you once were, but as a person who can see what you've seen, and do what you've done, and can move forward with hope for a better life. We know you will get through the anger and the fear, the self-loathing, the depression. We are with you as life partners because we know you're strong. Let us in. Let us know when you're hurting. Talk to us. You can be vulnerable with us and we will still love you. Some of us have learned to walk lightly around you. Some of us are angry because we couldn't fix what was wrong for you. Some of us have gotten used to not having you in the now/present when you're with us, and we've gotten used to being alone. We spend our lives as first responders' partners checking in with you when you walk through the front door. We look to see your face, your expression, the set of your shoulder. We try to gauge what kind of day you've had, what you've been through, what you've seen. We're good at that. Most of us don't expect you to share your job experiences with us in detail. You often protect us from that. What you may have discovered here [at WCPR], how it has changed you, we want you to share that with us. Take it slowly. Hold us first, tell us you love us. We are about to be reintroduced to someone we might have thought we lost. Be patient with us. We want to be there with you. (GB, personal communication, 2012)

14

RESILIENCE AND THE POLICE FAMILY

Policing is a family occupation; what happens at work spills over to an officer's spouse and children. Conversely, what happens at home spills over to work. An officer's home life and the support of a positive significant relationship are key to buffering work stress and maintaining a sense of well-being on the job.

This chapter looks at the risk and protective factors that affect family resilience, including discrimination based on race, gender, and sexual orientation. The resilience model provides a diagnostic framework as well as a map for potential points of intervention to help fortify resilience within the context of unique family dynamics.

Thriving and struggling police families both seem to differ from civilian families in significant ways (Greene & Kirschman, 2010). Just as it is a mistake for therapists to treat stepfamilies as though they are the same as biological families (Visher & Visher 1996), it would be a mistake to treat police families without acknowledging and understanding the police subculture and how it permeates family life.

> Rick was driving on the freeway with his pregnant wife when a car cut them off. He chased the offending driver and pulled him over to the side of the road. Rick's therapist confronted him with his own reckless behavior and poor judgment, but to no avail. Rick's identity was too

wrapped up in his persona as a proactive tough guy, which was exactly what his department and his coworkers wanted him to be. His exploits were well known to his superiors, who benefited from his exceptional arrest rate. Unable and unwilling to change his behavior, he divorced after the birth of his child, essentially choosing his work family over his real family. It was a poor choice. When a new chief took over, Rick was fired for excessive force.

Does the power of a subculture to influence and reinforce behavior completely explain Rick's extreme actions? Probably not. With LEOs, as with any other client, therapists need to address psychopathology when they see it and explore the influence of family of origin. We endorse the hypothesis we presented earlier, that many officers, similar to many therapists, come from families in which there was an absent, alcoholic, narcissistic, or otherwise dysfunctional parent. Policing can be an extension of the role the officer played in his or her family as peacekeeper, protector, or super-responsible child. Or, as one client said, "The job chooses us, we don't choose the job."

The problem of singular identity—the inaccessibility of any roles other than cop—and the police officer's paradox mean that overlearned street skills and attitudes are, at times, misapplied at home and are at the heart of why many cops have relationship problems (see Chapter 16).

Police officers need to create social and emotional distance in order to protect themselves from a steady diet of human tragedy. In contrast, intimate relationships require emotions and vulnerability (Paton et al., 2009). As retired FBI agent Jim Reese says, "We in law enforcement have become very adept at turning our emotions off. It is the 'on switch' that many of us cannot find" (Kirschman, 2007, p. 32).

Early childhood experiences and the relentless pressure to stay in role amplify the spillover from work to home. To focus solely on the pathological is to miss the point that even thriving police families struggle with spillover.

DEFINING RESILIENCE

Police family resilience can be defined as the ability to struggle well and bounce back in the face of adversity. Contrast this to the familiar, yet faulty notions of invulnerability, self-sufficiency, and rugged individualism found in the law enforcement culture. Resilient families buffer stress, share pain, and offer positive appraisal to each other. They are able to make meaning out of adversity, maintain an optimistic outlook, dedicate themselves to larger values and purposes, balance stability and change, and be flexible yet stay connected. They have sufficient social and economic resources, they are not facing a pileup of crises, and they communicate effectively using a range of emotional expression, collaborative problem solving, and conflict resolution (Walsh, 1999).

Building resilience requires modifying the relationship among the family, the officer, and the department, moving away from triangulation toward collaboration. This is a tall order, given the extraordinary demands that most departments place on their officers, and the fact that, as stated earlier, police work is an identity, not merely a job. According to Greene (1997), there are three components to building resilience in police families—the individual, the family, and the organization—each with its own set of risk factors, protective factors, and therapeutic objectives, as listed in Table 14.1.

It is one thing to diagnose and strategize interventions with the family unit and individual family members, but it is quite a different matter to influence your client's employer. To do so is probably beyond the reach of most clinicians and raises ethical issues concerning confidentiality, role conflict, and dual relationships.

Furthermore, bear in mind that not all law enforcement agencies treat their employees the same way. In our experience, some agencies have enlightened policies and are rich in resources, providing officers and their families with a range of supportive options such as counseling, flexible work schedules, and so on. Family-friendly agencies take family circumstances into account when making special assignments or assigning shifts. They understand that families have problems and emergencies and do not label an officer who has issues at home as disloyal or as having skewed priorities (White & Honig, 1995). Other agencies, particularly smaller departments with limited budgets, can provide little in the way of individual or family support. Some agencies can be said to operate with "emotional intelligence" and compassion toward employees and their families, while others are intentionally or unintentionally abusive. As we said in Chapter 6, administrative betrayal—feeling let down or abandoned by one's agency—is at the heart of much unresolved traumatic experience.

POLICE FAMILY NEEDS AND ASSETS

Oddly enough, therapists working with police families frequently have a better idea of what threatens family resilience than what supports it. Greene and Kirschman (2001) devised an online needs and assets survey adapted from McCubbin, Thompson, and McCubbin's (1996) work with military families. We were interested in the factors to which self-defined successful police families attributed their well-being. Selected findings from the 420

TABLE 14.1. Greene's (1997) Three Components to Building Resilience in Police Families

The individual	The family	The organization
Risk factors	Risk factors	Risk factors
1. Inability to identify feelings 2. Denial of emotional needs 3. Isolation	1. Limited knowledge of police work 2. Conflict between job and family priorities 3. Conflict between job roles and family roles 4. Isolation	1. Limited awareness of organizational stressors 2. Limited resources to deal with these stressors 3. Perceived discrimination
Protective factors	Protective factors	Protective factors
1. An effective communication style 2. Established systems of social support	1. Awareness of job-related stress factors 2. Negotiated family structure with clear roles and responsibilities 3. Conflict resolution skills 4. Multiple social support systems	1. Training to increase the understanding of job stress 2. Ability to recognize signs and symptoms of stress 3. Culturally competent management and supervision 4. Ability to identify and eliminate discriminatory practices
Therapeutic objectives	Therapeutic objectives	Organizational objectives
1. Develop and/or improve communication skills 2. Increase and/or establish multiple social support systems	1. Increase knowledge of job stressors 2. Increase communication in the family 3. Increase conflict resolution skills 4. Increase family support systems	1. Increase understanding of job-related stressors 2. Develop early warning identification and support systems 3. Increase activities to support women and ethnic minorities 4. Conduct seminars about wellness and communication skills 5. Work with peer support and chaplaincy programs 6. Provide spousal and family support academies or programs for new and veteran spouses 7. Use computerized tracking systems to identify officers at risk 8. Conduct in-service training for command and supervisory staff regarding job stress and discrimination 9. Make confidential, low-cost, culturally competent counseling available for officers and their families

respondents are summarized below; some are predictable, others show how far from our traditional view of family life police families can be.

- Officers working in large departments (200+ sworn employees) had greater positive perceptions about their work environment than officers in small departments, possibly due to more opportunities, variety, and resources. Personnel in small departments were most at risk due to the lack of available resources and reported themselves to be more dependent on their families for support.
- Higher-ranking officers reported more work-related problems than line-level officers.
- Family well-being was correlated with the family's appraisal of the work environment as supportive, predictable, and available in times of need.
- Using McCubbin's categories, self-defined successful families were "pliant," meaning they scored high on flexibility and could change rules, boundaries, and roles to accommodate changes inside and outside the family. They had open communication and were willing to compromise, shift responsibilities, experiment with problem solving, and actively include all family members in decision making.
- Successful families also scored low on bonding, meaning they were independent, did not depend exclusively on each other for support, developed and used other support systems such as friends and extended family, may prefer confiding in others, emphasized going their own way, and were satisfied with a low level of attachment.
- Females, both sworn and civilian, wanted only slightly more flexibility, predictability, family mealtime, and connections with extended family than did male respondents.
- Females, more than male respondents, found that expressing feelings and seeking understanding through personal and professional relationships outside of the family (e.g., talking with others in the same situation) was helpful.
- Males and females were matched in the sense of control they had over work and in their commitment to the police mission.
- The most frequently endorsed coping style was investing time with children and family.
- Accepting and fitting into the police lifestyle was more helpful to officers than spouses, but not especially helpful overall and less helpful than self-development and building relationships.

Despite the limitations of an online survey, there are several implications from our findings that are useful to the community clinician.

- The pliant lifestyle should be normalized. This is best done in family orientations or spousal academies where veteran spouses talk about how they coped with shift work, crying babies, missed holidays, guns in the home, and so on.

- Spouses need direct information about department resources such as spousal academies, department-sponsored social events, and peer support and chaplaincy programs because they may use them more than officers. We know from experience that officers do not reliably bring this type of information home.

- Young families are most at risk for the nonenforcement spouse to become isolated and overwhelmed with child care responsibilities.

- The coping style most endorsed—spending time with children and family—is characteristic of single parents, suggesting that the couple relationship may suffer even as the relationship between parents and children prospers.

GOALS AND STRATEGIES OF POLICE FAMILY THERAPY

In our opinion the goal of family therapy is to strengthen resilience and fortify the family against the negative spillover from police work. To do this, the community clinician will first need a solid grounding in couple and family therapy. In this book we cannot give you that grounding, but we will highlight issues and suggest therapeutic objectives that are unique to the LEO subculture. To do this we have adapted the goals suggested by Borum and Philpot (1999) and added strategies that work well with this population.

Goal: *Strengthen the boundary around the couple, relative to the departmental boundary, by getting the couple to commit to spending more time together and working to build a sense of connection between partners.*

Strategies

- Use the calendar. Schedule time to talk about non-work-related issues; assign regular "welfare checks" when both partners have equal time to talk about what's going on in their lives; assign date nights and family days. Gilmartin (2002) believes that officers are more likely to engage in scheduled events that are written on the calendar than to do things spontaneously. When something is canceled at the last minute, help the family negotiate a system of rain checks to make up for the missed event.

• Make switching gears between home and work a conscious process. Create images that make the officer feel safe and protected (work mode) and connected and cared for (home mode). Develop rituals that represent and anchor each mode.

> Terry and her therapist spent a session working out cues to help her shift gears from work to home and back again. At the beginning of her shift, Terry took a moment to examine herself in the mirror, take inventory of the tools she carried on her duty belt, and silently say the "not today" mantra she learned in an online street survival seminar. "Not today, not on this shift, not on this call, not on this stop—I will not be caught unaware" (Smith, 2011). At home, her visual trigger was the flower wreath on her front door. As she pulled into the garage, she repeated the phrase "Mommy's home" to herself and took a few calming breaths.

• Ask the couple to discuss ways to fortify the boundary between home and work without creating an artificial, impermeable barrier where the officer feels he or she can never talk about what happens on the job (see Chapter 16). Aim for balance between work and family, work and rest. Point out that people with busy lives don't "find" time for outside activities, they "make" time (Miller, 2007b).

• Miller, a police psychologist, suggests that officers try "dosing" family time by first setting aside a few hours for a relatively easygoing, enjoyable outing and then incrementally increasing the time in subsequent activities. He recommends varying events by sometimes devoting time just to the kids and other times just to the spouse. He points out that when an officer is proactive in setting family time, the family won't feel as if they have to chase their officer down, and the officer may actually end up with more free time (Miller, 2006a).

Goal: *Increase intimacy by reducing triangulation through direct and positive communication.*

Triangulation is tricky. When spouses blame the job for their unhappiness, they put their mates on the defensive for loving a sometimes risky, often demanding job. Conversely, when officers use work to escape friction at home they risk prolonging their problems. Cops can be heard complaining about their spouses to other cops, while spouses may feel more comfortable sharing family problems with friends. Figuring out when and how this vicious cycle got started is more fully explored in Chapter 16.

Clinicians must also avoid getting drawn into triangulating with the officer, forming yet another alliance from which the spouse is excluded. Jana Price-Sharps (2011) recommends using a joint therapist method that she calls the "union rep style" when working with police couples. In her method, each individual has a therapist. Both therapists meet with the couple for the first session, followed by two individual sessions and another conjoint meeting. The advantages are that each client has an advocate, clients receive individual coaching about the best way to address problems in the four-way meetings, and each has an opportunity to debrief with his or her own therapist afterwards. The therapists can coordinate sessions, exchange information about family dynamics, and avoid triangulation, manipulation, and dishonesty.

Strategies

• John Gottman (1999) claims that one of the most common bids for attention and connection in couples is the simple question "How was your day?" An innocuous question, unless you're a cop. Shift work also complicates the question. Police families working different shifts have to get creative about communication and take advantage of electronic messaging, although the old-fashioned methods still work. Therapist Guy Shiller recommends using Post-it notes, which are consistent with the short, terse style cops use on the radio. One of his patients told him that she was frustrated because shift work was wrecking her sex life, so before she left for work she would leave a post-it note on the bathroom mirror for her sleeping husband saying "think sex" (Kirschman, 2007).

• Encourage the couple to make a list of nice things they can do for each other. This may not be as easy as it sounds. Cops, who have no trouble commanding people on the street, can be surprisingly reluctant to ask for what they need at home (M. Dunnigan, personal communication, October 9, 2012). Normalize the fact that just because people love each other, this doesn't mean they can read each other's mind. Nor does being a cop mean you automatically know what other people need. When necessary, we ask LEOs if they know about the platinum rule: Do unto others as they would have you do unto them. This is actually a principle involved in hostage negotiation: give the hostage taker what he wants in exchange for releasing hostages, not what you think he should have.

Goal: *Help the couple gain insight into basic influences in their relationship.*

Strategies

• One strategy is to move the conversation from law enforcement to gender differences. Law enforcement families readily relate to the theories about how men and women communicate differently. Learning about brain physiology, whether it pertains to gender differences or responses to trauma, is useful. Like other psychoeducational approaches advocated throughout this book, information seems to reduce personal blame and defensiveness and adds humor to the situation—always a plus when working with cops.

• We have had success, especially with spouses, using material about codependency. The concept of codependency is useful in helping someone set and hold boundaries. For example, we have used the *Substance Abuse and Recovery Workbook* (Liptak & Leutenberg, 2008) as the basis for self-assessment and group discussion during spousal retreats.

Goal: *Teach basic communication skills.*

Strategies

• These would include I-messages, problem solving, negotiation, conflict resolution, assertiveness, forgiveness, and appropriate self-disclosure. Such skills should be among the basic tools of every clinician. The goal is to reduce reactivity and encourage active listening.

• Some LEOs struggle with alexithymia, the inability to put feelings into words. This may contribute to their communication difficulties as well as their somatic problems. It can help to provide officers with word lists describing various emotions. Families and friends want more than terse replies that resemble the unadorned communications put out over a police radio (see Chapter 16). The ability to express emotions is also useful for filling in the blank spots in an officer's recollection of a critical event (Honig & Sultan, 2004). Some officers have artistic abilities and are able to express their reactions through creative therapies and journaling. Be careful here: Asking officers to participate in an art project or sand tray play may make you seem like a "new-age earth biscuit."

Goal: *Expand the couple's social interactions beyond other police families and their families of origin.*

Miller (2007) advises police officers to turn off the "cop channel—all cop, all the time"—and involve themselves with nonpolice friends and activities.

As police officers age on the job (see Chapter 4) they often develop a we–they mentality with the public. This is the fallacy of uniqueness, that only cops can understand each other. Public scrutiny is one of the givens of the job. Cops avoid socializing with non–law enforcement folks because they are accustomed to seeing the worst in people. They have no illusions and a lot of cynicism. They know that the reverend beats his wife because they've been called to his house on a regular basis. They've arrested the town's beloved librarian for drunk driving and had to cite the president of the Kiwanis club for shoplifting. When they look at the Little League coach, they see a child molester. They take the risk of running the license plates of their daughters' dates to check for criminal history, which is strictly prohibited, because they've see too many victims of date rape. And they're tempted to do the same for the caretaker who attends to their elderly parents because last month they took a report from an elderly man who lost his savings to an unscrupulous home care aide.

Strategies

- Cops get tired of living in the limelight, particularly when they encounter more criticism than praise, more antagonism than respect. It may not seem like cops need lessons in assertiveness, but if they are to expand their social circle beyond other first responders, they may need coaching to prepare themselves to respond calmly or with appropriate humor rather than overreacting to intrusive questions or unwarranted criticism. Antici-pating, visualizing, and rehearsing a lighthearted reply like "Sorry, I'm off duty," or "That's above my pay grade" will be helpful.

- We always advise police families to keep their non–law enforcement friends, even if this is difficult due to scheduling problems.

- We encourage families to participate in community activities, spiri-tual communities, team sports, and recreational pursuits the whole family can enjoy.

- We ask bluntly, "What hobbies did you once have and what keeps you from participating in something you once loved doing?" We try to problem-solve obstacles and then make reengaging in these activities part of an action plan.

SOME WORDS ABOUT DISCRIMINATION

As Greene (1997) points out, discrimination is a risk factor that can threaten anyone's resilience, including that of majority white males, who can feel themselves victimized by changing social mores (Kirschman, 2007). Being the victim of discrimination or merely being a statistical minority can amplify the stress of the job. Toch (2002) asserts that emerging differences in reported stress levels among senior officers in his study can be attributed to the perception by female and minority officers that they have been targets of discrimination. Bringing a lawsuit against one's employer or fellow officers is exceptionally stressful. The plaintiff risks being shunned, harassed, or worse for his or her disloyalty. Policing is not a job where you can alienate your coworkers and then expect to work together amiably and feel safe. The drawn-out legal process that follows is often a nightmare for the officer and his or her loved ones.

It is beyond the scope of this book to do more than introduce the reader to the challenges facing women, minorities, gays, and lesbians in law enforcement.

Women in Law Enforcement

Women make up approximately 12% of today's police force, most at the level below sergeant. Ethnic minorities represent approximately 20%, and there are no available statistics on the percentage of gay and lesbian cops. Policing is largely a male-dominated occupation. These days blatant kinds of harassment are less common than subtler forms such as being shut out of opportunities for special assignments, discriminatory promotional processes, social isolation, failing to get credit for a job well done, and so on.

Women and men often police differently. For example, women are more likely to diffuse a potentially explosive situation verbally rather than physically. This can be misunderstood by male coworkers and trainers who want reassurance that women are capable of taking physical control of situations when needed and can be relied upon for backup and to keep their fellow officers safe—despite the fact that only about 10% of policing involves physical altercations, and the rest involves judgment, decision making, and problem solving, activities for which women are uniquely qualified.

Women who are LEOs face a dilemma unfamiliar to their male counterparts. A woman has to prove that she is as good as a male, yet when she shows herself to be aggressive, powerful, and tough, she may be regarded as pushy or strident. She must be one way at home and another way on the street. Male officers also need two sets of interpersonal skills, but the fluctuation between the two is less dramatic.

Women officers, like women everywhere, carry the lion's share of child care and domestic responsibilities (Hochschild, 2012; Toch 2002). Those who are single complain they have difficulty finding men secure enough to date a woman who carries a weapon and has powers of arrest. Finally, some studies indicate that women officers, though less prone to alcoholism than men and more willing to ask for help, are more at risk for PTSD (see Chapter 5).

Ethnic Minorities in Law Enforcement

There are thousands of examples of friendship, loyalty, and genuine affection between cops of all races. As with women, blatant harassment has largely gone underground to be replaced with subtler types of discrimination. Minority officers stand out from the group, in some departments more than others. The scrutiny that results adds strain to an already difficult job. As one of our former teachers said, "The easiest job in any workplace is to be a mediocre white male." Everyone else lives in a limelight that magnifies their errors and their achievements, setting them apart from others.

Some minority officers work in settings that tend to stereotype minority races as culturally and genetically criminal. There are too many tragic examples of undercover or off-duty minority cops being shot by fellow officers who mistook them for suspects. Consider the cost of listening to racist remarks about one's own people or having one's own community regarded as a combat zone or a place to increase arrest statistics. And how high is the price a cop pays for complaining, or for stuffing his or her feelings in the interests of getting along?

Gays and Lesbians in Law Enforcement

Gay men in law enforcement are victims of a staggering number of virulent stereotypes and insults. Gay men, like women, are suspected of lacking such "manly" attributes as courage, bravery, and loyalty. There are some in law enforcement who see themselves as the thin blue line that holds back moral decay. To them, homosexuality is a sin, and homosexual officers are immoral and don't belong in law enforcement. Gay cops seem to suffer more indignities than lesbians. Lesbians are less threatening to the status quo. Some men who are repelled by gay men are titillated by lesbian sex. Lesbians, it appears, are stigmatized more for their gender than for their sexual orientation.

KEY POINTS

- Create a "map" for therapy. Cops will be most comfortable with a structured game plan.
- Have handouts for the family to take home. Suggested topics are communication skills, how to get the most out of therapy, what to do about secrets.

- Openly discuss the pitfalls that sabotage therapy: affairs, lies, and manipulation.

- Be prepared to accommodate shift changes or last-minute schedule changes to avoid having the officer drop out. Because it's rarely possible for officers to say no to their superiors, schedule changes provide an easy out for an officer who wants to avoid a therapy session, and thinks it's okay if his or her spouse goes alone.

15

GIVENS AND PARADOXES

If you think it's tough being a cop, try being married to one.
—BUMPER STICKER

There are certain givens to police work, dimensions of the job that won't change. Families can adapt to the givens, but they can't avoid them. Arguing about them only creates conflict and makes officers feel guilty about loving a job that creates stress for the family. Something similar might be said about the police officer's paradox, a phrase first used by a colleague to describe the fact that the skills a good cop needs and works hard to develop can be damaging to the officer's personal and family relationships. This chapter investigates both.

THE GIVENS

Dealing with the givens in therapy presents the clinician with a dilemma. Just how much adjusting should a family do to accommodate the police lifestyle—a lifestyle once compared to a "greedy mistress" (Niederhoffer, 1978)? There is no ready formula for this. The objective is to help the family fix the problem, not the blame. (Blaming the department is futile. Neither cops nor their families have much, if any, control over departmental policies.) Much depends on how much goodwill family members have left for each other by the time they seek counseling.

Be prepared to hear a lot of complaints from both parties in a couple. The nonenforcement spouse may complain that his or her cop is cold, controlling, doesn't show emotions, never talks about work, always talks about work, cares more about work than family, is sarcastic, denies being troubled, treats the family like "perps," expects perfection, won't tolerate disagreement, is judgmental, antisocial, criticizes everything, is always right, never asks anyone else's opinion, and is preoccupied. The LEO may complain that his or her mate starts in with problems the minute the officer walks in the door, talks too much, doesn't listen, asks stupid questions, doesn't understand the job, doesn't want to talk about the job, is jealous of the job or resentful of the job, gets scared or upset when talking about the job, pressures the cop to talk, thinks cops are callous, and doesn't get cop humor.

The givens discussed in this chapter are public scrutiny, playing second fiddle to the job, unpredictable and unwieldy schedules, and worry about safety. Because every family is different, there is no one-size-fits-all response to these givens. Once anger subsides and family members restore trust and confidence in each other, they can get creative. In other words, if the clinician can help the family create a safe space in which a solution is possible, almost any solution will work.

Public Scrutiny: Living Life in a Fishbowl

Most people have a great deal of respect and admiration for police officers. That's not the problem. The problem is that police officers stand out in our culture in a way that people in few other occupations do. So do their families. Think for a minute how children might feel when their classmates tell them in no uncertain terms that their mother will be killed because she is a police officer and that's what happens to police officers, or at least the ones they see on TV. How do kids feel when their teachers hold them to a higher standard just because their parents are police officers? Imagine what it's like to read about your spouse in the newspaper, to see the person you know to be a warmhearted, gentle partner described as sadistic and brutal. What must a family go through, knowing that the neighbors are reading the same newspaper? Even if the neighbors don't say anything, how could anyone help but wonder what they're thinking?

> Alice shot and killed an emotionally disturbed man who lunged at her with a large knife as she was interviewing him in his small hotel room. Almost immediately, the dead man's family began a public relations campaign, idealizing their son as a hardworking college student, despite his long police record and multiple involuntary mental health holds for violent behavior. They enlarged photos of Alice and created

placards and billboards calling her racist. It was hard for Alice or her family to go anywhere in town without being taunted by members of the public who demanded that she not only be fired, but that she move. Her children began having nightmares. As much as she reassured them that she had done nothing wrong, they remained anxious and fretful, worried about their own safety and panicked that their mother might go to jail.

Alice consulted a therapist for help calming her children. She was thinking about moving, but worried that changing houses and schools would further disrupt her children's already disrupted life. Unfortunately, the first therapist Alice consulted focused primarily on the details of her shooting and questioned her motives in what Alice felt was a slightly accusatory manner. She was already conflicted about having to kill the suspect and was feeling judged by people who didn't know the whole story. The therapist appeared not to take Alice's fears seriously and thought she was overreacting. Rather than questioning Alice's decisions, he should have worked to establish a therapeutic alliance. He needed to create a safe environment for her to talk and help her with her children's anxieties, which were her primary concerns. His greatest mistake was to confuse the mandates of Alice's job, one of which is to go home safely, with some defect in her personality.

The second therapist Alice consulted was content with only the briefest description of the incident. She focused on Alice's children's welfare and asked questions about their growth and development. She shared information about how trauma affects kids and helped Alice plan for the future. When her children were calm and behaving more or less normally, Alice was able to talk about her own fears and complex feelings.

Police work is compelling. Witness the numerous TV shows and movies about cops, most of which distort and mythologize police work and police officers. Some people are genuinely interested in what a police officer does, but many are confrontational or only interested in the spectacular. The question "Have you ever killed anybody?" is a common irritant. Even family gatherings can be stressful.

Ed had been part of a high-profile incident in which two of his fellow officers were murdered, and he in turn killed the suspect in hand-to-hand combat. His relatives asked him over and over to tell them what happened. They regarded him as a hero, which he was. But, unbeknownst to them, every time he retold the story, he had a nightmare. His wife, Betty, finally had to tell the family to stop asking for a replay. They might be able to turn it on and off like a TV show, but Ed couldn't. At the same time Betty was running interference for Ed, she had to suppress her own emotions and often seethed inwardly that her family did not seem as interested in her well-being as they were in Ed's. No one asked how she was faring while trying to support Ed, who was both traumatized and grief stricken. No one knew how deeply this tragic incident frightened their youngest son or how much teasing their older son was facing at school during the highly publicized investigation. (Adapted from a training video produced by the California Peace Officers Standards and Training Television Network, 1994).

Police officers and their families don't have to be involved in shootings or headline-making events to be exposed to the public eye. We've heard many stories from officers who have been approached on the street or in restaurants, or even interrupted at home, by a parent who wants the officer to warn a misbehaving child to straighten up or be arrested and go to jail. Such intrusions into a police officer's private life are common. Therapists also get cornered for advice, but rarely, if ever, are we cast in the role of the tough guy. Teaching a child to fear the police rather than respect them does not bode well, for the officer or the child.

Playing Second Fiddle to the Job

Cops are most comfortable socializing with other cops because they can relax without having to be "perfect" or politically correct. Most police families are part of a supportive, tightly knit social network. On the downside, these gatherings may be dominated by shoptalk that excludes and isolates spouses. Surrounding oneself and one's family with other law enforcement professionals is a risky business because it narrows one's perspective and is self-reinforcing. It is as though an officer's entire existence centers around his or her work, and other roles, such as father, mother, hobbyist, or volunteer, fade into the background. This only serves to reinforce the feeling that being a cop is an identity, not just a job, and that no one but another cop will ever understand. Still, to many, hanging out with other police families is better than having to dodge civilians' annoying, uninformed questions, requests for favors such as fixing a traffic ticket, or challenges about police behavior.

Michelle Perin writes for the website *PoliceOne.com*. She knows firsthand the experience of being treated as though her life was less interesting and she was less important than her police officer husband.

Many officers and their families struggle with separating the personal from the professional. What we face most often are the constant questions or requests for advice from people when they learn he is an officer. I stand quietly by his side waiting to go mix and mingle at a party as he explains why an officer had a right to give this friend a ticket, how a civil case was different from a criminal case or why a recent police shooting across the country was or was not justified in his opinion. I doubt a trash collector's wife has to listen to queries about the best way to get out of putting their can at the curb at the right time of morning. (Adapted from Michelle Perin, *PoliceOne.com*, January 11, 2011)

Interacting with family and non–law enforcement friends is essential to a balanced life, for officers and their families. Yet, over time, as described in Chapter 4, some officers withdraw from their formerly wide circle of social contacts. Shift work makes interacting with 9-to-5 workers difficult. But perhaps the greatest impediment is a mindset that divides the world into two camps: us and them, cops and "everyone else." With few exceptions, members of the "everyone else" group are viewed with cynicism.

Anne asked her husband, Bob, to meet their new neighbor, who was mowing his lawn. Bob went to the door, opened it, looked over at his neighbor, and stepped back inside. "Forget it," he said. "The guy's an asshole."

Such instant judgments, based on next to no information, are work tools that officers need to stay safe on duty, but they are damaging to officers' personal lives and off-duty relationships. Often they are highly entrenched. Clinicians can and should endorse the fact that healthy people are invested in more than their work (Gilmartin, 2002) and have multiple roles in their community, including being a good neighbor. The officer client is apt to react defensively, so proceed slowly. Gently challenge these instantaneous reactions and get the client to slow down and do a little detective work before determining that someone is hostile, stupid, or criminal. Help the family deal in advance with intrusive or critical comments about police officers. Work on developing some lighthearted ways to end a conversation without starting a fight (Kirschman, 2007). At the same time, validate the fact that police officers and their families are not public property and have a right to protect their privacy.

Shift Work, Long Hours, Separations, Deployments, Unpredictable Schedules, and Unpredictable Moods

In Chapter 7 we discussed the impact that the intrusions and inconveniences of shift work, long hours, and last-minute schedule changes have on family life. Now, add the effect of long-term separations generated by deployments to two wars. Military service is a common steppingstone to law enforcement. Many law enforcement professionals are in the National Guard or have served in the armed services. Think, too, about the rising number of natural disasters requiring police response and the extra duty generated by the threat of terrorism. It is startling to realize how much of ordinary life police families sacrifice for the job, and how self-reliant those waiting families must be. We cannot emphasize enough the need for police families to have multiple support systems including friends—both law enforcement and civilian—extended family, and spiritual communities. They also need to know how to turn off the gas or fix a frozen pipe. If they can't handle small home repairs, they should, at least, know whom to call.

Someone once described police work as 3 hours of boredom, followed by 2 minutes of terror, concluding with 6 hours of report writing. Every shift is unpredictable, which may be part of the allure of police work. Most cops would never consider working a job without variety or excitement. But while variety is the spice of life for most LEOs, unpredictability is hard on families. Small children need consistency. Changing schedules at the last minute is not only inconvenient, it sends a message that the job comes first.

By the time Laurie and Andy went to counseling, they were furious at each other. They had three little children at home and not a lot of discretionary money to spend on babysitters. Andy was routinely late getting home. Laurie tried to wait dinner for him because she felt that families who ate together were stronger and healthier. She resented Andy's allegiance to his work, and Andy, who was a rookie, feared that going home before his squad mates did was a sign he couldn't be counted on. He and Laurie argued about this to no avail. They were dedicated to each other, but their relationship was severely strained.

The combination of anger and exhaustion had limited their ability to think of creative solutions. Their family counselor, skeptical at first of Andy's excuses, asked Andy's permission to go on a ride-along with someone else in Andy's department. He saw instantly how quickly things could happen at the end of a shift and observed that no one went home until everyone's work was finished. If someone had a long, complicated report to write late in the shift, his squad mates stuck around to help. The counselor then suggested that Laurie go on a ride-along, something she'd never done before. Andy stayed at home with the kids. It was an eye-opening experience for both of them. Andy had no idea how stressful it would be to manage three hungry children by himself. Laurie could see that coming home to a houseful of crying children had less appeal than staying at work. At this point, Laurie softened her attachment to the ideal of family dinners, and Andy was more attentive about phoning home when he was going to be late.

When she could, Laurie waited to have a late dinner alone with Andy. Andy, on the other hand, realized he was putting work before family. He talked it over with his squad mates and was surprised at how supportive they were, especially the ones who were divorced.

Time is not the only unpredictable factor. It's also difficult to predict what kind of mood an officer will be in when he or she returns from work. Will he be exhilarated after a good arrest or bummed out after a poor performance evaluation? Will she be tired after taking calls without a break or withdrawn and moody because of something that happened that can't be discussed. Clinicians can assist police families to work out some homecoming habits. Everyone unwinds differently. Stay-at-home parents may need to hand off a child and have some adult conversation, while law enforcement spouses don't want to be hit with problems the minute they come in the door—they've been problem solving all through the shift and need a break. Cops who arrive home when everyone else is asleep and the house is dark may need a sense of welcome and belonging. Clinicians can work with officers to develop a conscious strategy for shifting gears between home and work.

As we've mentioned before, one strategy is to get the officer to visualize a series of self-images associated with work (strong, confident, objective, rational, emotionally controlled) and another series associated with home (affectionate, accessible, caring, playful, patient). Then create small rituals or anchors that serve as triggers to change from cop mode to home mode and back again as needed.

Long deployments need their own special homecomings. Ideally, the department has kept the family informed via a telephone tree, hotline, or debriefings. Otherwise, the family is on its own, relying on texting, e-mail, video chats, and so on. This may be difficult, depending on the location and nature of the deployment. It takes time to return to normal after a long deployment. The officer may be exhausted, cycling between wanting to rest and wanting to talk. Children may be alternately shy around a parent they haven't seen in a while and simultaneously eager to share experiences they had while the parent was away. Spouses may want acknowledgment for having held down the fort and assumed all the domestic responsibilities. Departments are wise to include family members in formal ceremonies honoring officers but often forget to do so. Families are wise to develop their own rituals and rewards to mark the transition home and to cash in any "rain checks" they may have made for missed occasions.

Worry about Safety

As we've said earlier, police work doesn't even rank among the top 10 most lethal jobs in America. Power line installers and repairmen are more likely than cops to die on the job. However, statistics are cold comfort to a frightened spouse, irrelevant to a grieving family, and barely reassuring to a rookie who is trying to anticipate how it might feel to fight for one's survival, to have a close brush with death, or, unlikely as it may be, to take another person's life. It is the police culture that teaches them how to think and feel about (and respond to) fear, death, dead bodies, and human tragedy (Koch, 2010).

Police families have no such *in vivo* classroom. They must learn by trial and error to manage their anxieties and protect themselves from secondary traumatization. One terrible incident sends shock waves throughout the entire community, causing officers and their families to ask, sometimes silently, sometimes aloud, "What if this happened to me? What if this happened to us?" The pageantry of police funerals demonstrates not just solidarity and respect but a profound acknowledgment of shared risk. One way to work with a worried spouse is to hit the problem head on. Forewarned is forearmed.

> Mary Jo was so terrified that her husband, Karl, would be killed on the job that he had stopped telling her what he did at work, because she would cry and beg him to quit. Mary Jo's therapist reviewed the statistics cited above, but it had no effect. Frustrated, she approached the problem from a different angle and asked Mary Jo to imagine that Karl was dead. Mary Jo protested that she didn't want to talk about this. The therapist persisted. If Karl was killed or even hurt in the line of duty, who would Mary Jo want to break the news? Mary Jo started to cry. "What would Karl want?" the therapist asked. "To be buried, cremated, have a memorial?" Mary Jo didn't know. Where were the deeds of sale for their house and car? Where did Karl keep a copy of his life insurance?
>
> It was a tough session, but it worked. Mary Jo went home and asked Karl these same questions and more. Together they assembled a file of important papers, including a will and an advance medical directive. It didn't eliminate Mary Jo's fears, but it did give her confidence in her own abilities to manage given the unlikely possibility that Karl would be killed in the line of duty. Avoiding the subject had the paradoxical effect of increasing her fear. Facing it directly took away some of the emotions.

Few of us want to think about our own deaths, especially young people who may feel invincible or be in that stage of adaptive denial mentioned earlier. You may get some pushback, but encourage the family to discuss end-of-life issues. This is altruistic self-interest. Nothing complicates grief worse than discovering that your husband has left everything to his first wife. Or having the person your spouse hates most be the one to break the news or speak at a memorial. All adults in a police family should know where to find important papers, financial records, and telephone numbers. Some departments require officers to do this, but rarely, if ever, are they required to include their families.

On-the-job injuries are far more likely than on-the-job deaths. Every year there are thousands of line-of-duty assaults on police officers. There are many ways for cops to get injured: the human body isn't designed to carry 10 to 15 pounds of gear around the waist, get in and out of a patrol car dozens of times a day, or chase someone 15 years younger down the street and over a fence. Even working out to stay in shape has its hazards.

Many cops make poor patients. They don't do well with confinement. They may be anxious about being declared unfit for duty and losing their jobs. Cops often joke about the sweet deal injured officers have getting 50% of their salary tax free for life. It's as though they have put something over on their departments. In our experience, money doesn't compensate for an unplanned, unwanted premature retirement. Nor does it compensate for the seemingly endless hassle of dealing with the workers' compensation system, which can be the most heartless of bureaucracies. The appeal of tax-free money doesn't offset a police family's fears about managing on half a salary, or an officer's anxiety over changing careers and identities in midstream, losing fraternity, feeling like damaged goods, or facing the future with limited physical ability. Clinicians can be useful working with disabled officers and their families, helping them to manage their anxieties, deal with depression, face reality, and plan for the future.

THE POLICE OFFICER'S PARADOX

To function effectively in our job you must annihilate, smother, and suppress normal emotions like fear, anger, revulsion, and even compassion. To do otherwise is to invite overwhelming doubt or hesitancy when decisive action is required. The penalty for your achieved competence is a mind set that might as well be a foreign language to your social contemporaries. We are . . . victims of our own success. When these same normal and appropriate emotions . . . surface in personal relationships, we automatically shut down and wonder why, over time, the people we care about the most complain that we are aloof, cold, and uncommunicative.
      —CAPT. (RET.) AL BENNER, PHD (in Kirschman, 2007, p. 28)

The same work skills that make a good police officer can damage that officer's relationships with friends and family. How ironic that what contributes to success at work, when misapplied, or applied in the wrong setting, can create an avalanche of problems in the officer's personal life. Police trainers rarely warn cops of the unintended consequences of learning their jobs well. And they almost never reveal the inconvenient truth that being good on the job sets them up for trouble at home. Joel Fay learned this lesson the hard way, on his own, as he went from idealistic young soldier to wary cop. His personal journey forms the basis for this discussion.

Joel's Story

"When I was 18 years old I joined the Army. I remember marching around a large field practicing right and left turns, all the while shouting 'Kill.' It was the Army's way to turn me and a bunch of other guys who had never killed anything bigger than a bug into soldiers. I recall thinking, 'When this is all over, I hope we get to march around the field shouting, "Don't kill!"'

"In the police academy we didn't shout 'Kill,' but if we were wrestling with each other in defensive tactics class and losing the fight, the instructors would yell, 'If you lose the fight in here you're going to die out on the street.' That message was drilled into us over and over, especially when we were exhausted from running or unable to do one more push-up. 'If you give up now, you'll give up in the field and it will kill you.' The message was simple and we learned it well. There are people out there who, given the opportunity, will kill a cop. The problem is I never knew who those people were, and I never knew when I was going to encounter them.

"Suppose, on the day you finished your degree in social work or psychology or counseling, the commencement speaker at your graduation announced that one or more of your clients might try to hurt or kill you sometime during your career. The speaker, an eminent professional whom you held in high regard, couldn't say for certain which client was dangerous or when that client might show up in your office, only that it was certain to happen. Even so, the speaker emphasized, it was important to remain empathic and open to all your clients. In closing, she warned against bringing these concerns home to your family, because they had enough to deal with and having you talk about these issues would just add unnecessary stress. Would you have changed careers? Could you and your family have lived with this level of stress for 25 years?

"My options were clear. If I was going to run into people who wanted to hurt me, most of whom were probably bigger and stronger than I was, I had to learn command presence, which meant that I had to act tougher than I felt, so that these bigger and stronger folks would think twice before taking me on. I couldn't show them that I was afraid. I had to project confidence. It was like partnering with

an inflated version of myself. On the other hand, it allowed me to walk into chaos and establish control simply by my authoritative bearing. Command presence was as vital to my police work as any piece of equipment I owned. It was also very seductive.

"Whereas my Army training was obvious, direct, and restricted to battlefield duty, my police officer training was subtler and began to infiltrate my personal life. It started out with the warning never to let my guard down. To do this, I learned to shut off my emotions. I could look at somebody who had just jumped off the roof of a six-story building and not be the least bit curious about why the person had jumped. I was able to simply hand a mother who had been kidnapped and raped in front of her children a card with the phone number for a rape crisis center and then walk away emotionally unscathed. I believed then that if I allowed these incidents to touch me personally, I could not be effective. I still believe this.

"Of course, some cases made me sad and some were frightening, but you couldn't tell by looking at me. I got good at pretending not to feel, laughing at heartbreaking situations, and hiding my true feelings. What I didn't learn was how to detach from tragedy, yet be emotionally present for my family.

"After 5 years on the job, I also began noticing that I didn't like a lot of people. I mean I didn't like whole groups of people. Every day at work I would meet people at their worst, and every day I would console a victim or arrest a suspect. The world began to look like two large groups—suspects and victims. When I confided this to a more senior officer he said, 'Yup, and today's victims will be tomorrow suspects.'

"All these changes weren't just happening to me, they were happening to all of us. A friend of mine told me that soon after he was married, his wife wanted to know why he carried disposable gloves in his pocket. He explained that some of the people he met each day had urinated or defecated on themselves and he had to search them to make sure they didn't have any weapons. His wife was amazed. She knew the type of work he did, but she never stopped to think about the details.

"Another friend responded to a suicide, along with the coroner. The coroner explained that he could determine how long the person had been dead by examining the number of generations of maggots in the body. 'Simple math,' he said. 'You just count the generations and multiply that by the life cycle of the maggot.' That night at dinner, my friend's wife asked him how his day went. 'Fine' was

all he could say. The conversation moved on to other topics. He chimed in as best he could, all the while thinking about maggots and their life cycles. He said he didn't think his wife noticed that he was quieter than usual, but he wasn't sure.

"*As the years passed, there were times when I didn't like myself, moments when I realized that I didn't know who I had become. Sometimes I wondered, 'If this continues, where will it lead?' These moments were painful enough for me to realize that things were going in the wrong direction. The psychological dissonance between who I believed I was, who I thought I was becoming, and who I wanted to be was so great that I sought help before I caused lasting harm to myself or the people I loved.*

"*I became a psychologist while I was still a cop. Being a psychologist made being a police officer a lot harder—not because I was smarter or had more education, but because my psychological training forced me to see people differently. I could no longer separate myself emotionally from the citizens I encountered on the job. I started to see people as something more than their problems. I was curious as to why somebody would engage in behavior that was clearly against his or her best interest. And while police work encourages black-and-white thinking, I was starting to see shades of gray. This made it difficult for me to arrest somebody and probably made me a less effective officer. The protective shield of social distance that I had worked so hard to establish began to erode, leaving me more vulnerable, emotionally and physically.*

"*The long-term challenge for police officers is to find a way to maintain humanity in the face of inhumanity, to stay connected when disconnection makes a lot more sense, and to show compassion when confronting people who have none. It is no easy task to balance the need to detach and the need to connect.*

"*There is a poster on the wall of a police department where I sometimes go to teach. It shows a burly cop in a bulletproof vest. The caption on the poster says 'This can't protect you from yourself.' When I talk to LEOs about the police officer's paradox, I show them a photograph of a SWAT team dressed in Kevlar helmets and high-threat tactical vests. I point out that the officers are protected physically and emotionally, that their gear puts them in a tactical frame of mind, and reminds them that staying safe is their top priority. And then I ask the class what happens when these officers go home and their loved ones want to connect emotionally. They*

may have taken off their vests and their helmets, but can they allow
themselves to become emotionally vulnerable? We talk about the
differences between being vulnerable at work and vulnerable at
home. I tell the class that I eventually came to understand that
what makes me vulnerable also makes me accessible. And when I'm
accessible, I'm able to connect to the people I love and need and they
are able to connect with me."

DECONSTRUCTING THE POLICE OFFICER'S PARADOX

There are three main components to the police officer's paradox: hypervigilance, cynicism, and emotional control.

Hypervigilance

As said in Chapter 13, the threat of danger is a police officer's constant companion. The reality of it is reinforced by the almost daily reports of LEOs who were injured, narrowly escaped death, or were killed in the line of duty. Heightened awareness of the potential hazards of police work is how cops stay safe. It may also promote neurological changes in the brain that accelerate the fear response. While some officers may have a higher baseline of stress chemicals like cortisol in their systems and are more vulnerable to hypervigilance, the actual and potential dangers of the job can make any cop reactive to the possibility of danger. This is especially so in the aftermath of a critical incident. Untreated and unacknowledged hypervigilance disrupts an officer's ability to relax even when safe. It reduces his or her comfort in unfamiliar situations or circumstances, such as crowded sporting events or foreign travel, where the officer can exert little control. Maladaptive efforts to cope can affect the family by limiting their participation in wholesome recreational pursuits.

Cynicism

Cynicism, expecting the worst of people or suspecting others of having ulterior motives, is based on job experience most civilians don't have. Officers see how acts of kindness or compassion can lead to victimization. They spend hours with the good Samaritan who opened her door to someone asking for help, only to be raped and beaten. Cops are lied to about everything from child sexual abuse to running a stop sign. It only takes one or two instances of being lied to before an officer decides the way to stay safe and keep his or her family safe is to trust no one and take nothing at face value.

Such a cynical worldview has a great impact on family life. Civilian and law enforcement spouses begin to occupy separate worlds. In the worst-case scenario, the civilian spouse regards his or her LEO partner as controlling. At the same time the LEO spouse thinks non–law enforcement family members are naive, idealistic, uninformed, and in peril of being victimized. It doesn't work to argue with cynicism. Cops have seen more than you have, and they see it up close in vibrant color. It is progress to move an officer from being suspicious to being skeptical.

Emotional Control

As we've said, policing is about control: control of self and control of others. The problem arises when emotional control is so overlearned or so habituated that the officer's emotional life becomes constricted, and he or she cannot open up to family or friends or find private ways to express normal feelings of fear, sadness, anger, and so on, even when it is safe to do so.

KEY POINT

- One of the occupational hazards of law enforcement is self-inflation—thinking that you know more than any civilian, including your family, and thinking you are more important. Not only is this inaccurate, it is damaging. Use common clinical sense. Avoid aligning with any one member of the family. Make clear from the outset that you understand that everyone in a police family will be called upon to sacrifice, compromise, and be flexible. Everyone will have to adjust to the givens and the paradoxes, and everyone should be rewarded for doing so. The idea is not for the family to work around the cop's needs or to sacrifice its own needs to the pressures an LEO encounters on the job. The goal is to work together to ensure that, as often as possible, everyone's needs are considered.

16

"WHY DIDN'T YOU SHOOT HIM IN THE LEG?"

Police Family Communication

> When I act [like a cop] at home, my family either responds to
> me as pompous or refuses to take me seriously. All of this sets
> into motion a destructive spiral. As my family pulls away,
> I accuse them of not caring.
> —RICHARD N. SOUTHWORTH (1990)

Trouble with communication is one of the most common complaints registered by police families. This chapter describes the challenges of communicating well and suggests some ways therapists can be helpful. We also describe the special challenges that arise when officers and their families are struggling to overcome traumatic situations. Every family and every couple has its unique communication preferences. And the divide between enforcement and nonenforcement styles is often amplified by gender differences and individual degrees of extroversion and introversion.

Police officers have two families, their work family and their real family at home (see Key Points). This is both a blessing and a burden, necessitating two sets of interpersonal skills, one for the job and one for home. Family members, as well, need strong communication skills. After all, they are married to trained interrogators who may think they know everything and are reluctant to talk to their families for a variety of reasons. Communicating well in a police family is a challenging enterprise, even for well-adjusted families.

> Melissa is a 10-year veteran and single mother of two working as a detective in a small city. One winter, in the middle of a blizzard, she was called in to investigate a rape. Her mother was incensed. "Can't you deal with it tomorrow?" she asked. Another evening she returned home late after assisting at the suicide of a young man. Her mother asked if she had actually seen his body. When Melissa told her that she had not only seen his body, she had helped cut him down and photographed the scene, her mother abruptly changed the subject.

No wonder police officers stop talking to their families. Whenever a police officer talks about his or her work and family members react with fear, disgust, disbelief, or querulousness, communication becomes stilted or nonexistent.

> When a teenage boy shot himself in the head, Phillip was first on scene, followed closely by the boy's mother, who had been searching for her son. She screamed at the sight of her son's body, grabbed Phillip, and buried her head in his chest, sobbing. Phillip had no choice but to put his arms around her and offer words of comfort until other family members could be located. It was a long and painful wait. Phillip had a son the same age, and his heart was breaking for this mother's grief and guilt. When he came home later that night, his wife was in bed. "How was your day?" she asked. "OK," he answered. "Go back to sleep." The next morning she asked him if everything was OK. His answer was abrupt. "I told you everything was OK, didn't I?" At dinner the following day, she tried again. He was ready then to talk about what had happened and how terrible he felt for the grieving mother. His wife looked relieved. "I'm glad," she said. "I thought your bad mood was about us."

TELL ALL/TELL NOTHING: WHAT, WHERE, WHEN, AND HOW TO TALK

Deciding what to tell the family is a genuine dilemma for police officers. We encourage couples to talk about their preferences regarding communication early in their relationship. Clinicians can teach basic communication skills, but the family needs to sort out for themselves what works best in their household. We believe officers should not make unilateral decisions about what and what not to share. The desire to protect the family from tragedy is admirable. Trouble comes when that desire is not properly explained or mutually negotiated, leading to isolation and feelings of abandonment on all sides (Woolley, 2007). Couples need to discuss the following issues and come to some agreement about them.

What to Talk About

It's common for cops to get caught in black-and-white thinking, believing they have to tell everything or nothing. In most instances, the nonenforcement spouse simply wants to know if the officer is in a bad mood because of work or because of something else. Are they mad, sad, or tired? If they're mad, who are they mad at? Children, especially, are sensitive to their parents' moods and prone to blame themselves or make up something worse than the truth.

We encourage officers to talk about their feelings and keep the details to themselves, unless their spouses have expressed a particular interest in them. We give the same advice to fire fighters and emergency medical personnel, who see a lot of gruesome and tragic accidents or medical emergencies.

> John rolled on a multifatality accident in which two small children died because their parents were driving drunk and didn't secure the children's seat belts. There was a lot of blood, and the children's bodies were badly mutilated. When he got home John hugged his kids and asked to speak to his wife privately. He told her that he had had a terrible day and saw something he hoped never to see again. He briefly described the incident as a fatal accident involving children and said that he felt fearful for his own children, anger at the selfishness of the drivers, sadness for the two innocent children, and anxiety over the fragility of life. He did not supply any details about the scene, the mutilated bodies, or the screaming parents. He knew from previous discussions with his wife that she was especially emotional about child victims and preferred not to hear any gruesome details.

Dealing with Secrets

On occasion an officer may be involved in an investigation or task force action about which he or she is sworn to secrecy. Sometimes the officer is undercover and, for safety reasons, must keep all aspects of the undercover assignment confidential. In rural areas, an officer may be investigating a family friend, a neighbor, or a local merchant.

There is evidence that the owner of the salon where Jack's wife, Lisa, always gets her hair cut is selling drugs out of a back room. Jack would prefer Lisa not go there anymore, but he doesn't want to arouse the owner's suspicion, since everyone knows Jack is a police officer. He's afraid to tell Lisa about the investigation for fear she'll inadvertently say something to the owner, whom she considers a friend. Lisa doesn't have the same information or the same training Jack does and is likely not to believe that her friend could be involved in criminal activity.

Jack has a huge dilemma. Should he tell Lisa and swear her to secrecy so that she will not get involved in any pending danger? Even if Lisa swears not to tell her friend, the suspected drug-dealing owner, wouldn't she be tempted to tell some other patrons in order to protect them as well? But if the owner starts suddenly losing customers, won't he start asking questions?

What do you think Jack should do? As his therapist, what would you recommend? Jack needs first to examine his department's regulations to reaffirm the policy about discussing pending cases with family members. He then needs to consult with coworkers and peer support members. If Jack determines that he cannot reveal any aspect of the investigation to Lisa, he has to do something to protect her, protect the investigation, and buy some time. Perhaps he can find a way to treat Lisa to a haircut at a new beauty salon that has been getting rave reviews but is a little pricey. The bottom line, when it comes to secrets, is that LEOs should do the exact same thing that clinicians should do when confronted with a sticky ethical issue: review the relevant legal or ethical points, consult with coworkers, and document the decision.

When to Talk

As we've said before, most cops hate being hit with problems the minute they walk in the door. They have been problem solving all day and need a break. They may be so reluctant to engage in meaningful communication that they appear disinterested, passive, or withholding when in fact they are simply tired of dealing with problems. On the other hand, many spouses have been stuck with child care all day and can't wait to hand off the kids or get help with the broken washing machine. It's the classic arsenic hour as described by Virginia Satir (1983), when everyone needs something and no one has anything left to give. How, when, and where families reconnect is different for every household, especially those affected by shift work. The point is that they take a problem-solving stance toward deciding when to talk, make some mutual agreements, and reevaluate them at some point in the future.

Where to Talk

Some males prefer to talk while doing something else, like walking the dog. Some females want physical closeness when talking about difficult matters and prefer to talk in bed or in the car. Gender differences affect all of us, regardless of occupation.

How to Talk

As we've said, police officers are professional problem solvers. It's what they do all day and what they're paid for. Having a bad day? Call the cops. Having a good day? Call a florist. Problem solving is a cop's default position, and while this behavior is frequently influenced by gender socialization, it can create issues at home, when one partner wants only to be heard and the other reflexively steps in and tries to fix things.

> Patty and Angie worked for the same department. Patty was a lieutenant and Angie was a supervising dispatcher. When something happened on the street, Angie would ask Patty what happened and get irritated if Patty didn't supply many details. Angie's interest in Patty's work and her desire to share left Patty feeling cross-examined. Patty, on the other hand, would wait patiently for Angie to volunteer information when she was disturbed about something, leading Angie to feel that Patty didn't care about her issues. When Angie had a problem, Patty tried to demonstrate her interest and concern by suggesting possible solutions, her reflexive problem-solving stance. This irritated Angie, who mistakenly felt that Patty didn't think she was capable of solving problems on her own. Now they preface their conversations by specifying what they want. Patty asks Angie, "Are you venting or do you need some specific help solving a problem?" Angie gives Patty options about when and where to talk, including the opportunity to opt out of describing an event in detail. Stonewalling is not an acceptable option. If Patty doesn't want to talk, she needs to give Angie a reasonable explanation for her behavior.

MYTHS OF COMMUNICATION

Cops have all kinds of reasons they don't talk to their families. Most of these are based on myths they hold and faulty reasoning. Here are some common myths:

"My home should be a sanctuary, free of conflict, politics, gossip, and gore."

There is, of course, a certain truth to this. We all need a break from work, a place to relax and let our hair down. But trying to create an impenetrable barrier between home and work isn't possible. The job follows a cop home. He or she only imagines that it doesn't.

When officers try too hard to shield their families from the unsavory and distressing details of their work, or to make their homes into sanctuaries separate from the pressures of the job, it creates a confusing and artificial separation. Such efforts throw communication off balance. Imagine being married to someone who may turn to you for support during a stressful period but at other times clams up and refuses to talk. The result is an "emotional seesaw" that takes its toll on everyone (Miller, 2007b).

> Ron had to clean up after a string of gruesome suicides. He didn't want to tell his wife about them for fear he would upset her with such gory images, so he told her he had been chasing bank robbers. It didn't take much for her to figure out that he was lying because he was still withdrawn and grumpy on the days he was pretending work was fun and exciting. Ron, like most cops, was good at putting on a game face when dealing with citizens and his fellow officers, but it didn't work as well at home. His wife found out what was really going on when she overheard him talking to a police buddy on the phone. She was hurt that Ron chose to talk to his friend and not to her and angry that she and the kids had to tiptoe around Ron's mood, not knowing why he was so grouchy and fearing he was upset with them. Moreover, she was conflicted about telling him any of this because she was afraid it would add to his troubles.

"My family won't understand: they'll be scared, angry, or disgusted, or they won't believe me."

It's sometimes hard for family members to understand the rush that comes from putting a bad guy in jail. What they hear instead is that the person upon whom they depend is doing something so dangerous that the potential consequences can jeopardize the entire family's well-being. Why would anyone chase a possibly armed person into an empty warehouse just because they stole thirty dollars' worth of auto parts? Sometimes even the cops wonder about this. The point is that when an LEO can't share the highlights of his day because his spouse is so frightened, the genuine communication required for intimacy closes down.

> Jack had an absolutely thrilling day, a high-speed pursuit that resulted in the major arrest of a big-time drug dealer. He was a rookie, and this drug bust was one of the high points of his career. He was elated when he came home and couldn't wait to tell his wife, who burst into tears

and begged him to quit. It was the last time he told her the truth about his work. At work, he could high-five with his buddies, who understood the thrill of the chase and the pride of getting a bad guy off the street. But at home, he felt guilty about loving a job with so much risk. Gradually he stopped talking to his wife about work, or he made up stories he knew wouldn't upset her. His wife sensed what he was doing and felt bad about not being able to control her anxiety.

"Talking about something will only make it worse."

This myth is shared by a lot of people, not just cops. How many of us were warned not to air our "dirty laundry" in public? It is common sense to avoid talking about things that are upsetting, although some research suggests just the opposite. Officers who do not discuss their traumatic experiences with their marital partners actually experience more, not less, distress (Davidson & Moss, 2008).

> Stan had been keeping secrets his whole life, including the fact that he was physically, emotionally, and sexually abused as a child. He was the model of rugged individualism until things stacked up so high he fell apart. His greatest fear was that once he began to tell his therapist about the abuse, all the tears he had worked so hard to suppress would overwhelm him and he wouldn't be able to stop crying. That would have been true in a traditional 50-minute session, but his therapist arranged to give Stan as much time as he needed and promised to "put him back together" before their time was up. Stan, as he predicted, had a major abreaction during the session. But he also discovered the healing value of sharing shameful secrets and feelings. At his next session, he and his therapist worked out a game plan for Stan to talk to his wife, including how to preface the discussion, how to explain why he had kept so many secrets, how and when to ask for a break if he got too upset, and what he and his wife might need as follow-up.

"I'll lose control and get emotional in front of my family."

This is a corollary of the previous myth. Cops are supposed to solve problems, not have them. An overabundance of machismo leads to the blunting of affect, overreliance on physical power, an inability to admit weakness, an inability to ask for help, difficulty addressing relationship concerns, and an endorsement of rigid gender roles (White & Honig, 1995). As we said earlier, suppressing emotions and hiding any sign, real or imagined, of weakness is part of the police paradox. The emotional tools necessary to be a good street cop too often backfire on the officer at home and in personal relationships, when overlearned (and overrewarded) work habits—such as controlling behaviors, perfectionism, overprotectiveness, cynicism, and emotional blunting—are used on the wrong people and in the wrong context. This doesn't make them easy to change, but using a psychoeducational approach opens up the possibility for change and gives the therapist and the family some ways to intervene.

> When Sylvia came home wearing "the face," her kids and her husband learned in counseling that she needed space to decompress because she had had a bad day at work. After a while, the same metaphor became the way the family brought Sylvia's attention to her behavior. "Mom," her kids would say, "you have that face again." It was a signal for her to lose her cop persona and just be Mom.

"I'm sick of talking about this at work. I don't want to talk about it anymore."

It's always a good idea for families and therapists to ask officers if they want to talk about an event that happened at work. When the answer is "no" or "not now," it may simply mean the officer has gone over the incident repeatedly at work, sometimes formally in a tactical debriefing, or informally because it's all anyone is talking about.

> After an officer was killed in the line of duty, everyone on duty was held overtime and everyone off duty was called in to work. Some were looking for the suspect, others were containing the crime scene or interviewing witnesses. Everyone was tired, hungry, emotionally overloaded, and needed a shower. Rather than releasing them to go home, a well-meaning but ill-advised superior officer, probably acting out of his own anxiety, convened a psychological debriefing and caused a mutiny as the exhausted officers stormed out.

Timing is everything. Officers should be able to talk when they're ready. This is why mandatory critical incident debriefings require officers to attend but not to talk. Sometimes LEOs are still processing their reactions and actually don't know what to say. Families are advised not to take this personally, but to check back with their officer or take a rain check. Officers are advised to explain their reluctance to talk rather than just stonewall. Every incident is unique and must be handled on a case-by-case basis. Some "events" are not truly over for the officer for months or even years as they are called to testify in court or continue to encounter suspects and suspects' families on the street.

"Only another cop will understand."

This is one of those myths with a kernel of truth at the center. It is unreasonable to expect that members of an officer's family will understand what the officer goes through unless they are cops themselves. We have to remind officers, just because someone loves you doesn't mean that they can read your mind or know what you need. When taken to extremes, confiding only in other cops creates emotional distance in the family, leaves family members feeling rejected, and sets the officer up to receive only confirming feedback from those who by and large share a similar mindset and point of view.

This bears repeating: One of the occupational hazards of police work is self-inflation—discounting the opinions of civilians, including one's own family, because they are considered naive. It's true that police officers see more of the dark side of life than the rest of us ever will. On the other hand, officers are prone to making sampling errors, judging all of humanity by the small percentage of people they see in their work. This is unfair, inaccurate, and needs to be challenged. Therapists can assist family members to determine how, when, and where to best challenge entrenched negativity, cynicism, and intolerance.

"Talking is a waste of time unless we're solving problems."

Sometimes this relates to gender. Many women enjoy talking for its own sake, while men, in general, endorse conversation as a functional enterprise. Sometimes, it relates to habit and style. Remember Patty and Angie (see above)? Patty couldn't understand Angie's need to ventilate her problems if she didn't want help coming up with a solution. Like many LEOs Patty had a "dispositional mentality"—solve problems and move on.

TRAUMA AND FAMILY COMMUNICATION

Cops talk to people all the time. No problem. It's us families that are left with the broken part.

—POLICE WIFE

Family is the officer's true first responder and primary supporter. Cops are good at putting on a game face at work, so it's their families who know they are having nightmares, thrashing in their sleep, or are short-tempered with the kids or fearful of being in crowds. The love of family is a critical component for healing. Ironically, that same love and compassion is the family's Achilles' heel. It is unbearable to watch someone you love suffer physically or emotionally, incredibly frustrating not be able to help or to understand what that other person is feeling. Children are especially affected by their parents' moods. The natural reaction of most families is to worry that they are doing something wrong and should try harder.

Families need help distinguishing between what they can do to help and what is beyond their control. They need to know when to seek professional help for themselves or for their loved one. Most of all, they need not to become hostages to trauma. Sometimes this involves a delicate balance. As the following example shows, neither love nor devotion can compensate for another person's suffering. When families ignore their own needs for recreation, socialization, and comfort in the hopes that they will hasten their loved one's recovery, they risk damaging their own well-being. They should be advised to take as good care of themselves as they do of their injured LEOs and not let themselves be negatively affected by the anger and irritability that so often accompanies trauma.

> Edgar wouldn't talk about what happened except to say that it was bad. Any disagreement or misbehavior from his children set him off. He was withdrawn. His drinking increased. He stopped going to ball games with his son. At first his wife, Amy, felt bad for him because he was suffering so much and was so changed from his normally cheerful, outgoing self. All she wanted was for things to return to normal in time for the holidays, which was a big deal for their family. Edgar was too depressed to participate in any holiday activities. He didn't want to go to church, he didn't care about presents, and he refused to go to any parties. Rather than going on their own, his family felt obliged to stay home with him because he was so miserable and they were so worried. Amy suggested he go for counseling, but Edgar thought that repeating the story would only make him feel worse. He stopped her from going because he didn't want anyone else to know how bad he felt.

Edgar and Amy's scenario illustrates just how much traumatic incidents affect family life—not just in the present, but sometimes for years to come. Posttraumatic stress injuries are intergenerational. Many clients discover in therapy that their own parents were dealing with undiagnosed, sometimes combat-related, PTSD (Danieli, 1994).

Edgar would have been way better off talking to Amy, and Amy would have benefited from counseling even if Edgar wouldn't go. She might have learned that her wish for a return to normal was probably unrealistic, and a poor benchmark by which to judge Edgar's recovery. It's better for families to look toward a "new normal" with specific, measureable, and achievable goals than to wish everything would be the way it once was. Clinicians can be very helpful assisting families to negotiate more reasonable, realistic, and progressive expectations.

When trauma strikes, family members will need support systems of their own as they struggle to support their officer. The family is not a bottomless resource (Regehr & Bober, 2005, p. 113). Ideally, departments should offer the same counseling benefits, peer support, and critical incident debriefing services to families as they offer to their police officers. But they don't. Behind every trauma victim is a nearly invisible family whose lives are also deeply affected and for whom few services exist (Kirschman, 2007).

> Brett was devastated after shooting an unarmed person who had a cell phone, not a gun, in his hand. It was a tragic incident, and Brett felt horribly guilty. His family tried in vain to persuade him that he had done nothing wrong and nothing bad would happen as a result. Brett's response was to feel that they didn't understand what he was going through, including the risk of lawsuits, disciplinary action, and so on.

Families cannot and should not provide tactical feedback unless they are trained law enforcement professionals themselves. What they can do is reassure their officers of their love and loyalty. They can help their officers separate their work behavior from who they are as human beings. And they can provide healing witness by listening without judgment and normalizing their LEOs' reactions.

Occasionally families will want to watch a video of their LEO's critical incident or listen to the dispatch tape. In some cases this is helpful, in others it may be traumatizing. It is useful to inoculate the family against what they will see or hear, predict possible responses, and plan in advance how they will deal with the aftermath. We have no hard-and-fast rules about this. The best a clinician can do is to provide as much advance information as possible and let the family decide for themselves.

Once again, we emphasize the importance of not pressuring LEOs to talk before they are ready. On the other hand, we recognize how frustrating and alienating it is for family members to hear their loved one talking on the phone to another cop when he or she clams up at home. The reasons for this are many, and we've addressed them throughout this book: fear of frightening the family, a desire to keep home uncontaminated by work, a desire to talk with others who were there or who have had similar incidents, and so on. Trauma takes time to process and makes people become self-absorbed. A traumatized person often has little left to give to others. This is why families need extended support networks of their own.

Despite the picture we have painted thus far, in our experience the time following a traumatic incident need not be entirely grim. It can be a time of closeness for couples. We know many spouses who relished those days when their normally taciturn mates wanted to talk and share feelings. It can also be a time when the family heals by engaging together in pleasant distractions that remind them of the goodness and comfort in ordinary experiences, activities like board games, jigsaw puzzles, cooking together, and time spent in nature.

VICARIOUS TRAUMA

The concept of vicarious or secondary trauma is familiar to therapists but not to police families, who are frequently surprised to learn that someone who is indirectly exposed to a traumatic event can be damaged by it and become symptomatic.

> Sandy was teaching school when her husband, Ben, was shot. Fortunately, Ben's injuries were not serious, and he was expected to return to work in a few weeks. Sandy was not doing nearly as well as he was. She and Ben were deeply connected. She couldn't stop thinking about how Ben had been so close to death while she was happily talking with her students. Every time she tried to go back to the classroom, she had an anxiety attack. She couldn't talk to Ben about the shooting because it made her cry. Ben was her rock. Other women's husbands got hurt, but Ben was careful and never took chances. Sandy couldn't shake off her fear that something else bad would happen to him if he returned to work. Asking Ben to quit only created tension between them. Ben became impotent, and Sandy assumed that he didn't love her anymore. She felt like a failure as a wife and thought she was going crazy.

It is understandable that a frightened spouse might want his or her cop to quit work. But pressuring a cop to leave police work is more likely to create resentment than it is to create respect for anyone's concerns. The same thing holds true for therapists who suggest that the only way to cure trauma is to leave the job. We are not ruling out finding other work. We have encountered many officers who were "fried"—done, burned out, and finished after a string of events. But it can be more effective to explore their work histories in detail than to recommend that they quit—they are likely to conclude on their own that it is time to move on.

ADDITIONAL CONSIDERATIONS FOR CHILDREN

The unique challenges and benefits that cops' kids face deserve a book of their own. We have integrated some of them into various scenarios throughout this book. This section includes a few additional points for clinicians to consider.

Cops' kids face a lot of challenges that change as they grow older. Little children may be filled with pride as Mom or Dad comes to their school in uniform on career day. It's cool to go to the police station, sit in patrol cars, or be around guns. It's even cooler to think of Mom or Dad as heroes, able to protect them and everyone else, although it does feel a little weird to go to a restaurant and have everyone stare, or hear someone else's parents threatening to send their children to your table because your kind and gentle police officer father will make them behave. And what about the teachers who think you should be better behaved than anyone just because your mother's a cop? And how come your mother thinks so too? What happens when your father has to work overtime because there's an earthquake? Who's going to watch over you while he's out helping other people? And what happens to you if he gets hurt or killed?

> Greg was off duty driving his teenage son home from school when they passed a police car, light bar flashing, as the officer pulled a vehicle to the side of the road. "Nazi," his son sneered. Greg felt a rush of hurt, then anger. He tried explaining and defending the cop's actions, but when he got no response from his son he lost his temper. "Being a cop is what pays the rent, being a cop is what bought you a computer, being a cop is going to send you to college. So don't pull an attitude with me." They spent the rest of the ride and the rest of the day in silence.

Older children, like Greg's son, struggle with issues of authority and are prone to being teased at school. This can get especially difficult when there is headline news about a police action. Was Greg's son imitating his friends? At this stage in his development, being accepted by his peers may matter more to him than his family's approval. It will be a challenge for Greg and his son to survive his adolescence and keep their relationship intact.

Therapists can assist police families in discriminating between age-appropriate behaviors and serious acting out of the sort LEOs encounter every day on the job—drug addiction and gang violence. As we mentioned before, on the street noncompliance is often a prelude to violence. This, combined with a worst-case scenario mindset, places some officers at risk for overreacting to common disagreements at home and expressing themselves too forcefully. It is important for the clinician to distinguish between habituated, overlearned, and misplaced work behaviors and aggressive behavior that is prompted by a psychological condition or substance abuse. Greg's reflexive defensiveness was off the mark. It took his therapist to point out that his son's angry disdain camouflaged an underlying anxiety generated by his parents' deteriorating marriage and the imminent threat of divorce.

While some kids rebel against their LEO parent's public image, others can use it to help them out in times of trouble. Many of us have bragged about our parents—my dad can beat your dad—but when your father or mother is a cop such childhood taunts really carry some weight. Police officer parents need to caution their kids against relying on professional courtesies to get out of trouble when they are stopped for speeding, curfew violations, and so on. Instead, they need to take full responsibility for their actions.

It goes without saying that all parents are concerned about their children's safety. It's just that cops know too much and, as we've said many times, are overly attuned to the real and potential dangers around them. It's as though they are never off duty, and neither are the criminals.

Ricky and her dad were in a grocery store shopping for cereal when he spotted a wanted suspect in the same aisle. Her father grabbed her, spun her around, and pushed her toward the back of the store, whispering that they were going to stay there until the "bad man" left. Fifteen years later, Ricky can remember the incident as though it happened yesterday.

Children imitate their parents. An overly vigilant, cynical, apprehensive, and suspicious parent will likely raise a child who believes the world is a dangerous place. LEOs must carefully balance what they know about the world—particularly the terrible things that can happen to children—with safeguards and cautions that teach but do not alarm. What Ricky remembers about the grocery store incident is that while she felt scared, she also felt protected. The incident became a positive experience, one she and her father could share, rather than a warning about the perpetual dangers that lurk in innocuous places.

Finally, we need to say that most LEO kids love and admire their parents and grow up to be well-adjusted adults. Our attention to some of their unique circumstances is not intended to imply anything else. Perhaps the best way to say this is to quote a cop's kid.

Aiden is in his twenties. When asked what were the best and worst parts of being a cop's kid, he looked puzzled. "That's like asking what is it like having a father?" He thought for a moment. "All I remember is how much fun it was living with my father's K-9 dogs, and getting to shoot some cool guns at the range." He paused again. "I guess the thing you should tell the people who read your book is that the most important part of my dad being a cop was that he never acted like one at home. At home, he was just Dad."

KEY POINTS

- We use the term "real" family on purpose to refer to the officer's biological relatives or spouse. We do this with the belief that the work family is fickle. "Home," as the poet Robert Frost said, "is the place where, when you have to go there, they have to take you in."
- Education is key. Parents want to know how children react to trauma and when to ask for professional help (Kirschman, 2007).
- Guard against letting children assume prematurely adult roles such as comforting or protecting their parents or erroneously assuming responsibility for a parent's physical or psychic injuries.
- Emotion-focused therapy (EFT) is helpful when working with officers who may have difficulty identifying their emotions and accessing new ones (Greenberg, 2011).

17

THE FIRST RESPONDER
RELATIONSHIP

I went on a call involving a dead baby. The baby had passed
away in the night, most likely because of SIDS. . . . We still
had to go out to ensure that there wasn't something more
suspicious involved. Because I have children, the call was
hard to deal with. The parents were obviously very upset.
It was difficult not to put myself in their shoes. When I got
home, all I had to do was tell my husband what kind of a call
it had been and he knew just what to do and say to help me
deal with the fallout and "reset" myself.

—POLICE OFFICER

It is not uncommon for cops to marry other cops—or dispatchers, fire fighters, ER nurses, or other first responders. Many of these marriages work well because the couples share a unique culture and point of
view. There are also disadvantages to marriages between two first responders, such as child care problems, too much shoptalk, and living life in a
fishbowl. This chapter supplements the other chapters in this section by
focusing on issues unique to first responder marriages. In the end, what's
needed to sustain a healthy relationship is not so different for two cops
than it is for any other couple: putting family before the job, a diversi-
fied and extended social network, a range of interests and activities outside
of law enforcement, self-esteem, willingness to give and receive support,

the ability to be playful, patience to endure troubled times, an optimistic outlook on the future, satisfying work, adaptive coping skills, good communication, capable problem solving, time management, conflict resolution abilities, and good physical and financial health.

THE ADVANTAGES

We get it. We understand each other from a professional standpoint and know the stresses of the job. Heck, we even speak the same language—we can talk in Penal Codes and 10-codes . . . and not bother translating things into plain English. We have the same gallows humor about horrible situations—so we can laugh something off together and not seem like we're monsters . . . we're confident that if anything happens to us off duty while we're together, we trust the other . . . to respond appropriately . . . and not "nut up" like a civilian spouse might do.
—POLICE OFFICER SPOUSE

Communication between two first responders is likely to be a lot easier than that between a first responder and a civilian. Because they do similar work, there is no need to go into long explanations or answer a lot of technical questions. One cop would never ask another, "Why did you have to kill him?" They already know the answer because they've had the same training. Cops can listen to each other describe horrific or tragic calls without overreacting or becoming fearful, probably because they've been through a similar incident. What sounds frightening or grotesque to a civilian may seem like fun to another responder who shares an action-oriented bent and enjoys gallows humor. Cops benefit from one another's experience and can give each other feedback and advice that civilians can't supply.

Cop couples can help each other in practical ways. They can practice tactical skills together, help each other study for promotions, and consult with each other when making career decisions. Their combined salaries are generally enough to support a comfortable lifestyle, and those with kids can arrange shift work so that the children have one parent at home nearly full time. On an existential plane, cops see so much despair, random violence, and loss that they are well positioned to appreciate life and not take each other for granted.

THE DISADVANTAGES

There are a lot of challenges facing cop couples, though perhaps no more than those facing other dual-career couples, especially those with children. Because they share similar points of view and experiences, first responder couples are at risk for reinforcing each other when what may be needed is input from someone with a totally different point of view.

> Amber had a long list of complaints against her sergeant and her lieutenant, who were making her life miserable. She was on the verge of filing an official grievance. Her domestic partner, Eva, was very supportive and encouraging. She too had had problems with these same superior officers. They spent hours talking together, building on their mutual experiences. Months later, facing still more depositions with no end in sight, Amber and Eva both regretted not talking to some neutral third party who didn't share their viewpoint, someone who might have pointed out the downsides of filing a complaint or suggested other ways to proceed.

If police work is stressful, then cop couples have a double dose. They see each other too little, and the little time they have together can be filled with shoptalk. They have the same friends, the same interests, the same social outlets. Everyone knows their business, how much they make, when they go on vacation, with whom they eat lunch. They are the subject of rumors and gossip. Social situations can be especially awkward when one mate is a superior officer and the other is not.

> Dan was a corporal and Stephanie a lieutenant. Dan's buddies didn't know how to treat Stephanie in social situations. She wasn't just another cop, she was a superior officer. They felt inhibited in her presence and were careful about what they said and how they behaved. Stephanie felt like a party pooper. Dan missed hanging out with his friends and hated going to parties with Stephanie's colleagues because he couldn't relax. They fought about this at home. Dan accused Stephanie of ordering him around, and of taking out her frustrations with line-level officers on him. Secretly, they both worried that socializing separately could lead to infidelity.

We all need a break from work, a port in the storm. On the one hand, as we've said before, creating an impermeable barrier between work and home is impossible, and trying to do so can damage communication between couples. On the other hand, cop couples need to remember not to judge 90% of the world based on the 10% they encounter on the job.

> When Phyliss and Mel's 4-year-old daughter came home from day care complaining about pain between her legs, they went into overdrive. They had both investigated countless cases of childhood sexual abuse.

As a result, abuse was the first thing they thought about. They drove to the day care and literally began interrogating their daughter's teachers. They had a lot of apologizing to do after their pediatrician told them their daughter had a urinary tract infection.

Couples who work together have to consciously try to leave quarrels behind when they go to work and work behind when they are at home. Maintaining clear boundaries can be a challenge. How must it feel to over-hear someone in the locker room talking about your wife in disrespectful terms? What does it take to stay calm and focused when you have dispatched your husband to a call that turns violent and you have no idea if he's injured? How would you feel if someone hit the person you love with a beer bottle during a bar check? The normal human instinct would be to protect him or her. Depending on the circumstances, that may not be the safe or right thing to do. The use of force should be guided by objectivity and law, not fueled by emotion. This is why most departments will not allow couples to work the same beat or the same shift, let alone work as partners.

> Sheila noticed that her fiancé, Rick, drove by every time she had a car stop or got out of her vehicle to do a field interview, even though it meant leaving his sector. Rick had several more years of experience on the street than she did and worried about Sheila's safety. At home, he sometimes criticized how she had handled a call or lectured her on officer safety. Sheila responded with anger and defensiveness. She felt Rick was patronizing and didn't understand how difficult it was to be a woman in this job. This was a grave disappointment. Until she met Rick, her social life had been difficult. The civilians she dated seemed to be uncomfortable dating a cop and regarded her as an oddity. Their therapist helped Rick see that he was too involved to be objectively helpful. Rather than fret about Sheila's safety, he needed to focus on containing his anxiety. He learned to ask Sheila if she wanted his advice or feedback and to back off when she didn't.

Cops are used to being in control and supervising others. These are important work skills that can create trouble at home. Cop couples need to back down in an argument and learn how to negotiate and compromise. All couples fight. Somebody once said that every couple has at least 10 irreconcilable differences. Unlike street encounters, these conflicts and differences are not preludes to danger. Just as therapists can annoy their spouses by using their "therapy voices" at home, it is damaging and destructive for LEOs to use street techniques on each other. Cops don't get to make mistakes. When they do someone dies or gets hurt or sued or loses her job or makes the headlines. Home is a place to relax. A "my way or the highway" attitude at home not only shuts down communication but also stunts its growth by blocking out any information that doesn't conform with the speaker's opinion. That's why we often ask officers "Would you rather be right, or would you rather be free?"—meaning "Wouldn't you like the freedom that comes with shedding the burden of having to be right all the time?"

As we've said, first responders get used to suppressing their emotions at work. They are simply not permitted to have the spontaneous human responses that the rest of us would if we felt threatened or frightened or disgusted or sad. They have to stuff their feelings and do their jobs, no matter what. Like other overlearned or habituated behaviors, it's hard to turn things around at will and start expressing feelings the minute you walk through your own front door.

> Mike and Leslie each spent years working tough assignments—homicide investigation, child abuse, and victim services. They coped by covering themselves with emotional armor. They had to be thick-skinned and tough because if they weren't, their jobs would have been unbearable. They used to talk about work. Sharing the good and the bad with each other was a blessing. Sometimes they didn't have to say a word, they just understood the bad moods and left each other alone. They both agreed that showing emotions was a weakness. Neither could afford to display much feeling and then get up the next morning ready to go back to work. Shutting down was their way of coping. But over time, as normal problems accumulated, their inability to open up caused them to distance and disconnect from each other.

Mike and Leslie needed more than help with communications. They needed a way to deal with work and not let things build up. They needed an extended support system, rather than depending only on each other, because it was simply too much for them to carry. Mike began talking regularly with a peer supporter at work. Leslie met with some other women cops and also started therapy. Both realized they needed to bring more positive activities and wholesome people into their lives.

COPS' KIDS

Things change for cop couples when they have children. In most departments, the pregnant cop will be relieved of street duty around the fifth month and placed in a position that doesn't entail physical stress. (The regulations around maternity and parental leave vary from department to department.) Shift work makes child care a challenge. While some shift arrangements allow children to have one parent at home nearly all the time, the downside is that the parents may rarely see each other. Those with overlapping shifts will need 12–14 hours of child care on the days they both work. That's a long time for children to be separated from their parents. Sleep deprivation, a perennial problem for cops (see Chapter 7), is made worse by a colicky baby who can't sleep or small children who have to play inside.

Having children can change an officer's attitude toward risk taking and danger. What was once considered fun—a foot pursuit, a high-speed chase, serving a warrant—looks very different to a mother or father with small children waiting at home. When both parents are in police work, the potential for injury and the preparation for injury become a matter of concern. Making wills, advance directives, and so on, is a necessity.

Cop couples with kids need an extended support system. When disaster strikes, both parents will likely be called into duty. They need to arrange child care in advance and to prepare a disaster plan for the family. Each child needs to know where to go, what to do, and how the family will stay in touch when both parents are working. These days, disaster planning may include financial reversals as governments downsize their police departments.

> Heather and Greg worked for different departments. He was a fire fighter, she was a cop. Both were facing significant pay cuts due to the budget situation in their city. Heather had so little time on the job that she worried about layoffs. At home, their financial situation was all they talked about, precisely because they were both dealing with it.

STRENGTHENING THE FIRST RESPONDER RELATIONSHIP

Do the pitfalls of a first responder marriage outweigh the benefits? That depends on the couple, their coping skills, their department, and, as always, luck. The following questions may be helpful in sorting out strategies for helping a couple strengthen their relationship (Kirschman, 2004):

- Do your clients, independently and as a couple, have interests, hobbies, and activities outside of the emergency response culture?
- Does the couple spend sufficient time off together, with the children

and alone? Because everyone has different needs, is budgeting time a negotiable issue?

- Do they have a diverse social network that extends beyond other first responders?
- Are they part of a religious or spiritual community?
- How skilled are they at conflict resolution? Do they ever lapse into "cop mode," using intimidation or physical force? Do they know how to repair the damage done?
- Do they have enough positive activities in their lives to offset the negativity they both encounter on the job?
- Do they place limits on how much shoptalk is permitted at home?
- Does the couple have goals for the family and for themselves as partners and as individuals?
- What is the financial health of the family? Does either partner, or both, work excessive overtime or have a second job because they are living beyond their means?

KEY POINTS

- Balancing career goals and family goals is especially difficult for women. Despite changes in society, women still shoulder more domestic responsibilities than men (Hochschild, 2003), including child care, which is expensive and hard to come by, especially for shift workers.

- Both members of a cop couple need to set goals for themselves as individuals and as a family. They also need backup plans in case one or both of them get injured or need to take a premature retirement. All it takes is a blown knee or a torn shoulder for an officer to be medically retired, left to live on half of his or her previous income. Contingency planning is a must.

- Many cops are competitive by nature. Couples can avoid direct competition by specializing in different aspects of policing or working in different departments. They should never partner together or work the same beat on the same shift.

- A cop couple will need to adjust to help each other's careers. They should guard against letting others assume that they don't want to compete against each other for promotions or specialty assignments, or that the more important opportunities should automatically go to the male first. Women, especially, should not let others assume that they don't want to be considered for tough assignments after they become mothers. When both spouses work for the same agency, rules against nepotism will likely affect both officers' career paths.

- Some assignments are more stressful or dangerous than others (see Chapter 5). Whenever possible, the other spouse should try to secure a less stressful assignment.

Parents should anticipate the strain the assignment places on the family and plan accordingly.

- Cut down on department-sponsored social activities. The family should come first in off-duty hours, even if it means one or both spouses are less likely to be promoted because they are not being politically savvy.

- Because cop couples usually have busy and frequently changing schedules, they need a shared calendar to display everyone's activities in advance: vacations, school holidays, training days, shift changes, and so on (Gilmartin, 2002).

18

INFIDELITY, DIVORCE, AND DOMESTIC ABUSE

> ... what do you say to the woman who has been in a relationship with a cop who never communicates? Who cheats every time he has the urge. . . . What do you say to the family he left behind . . . ?
> —E-MAIL FROM POLICE SPOUSE

> Sorry for the long story. I am just scared and sad. Any advice would be greatly appreciated.
> —E-MAIL FROM POLICE SPOUSE

There is an enduring myth that cops are routinely unfaithful, divorced more than other occupational groups, and prone to domestic violence. Often, it is the cops themselves who perpetuate this myth. We are keen to present reliable findings to the contrary. Why would police families seek counseling if they believed they were doomed to divorce or domestic abuse? And why would any clinician agree to work with a police family when the odds of a good outcome were near impossible? This chapter sets the facts straight and describes work factors known to play a part in domestic discord that can escalate if not addressed. It also addresses the tricky issues around reporting domestic abuse.

INFIDELITY

Getting dependable data about infidelity is hard to do. Locker-room talk is hardly a reliable source of information. Police officers, like others who work long hours away from home and meet a variety of people, have ample opportunities to be unfaithful. Police groupies, "uniform junkies," and "badge bunnies" are rarely in short supply. And now that women make up approximately 10% of the police force, the close-knit bond among officers or between partners, not to mention hours training together or attending off-site conferences, has the potential to lead to romance (White & Honig, 1994). So does working closely with other first responders such as dispatchers, fire fighters, and emergency room nurses. Marital therapist John Gottman suggests that infidelity is the search for lost friendship. While this is not true for everyone, in our experience, people who work together or do similar work easily share experiences, a worldview, and a mindset that their civilian mates may not. (Couples who marry before one becomes a first responder may be at special risk due to lifestyle changes brought about by emergency services work.) What starts out as a friendship can evolve into an emotional affair where the two people involved share more, talk more, and are more emotionally available to each other than they are in their committed relationships.

Trauma also has the potential to raise the risk for infidelity when the psychologically injured officer looks for illicit sex to restimulate adrenaline or fight depression, or to counter feelings of inadequacy by finding someone who, at least temporarily, finds him or her a person of worth. Having PTSD does not excuse an individual for breaking her agreements with a loved one, but it is a factor clinicians should consider.

Miller (2006b) places individuals along a continuum from those who will never cheat, no matter the cause or the temptation, to those who have no hesitation about extramarital relationships. In between are those vulnerable officers with the same risk factors for infidelity as anyone else regardless of occupation—family conflicts, career disappointments, and low self-esteem.

Loss of integrity, guilt, divorce, and so on are not the only consequences for the police officer who has an affair. Sexual improprieties with coworkers or, worse, with citizens are potential career enders. Most departments have general orders regarding fraternization between colleagues, especially those of differing ranks, and prohibit interactions with citizens for sexually motivated reasons. There are always individuals willing to submit to a sexual shakedown, an exchange of favors in lieu of arrest or getting a ticket. Some victims, particularly rape victims or victims of domestic abuse, may express their gratitude for an officer's assistance in inappropriate, sometimes sexual, ways that can be danger-ously intoxicating. Such interactions can be considered abuse of authority under color of law (International Association of Chiefs of Police, 2011). We warn our cop clients not to believe the "press notices" they get—good or bad.

Repairing a relationship after one partner or both have been unfaith-ful is beyond the scope of this chapter, and no different than it would be for any couple. The point we wish to stress is that while police work can be used to justify infidelity, it is more accurate to say that infidelity, however often it occurs, is not so much a consequence of the job as it is a reflection of the people involved (Kirschman, 2007).

DIVORCE

As stated earlier, it is a common myth that the divorce rate for police offi-cers is substantially higher than it is for the general population. Anecdotal evidence suggests that if police families survive the first 3 years of marriage, their risk of divorce is no greater than that of other families and that second police marriages may be even more stable than first or second marriages in the general population (Miller, 2007b).

McCoy and Aamodt (2010) studied demographic variables collected from 449 occupations in the 2000 U.S. census data. Shift work, overtime, and weekend work were rated and found not to account for any variance in the divorce rate, although ethnicity, gender, and average income did. Con-trolling for race, gender, and income, the researchers found that the divorce rate for law enforcement occupations—meaning the percentage of respon-dents who were divorced at the time of the census, not the percentage of respondents who ever divorced—was 14.47% lower than the national aver-age of 16.96%, and lower than the rates for psychologists (19.30%) and social workers (23.16%).

A breakdown of the broad law enforcement category produced the fol-lowing divorce rates: police officers and sheriff's deputies (15.01%), super-visors (12.75%), detectives (12.53%), and railroad police (5.26%). Only animal control officers, fish and game wardens, and parking enforcement officers exceeded the national average. Correctional officers and supervi-sors had higher than average divorce rates, but they were lower or equal to the divorce rates of demographically matched peers. The three broad occupational categories with the highest divorce rates were dancers and choreographers, bartenders, and massage therapists. The three occupations with the lowest divorce rates were media and communications equipment workers, agricultural engineers, and optometrists.

DOMESTIC ABUSE

I have often heard that domestic abuse among those who are sworn to protect and serve is the result of the stress of the job. I have not read any research that supports this idea and I could not confirm it in my practice of over 25 years. Most officers do experience stress that is related to the profession but few are batterers. If domestic abuse was caused by stress than all of them would be batterers, which is not the case. Officers are trained to make order out of disorder and take control. When this behavior bleeds over into a police family it is more intense and, in my opinion, more deadly. Victims of police domestic abuse need special support and resources and cannot be treated like other victims.

—Dr. Lorraine Greene, former director of Behavioral Science,
Metro-Davidson Police; winner of the 2010 award by the Office
of Victims Assistance for her work with victims of domestic abuse

When do command presence and controlling behaviors at home become verbal or physical abuse? Are there work-related factors that the clinician should consider? This is not to suggest that work-related stress explains or excuses abusive behavior—clearly it does not. But if a clinician thinks there is any possibility of helping a police family repair the damage done by domestic abuse without putting anyone's safety in jeopardy, understanding these factors may be helpful in both diagnosis and intervention.

It is beyond the scope of this chapter to fully discuss the research on domestic abuse in police families—which has both critics and endorsers—or to review the basic principles for safely treating domestic abusers and their families. What we do want to explore are findings that may be unique to this population and unfamiliar to the community clinician.

A Brief History of the Problem

Recent studies suggest that domestic abuse is not widespread in police families, due to improvements in preemployment screening, improved background checks, and polygraphs that more effectively weed out most of the actual or potential abusers. It is important, however, to remember two things: (1) preemployment screening is a snapshot in time, before the individual is exposed to the job, and (2) the findings from preemployment screenings are valid for only 1 year. There is no question that in the past some departments have looked the other way, protecting abusive officers from their accusers. This has made it difficult to obtain accurate statistics about the prevalence of domestic abuse in law enforcement families. Who would readily admit to behavior that could result in job termination? The ability to study the problem is further compounded by disagreements and inconsistencies about the very definition of abuse, which exists along a continuum from overly controlling behavior to verbal abuse to physical violence.

Things have tightened up since the Omnibus Consolidated Appropriations Act of 1997, which mandates that anyone convicted of misdemeanor or felony domestic violence may not possess or use a firearm. In 2003, the International Association of Chiefs of Police wrote a model policy for handling domestic abuse committed by police officers. How well and how widely these guidelines are implemented is impossible to determine (Kirschman, 2007).

The Police Persona

We can't emphasize this too much: police work is all about control—control of people, situations, and emotions. LEOs work in paramilitary organizations, where they give and take orders without explanation. They expect compliance from citizens, and they are trained to use physical force and verbal intimidation to get the job done. Failure to take action when required is not an option. Physical and verbal confrontations become a routine part of their work. As a result, they can become desensitized to aggressive behavior in a way that their families are not. Consider the following exercise that we do at couple's workshops.

We start with an escalation-of-force scale where 1 equals no force and 10 equals lethal force. We then ask the officers in the room how they would rate intimidation—yelling, using nonverbal tactics such as glaring, assuming an aggressive stance, and so on. Most give it a 1 or a 2. Then we ask spouses how they would rate the same tactics if they were used at home. Most give it a 10 or, as one woman said, "that's when I pack my suitcase and head for the door" (Kirschman, 2007).

It is not uncommon to hear families complain that their officers talk to them like "perps" and treat the children as though they were delinquents. When this is brought to the officers' attention, they are often surprised to get this feedback because they are so used to talking to people with their occupational persona intact they don't notice that they are in "cop mode" at home. It's as though they've forgotten how to use their "inside voices," or they have difficulty slowing down and talking at a normal conversational pace using normal give and take. We advise officers to ask their families, "Have you ever felt afraid of me?" They are sometimes shocked at the answers they receive.

We recommend talking about abusive behavior and the police officer's paradox at orientations for new hires and their families. It is important to raise awareness of how work habits can be destructive to home life and to give intimate partners permission to speak out or seek help at the first sign their loved one is acting like a cop at home. We stress the importance for cops of developing two sets of interpersonal skills, one for work and one for the family, and of learning how to shift gears between work and home.

We also stress the importance for family members of knowing what constitutes abuse, and when, where, and how to get help in a timely way. In an ideal world, if time permitted we would also offer communication training, assertiveness training, and conflict resolution skills.

Prior Trauma as a Risk Factor

There is some anecdotal evidence that officers with acute traumatic reactions—subclinical or unresolved PTSD—may be at risk for violent behavior, especially those with a history of mental health problems, including previous trauma exposure and complaints of organizational stress. The following scenario, first published in *I Love a Cop: What Police Families Need to Know* (Kirschman, 2007), illustrates the complexities that can be involved in abusive behavior.

> Jules was recovering from injuries he sustained in a fight with several gang members. He was outnumbered and almost lost control of his gun. In the long minutes before his backup arrived, he was certain he was going to be killed. While he was resting at home, his young son snuck up behind him and leaped in his lap without warning. Jules reflexively reacted as though he were in a fight for his life and slapped his child in the face.

Is Jules guilty of child abuse? Was he caught off guard and, for the moment, blindly fearful for his safety, or was he consciously and willfully punishing his child for disturbing him? There are no easy answers. Possible patterns of abuse in each family must be carefully sorted and examined on their own merits, in consideration of current state law, and with attention to the safety of all concerned.

Work-Related Factors

The community clinician working with families should inquire about the following issues that play a part in domestic discord, and, if ignored, may escalate to domestic abuse. All of the following factors are amplified by substance abuse problems, ongoing mental health conditions, and a history of prior emotional or sexual abuse.

1. Work conditions. Some studies suggest that officers reporting high levels of job stress or job dissatisfaction are more likely to abuse their intimate partners by misplacing aggression or seeking to rectify low self-esteem by asserting their authority at home (Gershon, 2000).

2. Work assignment. Certain assignments, like narcotics, undercover work, and Internet child pornography, are inherently stressful and pull the officer away from his or her family (see Chapter 5).
3. Shift work. Officers working midnights or swing shift may struggle with sleep deprivation or be at risk for the overuse of caffeinated drinks and over-the-counter medications. Sleep deprivation can lead to poor judgment, low impulse control, and a short fuse (see Chapter 7).
4. Isolation related to shift work or to a tendency to socialize only with other cops.
5. Excessive hours: officers routinely working more than 50 hours per week or taking no leave time, and thus being unavailable to their families. (We are not talking about crises, cases of exceptional urgency, or special deployments.)
6. Poor coping strategies: rugged individualism, an inability to ask for help in a timely way, and an overly macho mindset for both males and females, with rigid gender-role expectations such as the belief that "a man's home is his castle."
7. The emergency responder's exhaustion syndrome (ERES; see Chapter 3): a combination of anger, isolation, depression, and exhaustion.
8. Using more than 19 days of sick leave per year.
9. Abusing alcohol and/or pain medications, leading to moodiness, poor decision making, and lack of impulse control.

WHEN COPS ARE VICTIMS OF ABUSE

Officers are not always the perpetrators of abuse, sometimes they are the victims. Colleagues have described counseling officers who are so tired of fighting with people at work that they are overly passive or disengaged at home just to avoid more confrontations. Officers may be reluctant to defend themselves when their intimate partners become physical, shoving or hitting—perhaps in reaction to the officer's emotional withdrawal—because they fear that any physical move on their part, even an effort to move away, will be reported per the Omnibus Act and they'll lose their jobs. Others are reluctant to protect themselves, fearing that their size and training gives them an unfair advantage over their mates. Anecdotal evidence suggests that when both partners are in law enforcement, there may be a higher than average incidence of domestic abuse.

Underreporting is common among victims of abuse, who fear that reporting will exacerbate the abuser's anger and place them and their children in more danger. When the victim is a police officer, the shame associated with not being able to defend oneself makes asking for help especially challenging. They may also minimize the abuse to their therapists because it is not as bad as what they see on the job.

REPORTING DOMESTIC ABUSE

As stated above, the Omnibus Act mandates that anyone convicted of misdemeanor or felony domestic violence may not possess or use a firearm, including police officers. Although it is intended to protect potential victims, some believe that this law may inhibit police families from reporting abuse. Police officers who cannot carry a gun cannot work and will, in many cases, lose their jobs. Police family victims may not only be reluctant to report abuse, but they may be afraid to seek counseling or talk about their abuse for fear the counselor will break confidentiality, in which case the victim not only risks retaliation from her abuser, but economic disaster, loss of medical benefits, and so on. Finally, some departments have seen a rise in bogus abuse complaints made by spouses seeking to gain advantage in divorce or custody battles. Proceed carefully when reporting domestic abuse; your first order of business is to make sure the victim or victims are safe. Then you, as the treating therapist, should seek legal and clinical consultation. Make sure you know the reporting laws in your state. In California, for example, police officers are mandated to report domestic abuse, but clinicians are mandated only to report child and elder abuse.

KEY POINTS

- Beware of blaming everything on the job. It is true that police work habits can be hazardous to home life and many givens of the job are not family friendly. It is also true that police work provides a ready-made scapegoat for a troubled marriage and an easy out for avoiding the task of managing differences with loved ones and learning positive ways to build, strengthen, and maintain a family (Kirschman, 2007).

- While there are some studies and people who disagree, we think it is a mistake to assume that police officers are by nature prone to domestic abuse or that individuals prone to aggression are naturally drawn to police work.

- Divorcing couples, in general, need a lot of help, guidance, and coaching, especially when children are involved. Because of shift work custody issues and child care can be a challenge (A. Buscho, personal communication, April 22, 2012).

Part VI

GETTING STARTED

The community therapist who is trying to reach out to police might find other first responder groups such as fire fighters, emergency medical personnel (paramedics, emergency medical technicians, and private ambulance staff), dispatchers, corrections officers, probation officers, parole officers, crime scene techs, criminalists, animal control officers, emergency room personnel, body handlers, and so on, initially more receptive than cops. The first chapter in Part VI provides a thumbnail profile of three of these groups. Think about the challenges these responders face and what services you might be able to offer. The second chapter focuses on strategies clinicians might use with law enforcement and other first responder populations to establish themselves as competent, helpful, and trustworthy.

19

SPECIAL CONSIDERATIONS FOR TREATING OTHER FIRST RESPONDERS

Question: What's the difference between a fire fighter and a cop?

Answer: When people wave to a fire fighter, they wave with all five fingers. When they wave to a cop, they only use one.
—ANONYMOUS JOKE

God made fire fighters so cops could have heroes.
—ANONYMOUS JOKE

Each of the following groups, and the list is far from all-inclusive, is deserving of a book of its own. That we have devoted only one chapter to so many first responders was a practical decision that does not reflect the respect we have for the important, and often difficult, work they do.

Every first responder population has its own unique challenges, despite obvious similarities such as courage, a propensity for physical action, the desire to make a difference, love of tradition, dedication to the job, and pride in their professions. These differences are obvious even as these professionals work together, often at the same scene and on the same case. The following are brief summaries of the significant issues facing each of these groups. The descriptions are merely starting points. We have more information and data about fire fighters than the other professions because they have been studied more. Consult the resource section on recommended reading for additional information. As you read, think about ways your role as a therapist might fit in and with which groups you might have a particular affinity.

FIRE FIGHTERS

Work Life

Fire fighters and police officers work in different, though overlapping, environments—with the exception of public safety departments, which rotate employees between the fire service and law enforcement. How well this works for the employees and the community varies, depending on whom you talk to.

Cops and fire fighters are under public scrutiny as they perform often dangerous, time urgent work. Both groups are active risk seekers whose work life alternates between excitement and boredom. The work of fire fighters, with the exception of emergency medical personnel, is largely physical, while police work is mostly cognitive and interpersonal. Both groups experience significant levels of organizational stress, often exceeding line-of-duty stress. Their families all contend with spillover from the job to home.

What is not commonly known is that 80% of all calls for service to a fire department are medical calls, many of which involve tragic deaths, grieving families, and intimate contact with victims. Unlike other medical practitioners, who work in sterile, controlled environments, fire fighter medics and emergency medical technicians (EMTs) do their work in the field—on highways, in bedrooms, restaurants, and so on. (In some departments, all fire fighters are cross-trained as EMTs, whereas paramedics are an independent unit within a department and have no fire suppression duties.)

Fire fighter paramedics have a heavier call load than their fire suppression colleagues, in part because there are fewer fires and because paramedics fill a gap in health care for the poor. Paramedics are susceptible to back strain and muscular injuries from twisting and lifting patients in an increasingly obese society. They are concerned about being exposed to communicable diseases and blood-borne pathogens. Compared to fire suppression work, some emergency medical service workers complain that their jobs are more tiring, less satisfying, and more psychologically taxing.

Fire fighting is a dangerous, and sporadic, pursuit. Going from zero to maximum levels of physical exertion is exceptionally hard on the body. The leading cause of death for fire fighters is heart attacks while fighting fires. Exhaustion and injuries are a fact of life for fire fighters: strains, sprains, muscular pain, cuts, burns, and inhalation of smoke, gas, or unknown toxic substances (Kirschman, 2004). Sleep deprivation is a chronic challenge. Even if there are no alarms during the night, fire fighters rarely get enough restorative sleep.

Because paid fire fighters, also known as career fire fighters, work in teams and live together, they feel like family, for better or worse. Volunteer fire fighters, who constitute 80% of the fire service, are generally located in rural areas and, with some few exceptions, live in their own homes. Although there is some interchange between volunteers and career fire fighters, the paid fire fighters are generally younger, better trained, better equipped, have a higher call volume, and are responsible for more lives because they work in densely populated areas.

There are a wide variety of schedules in the fire service. The predominant pattern is 24 hours on, 48 hours off, for a total of 6 working days per month. In contrast, police officers work about 26 days per month. The fire service schedule is one of the perks of the job, and many fire fighters have second jobs or side businesses. (Wildland fire fighters work during fire season, often camping out or flying to the scene of the fire.)

Living together in a firehouse has its up and downs. Every house and every shift seems to have a personality of its own. There are high levels of bonding, mutual support, and lots of practical pranks. On the other hand, as the fire service has become more diverse, living together in a multiethnic group that includes both men and women can be challenging. In the "old days" fire fighters needed only to be strong and willing. The modern fire service requires them to be interpersonally skilled as well.

One of the biggest differences between cops and fire fighters is their social mandate. The social mandate for law enforcement is to control situations and people who are out of control, put bad guys in jail, and restore the peace. They do other things, of course, but that's their main objective. The fire service mandate is to save lives and property, which also involves equipment maintenance and community education. It's a clearer, less complex goal.

People living in a democratic society are ambivalent, if not downright suspicious, of authority. Hardly anyone is ambivalent about the fire service. Fire fighters are our heroes. Rarely does anyone lie to them or try to hurt them. In a 2012 presentation, Gilmartin said that cops work in a profession based on "mistrust" whereas fire fighters work in a "trust-based" profession. They appear to have higher job satisfaction, aren't as wary of the public, and usually don't develop the kind of we–they mindset that cops often possess. Fire fighters sometimes complain that cops are too abrasive, while cops, only half in jest, accuse fire fighters of spending their shifts in recliners watching TV. Events following the September 11 terrorist bombings in New York reportedly led to serious conflicts between LEOs and fire fighters (Langewiesche, 2003).

The following incident illustrates how these differences can intrude into the workplace.

> A young woman lay mortally wounded on the sidewalk, shot by an unknown suspect in front of the nightclub where she had been celebrating her engagement. The fire fighter paramedics were waiting on the perimeter until the scene was secure before attending to the victim. The police, believing the shooter was in the crowd, locked all the patrons in the nightclub so that no one could leave before being interviewed. After the incident was over, the fire fighters were angry to learn there had been no suspect in custody, because that's what a secure scene meant to them. They felt vulnerable, out in the open, bending over the victim, their backs exposed while the shooter's whereabouts were unknown. The cops, on the other hand, complained that in the rush to get the victim to the hospital, fire fighters had bundled evidence, like bullet casings, with the victim and then later tossed everything away when they cleaned and restocked the ambulance.

FIRE SERVICE FAMILIES

Fire service work spills over to family life in ways that are both similar to and different from the complaints we hear from police families. In terms of shift work, the 24-hour shift is a long time for families to be separated or for one spouse to have continuous child care responsibilities. Fire fighters miss cherished family rituals such as dinnertime or bedtime, not to mention birthdays, recitals, and other important family occasions. Fire fighters can become overly anxious about their children's safety, especially those working emergency medical services (EMS), because of the constant stream of car accidents, bike accidents, playground falls, SIDS deaths, and so on to which they respond. They can be demanding that their homes be as clean and well organized as their fire trucks and medic vans, creating an impossible expectation that places extreme pressure on the family.

Fire service families, like police families, often feel that they play second fiddle to the job. Even on their days off, fire fighters can be preoccupied with work. When a fire fighter goes shopping, he looks first at the store construction, fire exits, and location of flammable goods and second at whatever he and his family came to buy. Before a vacationing fire fighter unpacks, she checks for the nearest fire exit and the closest fire extinguisher, and asks for a transfer if her room is not on a lower floor.

In Chapter 18 we cited divorce statistics from 449 occupations based on the 2000 U.S. census data (McCoy, 2010). At the time of the census the national average for currently divorced individuals in the general population was 16.96% while the fire fighter divorce rate was 14.08%, far less than the figures that get bandied about online and around the fire house dining table.

Fire service families are more integrated into the workplace than police families are. They sometimes come and go during a shift. They are invited to holiday meals, barbeques, and fundraisers. The we–they mentality that separates LEOs from their civilian spouses is far less intrusive.

Occupational Hazards: Alcoholism and PTSD

There is some indication that fire fighters have elevated rates of alcohol consumption. Concern about drinking in the fire station has generated a recommendation by the National Institute for Occupational Safety and Health (NIOSH) for immediate adoption of the International Association of Fire Chiefs' zero-tolerance policy for the consumption of alcohol within 8 hours of reporting for all activities and functions of the fire service, including training. Furthermore, alcohol is forbidden on the premises of any operational portion of a fire department (Alcohol Policy Alliance, 2009).

Alcohol has a long history in the fire service. Many volunteer departments operate like community centers and derive a substantial percentage of their funding from renting out the fire station for social events. A "cold one" after a hot fire was a long-standing tradition. In the past, many firefighters considered the fire station as their second home, a place to kick back and socialize with all the comforts they would have in their real homes. Some still do. It is ironic that people who so frequently see the tragic results of alcohol-related accidents would consider drinking on the job.

Fire fighters are compassionate individuals who enter the service primarily to help others. Paradoxically, their best days may be someone else's worst. Like police officers, they are exposed to more tragedy in a few months or a few years than the rest of us will see in a lifetime. Here's a small sample of the calls to which they are deployed: shootings, drownings, knifings, bombings, beatings, hangings, car wrecks, train wrecks, airplane crashes, falls, fires, explosions, electrocutions, overdoses, poisoning, suffocations, incinerations, heart attacks, dog attacks, seizures, chronic and acute illness, trench collapses, building collapses, sudden death, dismemberment, workplace violence, school violence, domestic violence, gang violence, and disasters, natural, unnatural, accidental, and intentional. This is not to mention the ever-present threat of terrorist activity including biochemical warfare, dirty bombs, and mass casualty incidents (Kirschman, 2004). As with other first responders, when the call resonates with the fire fighter's personal experience or the fire fighter can identify with or knows the victim, the risk for traumatization is greatly increased. This happens frequently on medical calls, especially those involving children.

The reported prevalence rate of PTSD in fire fighters varies widely. Much of the research has evolved from the Oklahoma City bombing and the attack on the World Trade Center. It is beyond the scope of this chapter to review all such studies other than to say that alcohol use seems to rise in this population following a catastrophic event (North et al., 2002). Other common coping strategies are gallows humor and overfocusing on the medical/technical aspects of the event. Exercise is helpful in reducing symptoms, as is social and psychological support from friends, family, and work peers (Berninger et al., 2010).

Some trauma specialists working with combat veterans theorize that the cultural imperatives of the military population, like that of first responders, may make those suffering from PTSD reluctant to endorse the DSM criterion of "fear, helplessness or horror." Instead, they may have other more dominant responses like anger (Murphy, 2012). Helping fire fighters and paramedics identify emotions is apparently more helpful than voluntary emotional expression in managing occupational stress (Halpern, Maunder, Schwartz, & Gurevich, 2012). This makes sense in light of a study of 225 U.S. fire fighters in which fear of emotion emerged as the strongest individual predictor of PTSD (Farnsworth & Sewell, 2011).

DISPATCHERS

You may know where you are and what you are doing. God may know where you are and what you're doing. But if your dispatcher doesn't know where you are and what you're doing, then I hope you and God are on very good terms.
—POSTER in a 911 dispatch center

Work Life

The job of 911 dispatchers or communicators is a tough one—lots of responsibility with little control. Call centers are the virtual heart of an emergency response agency, and dispatchers are the first responder's first responder. A dispatcher's job is to quickly assess an incident, often with incomplete information, and then send appropriate help, making certain that responding personnel have all the information they need to safely proceed. Dispatchers gather advance intelligence. Are there weapons on scene? Have the police been out to this location before and why? Does the caller or his family have a criminal history? Is this a medical or psychiatric emergency? What other units are available for backup?

Dispatch centers are equipped according to the available resources. Larger, better-funded agencies can supply their 911 call centers with the latest in technology and ergonomically designed furnishings. Staff members wear uniforms and are highly and continuously trained. Other centers operate out of small, dark, poorly ventilated rooms where communicators are tethered to their consoles. In the larger high-volume call centers, personnel are organized according to task: dedicated call takers receive incoming 911 calls, while dispatchers deploy emergency personnel—police, fire, utilities, and animal control. In smaller centers, the dispatcher handles both functions and may also be the chief's administrative assistant.

Occupational Hazards

Dispatchers do not face the physical dangers that field personnel do, but make no mistake, their jobs are exceptionally stressful and they are at risk for peritraumatic distress and PTSD (Pierce & Lilly, 2012). Imagine for a moment what it must be like to remain calm while listening to a wheelchair-bound man screaming for help as he burns to death or to give medical directions to a panicked mother who is performing CPR on her drowned child. What must it be like to talk to a caller who shoots herself while still on the phone? Or to soothe a child whose mother isn't moving after Daddy hit her? Or to calmly relay information to and from officers you have worked with for years, listening as they are pinned down under fire, some injured, some already dead. The human response to such stress is to run, yell, fight back. Cops get to do that on the street. But dispatchers must remain in their seats, cool and composed, focused on the task at hand, while literally swimming in their own adrenaline. When the crisis is over, the street personnel usually get a break, but not the dispatchers, who must continue fielding calls until, and if, someone can be found to replace them.

In what may be the only published study to date examining the relationship between duty-related trauma exposure, peritraumatic distress, and PTSD symptoms in telecommunicators, researchers asked dispatchers to identify their worst calls (Pierce & Lilly, 2012). The most commonly identified worst call was the unexpected injury or death of a child, followed in order by suicidal callers, officer-involved shootings (OISs), and calls involving the unexpected death of an adult.

The exposure to traumatic events is made worse for communicators in several ways. While field personnel have some limited control over the kinds of situations described above, the dispatcher has none. This can amplify feelings of helplessness. Without visual input, what is happening on the street is left to the dispatcher's imagination, which may be different from or worse than reality. One of the biggest stressors is not knowing what happened to the caller after help arrived. Was that mother able to revive her drowned child? Did the suicidal caller die? Many departments routinely include dispatchers in their after-action psychological debriefings, but many may not. Individual officers will often get back to the dispatcher who handled the call, but given the disposition-driven nature of emergency response, the opportunity to do this can fall between the cracks. Depending on the agency culture, dispatchers can feel like valued members of the team or second-class citizens. It is important to understand the unique organizational dynamics of the agency where your client works.

Dispatchers may also be at risk for PTSD because they are largely women, and women are known to be twice as likely as males to get PTSD. The reasons for this are not clear. Some suggest the difference is genetic. In our experience, dispatchers are very close to the first responders with whom they work, often referring to "my cops." They assume a great deal of responsibility for officers' safety, even though it's beyond their control. Officers who don't answer up when called create a lot of anxiety and anger. Finally, the sedentary nature of telecommunications can be harmful to health. The National Cancer Institute followed 250,000 American adults for 8 years. Those who were most sedentary (sitting 7 or more hours a day) had a much higher risk of premature death than those who sat less (Reynolds, 2012). One has only to spend time with communicators to see the high prevalence of obesity and the limited opportunities to eat well.

CORRECTIONAL OFFICERS

A consequence of putting men in cells and controlling their movements is that they can do almost nothing for themselves. For their various needs they are dependent on one person, their gallery officer. Instead of feeling like a big, tough guard, the gallery officer at the end of the day often feels like a waiter serving a hundred tables or like the mother of a nightmarishly large brood of sullen, dangerous, and demanding children. When grown men are infantilized, most don't take to it too nicely.
—TED CONOVER, *Newjack: Guarding Sing Sing* (2001, p. 234)

Work Life

Custodial care is the primary job of line-level correctional officers (COs), keeping themselves and society safe from inmates and inmates safe from each other. COs work in a variety of facilities: county, state, federal, public, private, civilian, and military. Approximately 70–90% have direct supervision over inmates, and the rest work in control rooms or provide transportation, counseling, and other support services. The inmates they guard can be juveniles or adults whose offenses range from minor to major. The security precautions they enforce vary both within and between institutions on a continuum from minimum to maximum. It's a stressful job being locked in with people whose primary objective is to get out.

Occupational Hazards

There are a variety of stressors confronting COs. As with police, organizational stress—supervisory demands, understaffing, shift work, mandatory overtime, lack of clear guidelines or procedures, paperwork, lack of promotional opportunity, poor morale, conflicts with coworkers, and so on—is high on the list. Add to that low pay and public stereotyping of COs as thug-like brutes who take delight in beating their charges.

The list of work-related stressors probably starts with danger. With the exception of police officers, the number of nonfatal violent workplace incidents per 1,000 employees is higher for COs than for any other profession (Finn, 2000, p. 2). Contributors to danger are overcrowding, understaffing, and the increased number of ever more dangerous gangs in the prison population. Some studies have found that COs working medium- or minimum-security areas have less stress than those assigned to high-security units, while other studies found no differences. To some, staffing an administrative segregation unit feels less stressful because inmates are locked down for the day. To others, the stress is higher because every inmate is a "potential time bomb" (Finn, 2000, p. 15).

A CO's day has the potential for escapes, emergencies, injuries, fights, suicides, and exposure to bodily fluids and feces, as well as communicable diseases like TB, hepatitis C, and AIDS—not to mention noise and bad odors. Many inmates are mentally ill and have needs beyond a CO's level of training. A CO is always at risk for being sued or threatened. Inmates have ties to their own communities and retain the ability to do harm. Thus the threat of violence to oneself and one's family is ever present.

The risks of working with an inmate population go beyond physical danger. COs are at risk for burnout, depression, anxiety, and stress-related physical and behavioral problems. Role confusion is a challenge, as COs may be required to assume multiple conflicting roles such as rehabilitation and custodial care. Overidentification with inmates is another risk, one that Gilmartin (2002) and his colleagues call the "Correctional Officer Stockholm Syndrome." A CO, especially someone with unresolved personal or work-related crises, may have more reliable contact with inmates than with friends or coworkers. This can lead to "loyalty slippage," where the CO's most viable support system becomes an inmate or group of inmates. The CO is then at risk for ethical breaches such as sex with an inmate, assisting in an escape, or improperly granting special privileges. The result can lead to the CO losing his or her job and family, and facing criminal charges.

KEY POINTS

- As always, the community clinician is advised to be a participant-observer before offering services or making incorrect assumptions about the needs of any of these occupational groups.

- To civilians, all uniformed personnel look alike, but the various groups look very different to each other. The community clinician needs to recognize that first responders are not a monolithic bloc; there are vital differences between and within groups.

- Toughness, peer bonding, resilience, the ability to remain calm under pressure, rugged individualism, and the rejection of outside support are the fundamentals that create fortitude in a first responder. Respect these elements and work with them, not against them (Greene, Kane, Christ, Lynch, & Corrigan, 2006).

- Organizational stress exceeds line-of-duty stress: a bad outcome (e.g., death of a victim) in a well-run operation seems to create less stress on responders than a positive outcome in a chaotic operation. What protects against traumatic stress is technically competent command staff who are concerned about the well-being of their subordinates and can express their concern in timely, effective ways (Kirschman, 2004).

- Do a "ride-along" in a 911 call center. Learn how it works. Avoid making impractical recommendations, like the well-meaning but ill-informed therapist who suggested dispatchers take time away from their consoles to do yoga. The dispatchers in this particular unit hardly had time to go to the bathroom, let alone do yoga. He was not invited back.

- Remember to include dispatchers in any services you may provide.

- Animal control officers are part of law enforcement. The stresses they face come from having to euthanize healthy animals and from exposure to animals who have been cruelly treated.

20

BREAKING AND ENTERING

> Anthropology demands the open-mindedness with which one
> must look and listen, record in astonishment, and wonder
> that which one would not have been able to guess.
> —MARGARET MEAD (1950, p. xxvi)

Nothing corrects for stereotypes and dispels myths like experience. You can read a dozen books about law enforcement as a profession, but the best learning comes from watching a real person do the real job. Here are four steps to help you learn more about law enforcement and connect with your local public safety agencies.

1. PUT ON YOUR ANTHROPOLOGIST'S HAT

The cultural competency of most clinicians is limited to race, ethnicity, gender, and sexual orientation. Far fewer of us have been required to study the world of work. If you want to be successful with law enforcement, the first thing you need to do is immerse yourself in the culture. At the risk of repeating ourselves, law enforcement, along with other groups of emergency responders like fire fighters and dispatchers, is a highly defined subculture with all the accoutrements of other subcultures: norms, traditions, identities, boundaries, and so on. Cops identify themselves as "blue," referring to the color of their uniforms. And while there are identifiable subgroups within the law enforcement culture, when push comes to shove, being "blue" trumps all.

> Professors from a local university were invited to give a diversity training to a nearby police department. The officers in the room were apprehensive and resistant. Past diversity trainings had been a disaster. This time promised to be different because the speakers were known experts in diversity. It took only 15 minutes for the supposed experts to antagonize the entire class by accusing them of racial profiling in traffic stops. When officers objected to being stereotyped and tried to explain how and why traffic stops were made, the experts labeled them as racist. Clearly the professors failed to do what they probably routinely preached to their students—study a culture before attempting to enter it, show respect, and understand that change comes slowly from the inside.

2. BE A SELF-STARTER

Reach out to the agencies in your area. What you're trying to do is get your foot in the door, increase your visibility, create trust, and generate opportunities for observation. The following are two main ways to do this: (1) participate in police/community activities and (2) volunteer your services.

Community Activities

• Attend a citizen's police academy. These generally meet once a week for several weeks and are great opportunities to learn about police operations and interact with personnel. A sample curriculum might include topics such as criminal investigations, evidence collection, firearms training, internal affairs management, emergency communications, sexual assault investigations, fraud and financial crimes, SWAT team operation, traffic enforcement, K-9 training, and stress management for law enforcement.

Some fire departments sponsor citizens' fire academies. Participants learn about fire science, get to suit up and fight a training fire, use jaws of life, and observe EMTs and paramedics at work. Police and fire departments work together and often respond on the same calls. While the two cultures are vastly different in many ways, as we've said, when you are accepted in one place, the chances are you'll get to be known in the other.

• Go on a ride-along. There is no better way to understand what LEOs do and to experience the changing rhythms of a patrol shift. Better still, go on several rides. Vary your schedule. What happens Monday nights on dogwatch (12:00 A.M.—6:00 A.M.) is different from what happens on a Saturday night. Observe the different dynamics between shifts or squads. Watch how cops behave during the shift day when the "brass" is around. Notice the different kinds of calls for service on swings and midnights. Ride during bad weather. See what it's like to direct traffic around an accident in a snowstorm. The cops will appreciate your willingness to be uncomfortable in the interests of learning more. If your local department doesn't offer ride-alongs, find one that does.

• Ride along with a fire department or medic unit. Notice how each shift and each "house" has its own unique "personality" and dynamics.

• Attend a police funeral. You will experience not just the tragedy, but the influence of tradition and the magnitude of bonding between officers, most of whom don't know each other personally.

• Tour your local detention center or prison. Correctional officers operate in a very different environment from patrol officers.

• "Ride-along" in the 911 communications center and watch the dispatchers at work.

Volunteer Activities

Volunteering is a great way to get your foot in the door and have the satisfaction of making a difference in your community.

• Find ways to help the department become more family friendly. Offer to talk to a spouses' group about managing the police lifestyle. Consider helping the department start a spouses' academy, family orientation, or support group. But be forewarned, this takes a lot of work, and there can be resistance from officers who want to keep their families separate from work.

• Join your local volunteer crisis intervention team. These teams are generally composed of trained peer support personnel—LEOs, fire fighters, dispatchers, and so on—who, along with volunteer mental health professionals, offer debriefing services to small underresourced agencies.

• Offer to teach classes in stress management to officers and civilian employees.

• Be a police volunteer: help file reports, do fleet maintenance, or assist with youth activities.

• Consider applying to be a reserve police officer. You will undergo a rigorous application process and be required to attend an academy that meets evenings or weekends to accommodate working people. This is a huge contribution of time and effort but with a big payoff. We know several colleagues who have taken this route.

• Sign up to be a volunteer fire fighter. This takes a lot of time and training but tenders the twin benefits of on-the-job learning and community service.

• Reach out to civilian employees. Next to families, records department employees and communicators are often the most underserved work groups in a police department.

• Many departments have in-house journals or newsletters and are looking for writers. Offer to write a column or a short article. The subjects can be psychological in nature, specific to law enforcement, or they can appeal to the general interest. Use your imagination; cops go to movies, read books, eat at restaurants, and use computers in their off time. Review some local restaurants, critique the latest technological advances, recommend your favorite books.

• Use your volunteer activity as an opportunity to barter for something that will help you learn about law enforcement. For example, in exchange for a module in stress management, barter your skills for a ride-along in a police helicopter, a tour of the detention facilities, or an invite to observe range training (A. Bisek, personal communication, November 12, 2012).

3. MATCH YOUR SKILLS AND INTERESTS TO THE UNDERSERVED NEEDS OF LOCAL LAW ENFORCEMENT

Very few police agencies employ a cadre of clinicians or have a behavioral sciences department. Those that do are typically large urban, state, or federal agencies. The vast majority of departments contract with clinicians for specific tasks that fall into one of the four primary domains of public safety psychology: assessment, intervention, operational support, and organization or management consultation. Because it is difficult to maintain a high level of expertise in all four areas, most clinicians specialize in one or two domains. One of the first things to consider when thinking about working with law enforcement is to identify which of these four areas interests you, falls within the scope of your abilities and state licensing regulations, or inspires you to get further training.

Assessment[1]

Most law enforcement agencies have a relationship with a psychologist or a psychology firm and refer all their testing to that person or organization.

---

[1] See also Chapter 8.

For many agencies this relationship is long-standing and based on a level of trust that has developed over the years. The bulk of the testing business is preemployment screening, followed by fitness-for-duty (FFD) evaluations, assessment for special assignments like SWAT, and assistance with promotional selection. If you are interested in working with law enforcement and meet your state's qualifications for conducting LEO assessments, you might get started by approaching a practice that specializes in law enforcement screening and selection.

Clinical Interventions

Clinical interventions typically include critical incident debriefings and psychotherapy services. One of the best ways to get started counseling officers is to join a provider panel for an employee assistance program (EAP) that serves police departments. Most law enforcement agencies offer EAP services to their employees. The number of sessions varies from one program to another and is part of a negotiated benefit. The reimbursement rate for providers also varies from program to program and is usually determined by licensure.

In our opinion, there is too little interaction and marketing of services between EAP providers and law enforcement agencies. This is a missed opportunity. Some of the activities described in the section on self-starting could well be an opportunity for program providers to make themselves known to the agencies they serve.

Operational Support

Activities associated with operational support include crisis and hostage negotiations, psychological autopsies, criminal profiling, counterterrorism, threat assessment, and training. These activities occur infrequently, require specialized training, and, at best, would be a small percentage of anyone's clinical practice. With the exception of training, few agencies would use an outside clinician for these purposes.

Training

Training requirements and opportunities vary in each agency. Some training is mandated by the state agencies that regulate law enforcement. Every state is different. Mandated continuing professional training (CPT) in California is largely tactical and beyond the expertise of most clinicians. Sample topics include arrest and control techniques, firearms tactics, first aid and CPR, and driver training.

Once mandatory training is completed, there is often little time or money left over. This, of course, depends on the size of the agency and its resources. Still, there are many topics that clinicians might propose or volunteer to teach and many formats ranging from short 10-minute "watch" trainings to be delivered at briefings to trainings lasting 1 or more hours. Many of these ideas will come from clients.

> Dr. Anne Bisek met a fire fighter client who was severely affected by the death of a child. She began researching the subject. Other than tactical information, she was surprised to find almost nothing about self-care in either the mental health literature or what was written for first responders. It was as though the topic was taboo. She began interviewing first responders and mental health professionals specializing in public safety, transformed what she learned into a 1-hour Power-Point presentation, tested it on some first responders, revised it, and then took it on the road. Clinical interventions and training on this subject are now a major part of her practice (A. Bisek, personal communication, November 12, 2012).

> Kirschman was working in the psychiatry department of a large hospital. Several of her clients were married to police officers. After listening to their fears and complaints, she put together a class called "I Love a Cop" and taught it at the local community college. At the time, there was little acknowledgment of the challenges facing police families. The class led to many opportunities for consultation and training with local police departments and eventually a book with the same name.

The following list is only a partial representation of the kinds of classes we have taught. Think how they might apply to your local law enforcement agencies.

- Crisis intervention (dealing with mentally ill citizens)
- Peer support
- Identifying deception
- Challenges facing LEOs who are returning combat vets
- Challenges facing those who supervise returning combat vets
- Stress management (acute and cumulative) for sworn and civilian employees
- Interviewing skills
- Peak performance
- Suicide by cop (victim-precipitated suicide)
- Self-care for cops
- Strengthening police family resilience
- Managing your career
- Preparing for retirement
- Dealing with the new generation of employees

- Preparing for promotion
- Management and supervisorial skills for sworn and civilian employees
- Dealing with grieving citizens (this is especially relevant for fire fighters and paramedics).

A Warning about Training

Police officers can be difficult to train. You will notice that officers coming in early head for the back of the room, and officers who show up late only reluctantly sit in front. Some put on sunglasses and read the newspaper while you're talking. As a rule, cops won't ask many questions, especially before lunch or a break, and this lack of interaction could be off-putting to a trainer not used to the police culture. Be sure to bring enough material to cover the entire training without a single question being asked. It isn't that LEOs aren't interested—it is the culture that discourages speaking up in class.

> Dr. Harvey is a very good instructor, energetic, funny, and stimulating. Most of his classes generate a lot of interaction. He was totally baffled at the lack of reaction he received from the 30 LEOs in his class on interviewing techniques. They asked no questions, didn't laugh at his jokes, and sat with stony faces. He was even more baffled to learn that the student evaluations were uniformly excellent with several comments that his was the best class they had ever taken.

LEOs are a fidgety bunch who are best served with hourly breaks. They prefer an interactive format to passive listening, like a lot of humor, and are easily bored, all of which means law enforcement trainers need to be thoroughly prepared, have lots of energy, be comfortable "smoking and joking" with students, and proficient using a variety of training techniques and multimedia formats.

> Chief (Ret.) Lucy Carlton and Dr. Sue Oliviera go with the flow in their popular classes for supervisors. Their classroom looks like a playground—round tables piled with small, rubbery toys, crayons, and scratch paper. They believe that their students listen better and learn more when they are allowed to fidget and encouraged to doodle.

Organizational/Management Consultation

In all but the largest law enforcement agencies, there are few resources and too little money for organization and management consultation. This is unfortunate because a well-run organization operates more effectively and generally has a satisfied workforce. There are a number of activities that a properly trained consultant, often a clinician, can offer to a police department. While we doubt this will be a robust enterprise for most readers, over the years we have facilitated or participated in the following kinds of interventions.

- Organizational development
- Long-term strategic planning
- Development of performance appraisal systems
- Assistance during promotional evaluations (scenario planning, rater preparation, etc.)
- Executive, supervisor, and management consultation
- Team building and conflict resolution
- Needs assessments
- 360-degree feedback exercises
- Community relations planning

A Word of Caution

The clinician who participates in interventions dealing with performance appraisal and promotional evaluations should not also be offering clinical services. If you have anything to do with promotions, however distant or technical, it is doubtful that LEOs will trust that whatever they disclose in therapy won't influence their future careers.

4. ENGAGE IN RIGOROUS SELF-ASSESSMENT

Not everyone is temperamentally suited to working with cops. It is one thing to read about the work. The idea of helping cops is interesting and exciting. But it is quite another thing to sit, face to face, with someone who is talking, in detail, about crimes against children, scenes of carnage, devastating traffic accidents, and violence of all types. Even those of us who have been counseling cops for years have trouble from time to time.

Is working with law enforcement a good fit for you? Many, if not most, cops will seek counseling for a number of commonplace complaints that aren't traumatic. Still, you are bound to hear some terrible stories. Would listening to them would harm you or be overwhelming? We ask this question because we have heard about clinicians who fell apart while working for EAP programs or volunteering to debrief emergency personnel after a disaster. They hurt not only themselves, but their clients.

John responded to a major disaster. He and his coworkers would meet with a mental health staff member at the end of each shift to talk about the day's events. After one particularly horrific shift he was talking to a therapist, describing in detail what he had seen and his frustration over not being able to save anyone. The therapist excused herself, left the room, and never returned. John told this story 20 years later, laughing about "how fucked up I must have been to make the therapist leave the debriefing." The reason he waited almost 20 years before seeking therapy again? He didn't want to harm another therapist.

Clinicians are compassionate people. We connect deeply with our clients and sometimes their stories move us to tears. This level of empathy can be wonderfully therapeutic. Unless your client is a cop. Cops are caretakers. If they feel their therapists can't handle their stories, like John, they will shut down.

Are Your Therapeutic Skills a Good Match?

Clinicians have many therapeutic approaches at their fingertips and, to reiterate, not all of them work with cops. Sand tray therapy may work well with some of your clients, but we doubt it will with LEOs. Asking your officer client to talk to a suspect as if he were sitting in the chair next to him is a time-honored gestalt technique, one we predict won't go over well with cops. Early childhood experiences may be crucial to the officer's issues, but don't go there until, and only if, you have established rapport and trust.

Does your personal style work for this population? Are you comfortable being casual and interactive? Is it OK for you to ask lots of questions rather than feeling you are the expert and should have all the answers? Is it OK with you to joke around with your clients and have them call you by your first name? How transparent and self-disclosing are you willing to be?

Do You Have Good Self-Care Skills?

Clinicians, like cops, are sometimes reluctant to get help when we need it. We think we should have the answers, and we feel embarrassed when we can't solve our own problems. Trust us on this, if you're working with cops, you will have hair-raising experiences and some sleepless nights. The decisions you make will have potential consequences that reach far beyond your office into the community. All of us belong to organizations (see the Resources) where we have instant access to hundreds of experienced colleagues. We ask for help when we need it. We check in with each other regularly and honestly. We debrief each other after every retreat and after every critical incident debriefing. We attend to our own mental and physical health and aim for a reasonable work–life balance. Our aim is progress, not perfection. We take care to practice what we preach to our first responder clients and our readers: "Please, take as good care of yourselves as you do the rest of us."

Appendix

RESIDENTIAL TREATMENT/
GROUP THERAPY

Throughout this book we have referred to our work at the West Coast Post-Trauma Retreat (WCPR; *www.wcpr2001.org*). This Appendix contains a detailed narrative description of this program in the hope that some readers will be inspired to start retreats of their own. If we can be of help in any way, please contact us at *wcpr2001@gmail.com*.

WCPR is one of only two such programs in the country. We exist due to the generous guidance of the founders and staff of the On-Site Academy in Westminster, Massachusetts. Over the years we have modified the On-Site program while remaining true to the overall goal of providing peer-driven, clinically guided assistance to first responders who have been involved in critical incidents that affect not only their ability to work, but also their personal and home lives.

OVERVIEW

The retreat began in 2001, and as of the publication of this book we will have completed approximately 100 sessions and treated nearly 700 clients. We hold 14 sessions a year with six or seven clients per session, plus three programs for spouses and significant others (S.O.S.). Even at this pace, we have a waiting list, and our retreats are filled months in advance.

Our staff-to-client ratio is about three to one. All staff, peer support providers, chaplains, and clinicians are volunteers; no one gets paid. The current cost to clients, their insurance companies, or their agencies is $3,000. The S.O.S. programs are underwritten by the Soroptimists of Marin County and are low cost.

The majority of our clients work in law enforcement, with the second-largest group working in the fire service. Most are males. Approximately 75% come from California, with the rest coming from out of state or out of country. They are referred by their departments, previous clients, therapists, or as a result of their own Internet searches for help. We screen them via telephone including an extensive standardized interview that will be repeated in more detail during the retreat. Our focus is on symptom severity, not diagnoses. Our exclusion criteria are active suicidality (although many of our clients have serious suicidal ideation), personality disorders, the absence of a work-related incident, and substance abuse (clients must have 30 days of sobriety).

PROGRAM COMPONENTS

The retreat lasts for 6 days. A typical day begins at 8:00 A.M. with a group check-in and ends at 10 or 11 at night. The tools we use have been described elsewhere in this book: group therapy, peer support, debriefing, cognitive-behavioral therapy (CBT), eye movement desensitization and reprocessing (EMDR), psychoeducation, nondenominational spiritual support, and ritual. Interactive psychoeducation classes are taught by clinicians and peers. Topics include the human response to stress, rescue personalities, the emergency responder's exhaustion syndrome (ERES), proper use of medications, forgiveness, tactical thinking errors, alcohol education, the influence of family history on current symptoms, and the influence of symptoms on current relationships. One night we have an Alcoholics Anonymous meeting run by recovering first responders. Clients conclude the retreat by making a 90-day plan for themselves with the assistance of an assigned peer who will stay in contact with them even after the retreat ends. We encourage and assist participants to transition into mental health treatment to continue their recovery work.

The use of peer first responders allows our clients to feel safe, builds trust, and creates a nonjudgmental atmosphere that facilitates self-disclosure. There are two groups of peers, colloquially known as "inside" or "outside" peers. "Inside peers" assist with the debriefing process. "Outside peers" support clients through informal discussions, self-disclosure, and assistance with a variety of activities and household tasks such as cooking, cleaning, and running errands. Most peers are returning clients. All activities, except the group debriefings, are conducted in an open area with all staff participating. The group therapy/debriefing process is held in a separate room, facilitated by two clinicians with assistance from the chaplain and two peers with advanced training. There are three meals per day, cooked by peers, plus a continuous supply of snacks. Every client gets a manual containing all forms, policies, a patient bill of rights, and copies of all PowerPoint slides.

DUAL RELATIONSHIPS

We take the issue of dual relationships very seriously. Policing is a small world. Lots of cops have worked together in a variety of situations that only come to light during the retreat. For example, two cops who work in different agencies may have gone through the police academy together or worked side by side on a multiagency task force. Because confidentiality is the cornerstone of our program, we take several steps to ensure that we handle these real and potential relationships in a careful, ethical manner. We read a script to prospective clients during the telephone intake explaining that if the client knows someone at the retreat he or she needs to tell us, and we will do everything possible to resolve the situation so that the client's anonymity is protected. Because many of our clients are referred by their therapists, who are also retreat volunteers, we also inform potential clients that we will make every effort to match them with a different clinician. We review the issues surrounding dual relationships once again on the first day of the retreat during the on-site orientation.

We also require staff members to sign a document stating that (1) they are aware of the multiple relationship issue, (2) there is no one else attending with whom, to their knowledge, they have a preexisting relationship, and (3) if they become aware of a preexisting relationship, they will alert a staff member within the hour. The staff member and the group leader/facilitator then discuss the benefits and liabilities of the staff member's attendance and decide what will be in the best interest of the client.

Furthermore, we read or send a letter to retreat clinicians stating that it is our policy not to pair clients with their own clinicians because this contributes to the efficacy of the retreat; provides a different clinical perspective that may be useful to the treating clinician; and helps our clinicians avoid multiple relationships. The retreat is a more intimate experience than the regular therapy hour, and it is our opinion that the purposes of the retreat and the outside therapy hour are best served when we can keep them separate.

Finally, we have several psychotherapists available who agree to consult on these issues and formulate a course of action in the event a multiple relationship might compromise our professional objectivity or judgment.

OUTCOME RESEARCH

We see WCPR as a return-to-life program, not a return-to-work program. Our major goal is symptom reduction. Even so, our results seem to indicate that symptomatic first responders can have a second chance at their careers. Consider the following analysis.

At the time of their retreats, approximately 47% of our clients were still on active duty. Approximately 90% of these clients were still working 1 year later. Of the 53% who were not working, 35% were already retired or very close to retirement. Of the remaining off-duty clients, 40% returned to work. These figures indicate that early intervention is more effective than waiting until the client is on stress disability leave. By the time a client seeks disability leave his or her symptoms have likely worsened, maladaptive coping skills may be more entrenched, the family resources may be stretched thin, and hope for recovery might have diminished, while feelings of betrayal have probably increased.

We assess clients' symptoms during the program and do follow-up assessments at 30, 60, and 90 days. Analysis of the Detailed Assessment of Posttraumatic Stress (DAPS) showed statistically significant reductions in scores on the following scales: Reexperiencing, Hyperarousal, Avoidance, Posttraumatic Stress Total, Impairment, Substance Abuse, and Suicidality. Analysis of pre- and posttreatment scores on the Symptoms Checklist 90—Revised (SCL-90-R) demonstrated that participants, regardless of occupation (fire or law enforcement), age, or gender, reported that their overall symptom severity decreased significantly by the end of the retreat. On average, each of the nine symptoms and three indices on the SCL-90-R decreased from a significant clinical level of psychological distress to within the normative range. Information about this research and other studies is available on our website, *www.wcpr2001.org*.

Resources

This section includes resources for both clinicians and clients. Starred items may be of interest to both. The resources listed are for information only and, with exceptions where noted, their inclusion here does not represent an endorsement by the authors.

RESIDENTIAL TREATMENT
FOR FIRST RESPONDERS AND FAMILIES

★ The West Coast Post-Trauma Retreat (WCPR) (*www.wcpr2001.org*) is a 6-day retreat in California (see the Appendix and the website for information, articles, and links). Spouses and Significant Others (S.O.S.) retreats are held three times yearly at minimal cost to retreatants.

★ On-Site Academy (*www.onsiteacademy.org*) in Westminister, Massachusetts, is a sister program to WCPR. It offers a variety of long- and short-term residential programs for first responders as well as nonresidential programs.

ALCOHOL TREATMENT: RESIDENTIAL

★ The Brattleboro Retreat Uniformed Services Program (*www.brattleboro retreat.org*) in Brattleboro, Vermont, offers inpatient and outpatient treatment for emergency responders struggling with addictions, substance abuse, and PTSD.

★ The Marworth Treatment Center in Waverly, Pennsylvania (*www.marworth. org*), offers an inpatient uniformed services program for police officers and fire fighters who need treatment for alcohol and chemical dependency.

★ On-Site Academy (see above) offers an extended care program for first responders with drug or alcohol problems.

SELF-HELP: ALCOHOL TREATMENT

★First responder—only AA meeting times and locations in the United States can be found at *www.policesuicideprevention.com/id24.html.*

SELF-HELP: GAMBLING

★ National Council on Problem Gambling (*www.ncpgambling.org*).

POLICE SUICIDE

★ The Badge of Life (*www.badgeoflife.com*) is a group of active and retired police officers, medical professionals, and surviving families of officers who have committed suicide. They maintain a website for the prevention of police suicide that is packed with information, research findings, links, personal stories, and free training videos about suicide prevention and wellness.

Hackett, D., & Violanti, J. (2003). *Police suicide: Tactics for prevention.* Springfield, IL: Charles C. Thomas.—The focus of this book is broader than the title indicates. Contents include the police culture, the supervisor's role in intervention, departmental denial of the problem, getting officers to seek help, family issues, and survivor issues.

Leenaars, A. (2010). *Suicide and homicide-suicide among police.* Amityville, NY: Baywood Publishing.

Violanti, J. (2007). *Police suicide: Epidemic in blue.* Springfield, IL: Charles. C. Thomas.

Violanti, J. (with O'Hara, A., & Tate, T.). (2011). *On the edge: Recent perspectives on police suicide.* Springfield, IL: Charles C. Thomas.—This book was written by sociologist and retired New York State trooper John Violanti, retired CHP officer Andy O'Hara, and Teresa Tate, surviving spouse and founder of Survivors of Law Enforcement Suicide (S.O.L.E.S.).

LEGAL ISSUES

AELE Law Enforcement Legal Center (*www.aele.org*) maintains a free law library including articles, books, and reports regarding police and public safety.

DEADLY FORCE ENCOUNTERS

★ The Force Science Institute (*www.forcescience.org*) conducts research and training about human behavior (physical and psychological) under high stress and in deadly force encounters. They offer a free bimonthly information-packed newsletter on their research and training activities.

★ Artwohl, A., & Christensen, L. (1997). *Deadly force encounters: What cops need to know to mentally and physically prepare for and survive a gunfight.* Boulder, CO: Paladin Press.—If your client has been in a shooting, this is the book to read.

★ Klinger, D. (2006). *Into the kill zone: A cop's eye view of deadly force.* San Francisco: Jossey-Bass.—David Klinger is a former cop turned college professor. His research, insight, and riveting case histories shed new light on what happens when cops find themselves face to face with dangerous criminals.

COUPLE AND FAMILY ISSUES

Creative Arts and Coaching Institute (*www.ca-ci.com*).—Award-winning police psychologist and test developer Robin Inwald's couple questionnaires have been normed on police families. The Couple Compatibility Questionnaire (ICCQ), which is completed by individuals about their partners or spouses, focuses on relationship compatibility. The Partner's Personality Inventory (IPPI) focuses on behavior patterns that may negatively affect relationships. Clinicians can use these and other instruments to create their own online testing services. For more information, contact staff at 866-508-2224.

★ Anderson, R. (2007). *Married to the badge: A wife's tale of survival.* Miami, FL: Blue Line Publishing.—A self-published memoir filled with stories of humor and heartache and advice. The author is married to an officer with the Los Angeles Police Department.

★ Egge, J. (2005). *Bullets in my bed: Surviving a law enforcement marriage.* Boise, ID: Legendary Publishing.—The author is married to a sheriff's deputy. Her easy-to-read book is part memoir, part self-help.

★ Farren, S. (2005). *The fireman's wife: A memoir.* New York: Hyperion.— Farren, a former paramedic, has written a smart, funny, and thoughtful memoir—good reading for anyone married to a fire fighter.

★ Kirschman, E. (2004). *I love a fire fighter: What the family needs to know.* New York: Guilford Press.

★ Kirschman, E. (2007). *I love a cop: What police families need to know* (rev. ed.). New York: Guilford Press.

★ Newman, V. (2011). *A CHIP on my shoulder: How to love your cop with attitude.* Mustang, OK: Tate Publishing.—The author is married to a California Highway Patrol Officer. Her book provides stories, positive thoughts, and simple wisdom about surviving and thriving in a law enforcement marriage.

Reese, J., & Scrivner, E. (Eds.). (1994). *Law enforcement families: Issues and answers.* Washington, DC: U.S. Government Printing Office.—A collection of theoretical papers regarding police families.

Wetendorf, D. (2006). *Crossing the threshold: Female officers and police-perpetrated domestic violence.* Arlington Heights, IL: Author.—Wetendorf is a longtime advocate for victims of police spousal abuse.

★ *www.wivesbehindthebadge.org* is dedicated to providing resources and emotional support to law enforcement spouses and families.

★ *www.policefamilies.com* offers free workshop outlines and PowerPoint slides for family orientations.

MENTAL HEALTH, STRESS MANAGEMENT, AND MEDICATION

Psychological first aid: Field operations guide, available at *www.ptsd.va.gov/professional/manuals/manual-pdf/pfa/PFA_V2.pdf.*

The National Institute of Mental Health has an easy-to-read, easy-to-understand guide to mental health medications on its website (*www.nimh.nih.gov/health/publications/mental-health-medications/complete-index.shtml*).

★ The National Center for Telehealth and Technology (*www.T2health.org*) offers free mobile apps for veterans that also apply to police officers, especially those with PTSD or stress management issues. The apps include BioZen (live biofeedback data that requires compatible biosensor devices); Breathe 2 Relax (portable stress management tool); PTSD Coach (educational tool for individuals who are experiencing symptoms of PTSD); T2 MoodTracker (allows users to self-monitor, track, and reference their emotional experience over a period of time); and Tactical Breather (can be used to gain control over physiological and psychological responses to stress).

Bartol, C., & Bartol, A. (2012). *Introduction to forensic psychology: Research and application.* Thousand Oaks, CA: Sage.—A comprehensive, easy-to-read overview of the many areas where psychology plays a significant role in the civil and criminal justice systems, including police psychology.

Bonifacio, P. (1991). *The psychological effects of police work: A psychodynamic approach.* New York: Plenum Press.—The author applies psychodynamic theory to the experience of urban police officers, exploring such topics as ambivalence, defense mechanisms, and so on.

Finn, P. (2000). *Addressing correctional officer stress: Programs and strategies.* Available from the U.S. Department of Justice at *www.ncjrs.gov/pdffiles1/nij/183474.pdf.*—Case studies from seven diverse, established, and replicable stress programs.

Finn, P., & Kuck, S. (2005). *Stress among probation and parole officers and what can be done about it.* Washington, DC: Office of Justice Programs, U.S. Department of Justice. Available at *https://www.ncjrs.gov/pdffiles1/nij/205620.pdf.*—This study examined the effect of stress on community corrections officers and identified promising stress reduction programs.

Finn, P., & Tomz, J. (1997). *Developing a law enforcement stress program for officers and their families* (NCJ 163175). Washington, DC: National Institute of Justice.—An excellent resource.

★Gilmartin, K. (2002). *Emotional survival for law enforcement: A guide for officers and their families.* Tucson, AZ: E-S Press.—Kevin Gilmartin is a former sheriff's deputy turned psychologist. Cops relate to his writing and his research. This book is important reading for anyone working with officers and is also a top choice to recommend to clients.

Greene, P., Kane, D., Christ, G., Lynch, S., & Corrigan, M. (2006). *FDNY crisis counseling: Innovative responses to 9/11 firefighters, families, and communities.* Hoboken, NJ: Wiley.—This wise, beautifully written book tells you all you want to know about FDNY fire fighters and their culture. Most of what you read applies to fire fighters and first responders everywhere. The advice to clinicians is invaluable.

International Journal of Emergency Mental Health. Special issue (2011): Stress and Health in Law Enforcement (Vol. 13, no. 4).—The journal is devoted to first responders' mental health issues. This special edition is packed with informative articles regarding cops.

Kitaeff, J. (Ed.). (2011). *Handbook of police psychology.* New York: Routledge.—This book covers a range of topics, many of which will be of interest to the community clinician.

Kurke, M., & Scrivner, E. (1995). *Police psychology into the 21st century.* Hillsdale, NJ: Erlbaum.—A collection of edited chapters covering the range of psychological and clinical services to law enforcement.

★Liptak, J., & Leutenberg, E. (2008). *Substance abuse and recovery workbook.* Duluth, MN: Whole Person Associates.

Marin, A. (2012). *In the line of duty.* Available at *www.ombudsman.on.ca/Resources/Reports/In-the-Line-of-Duty.aspx.*—An illuminating investigation into how the Ontario, Canada, Provincial Police and the Ministry of Community Safety and Correctional Services have addressed operational stress injuries affecting police officers. The problems and recommendations are applicable to police departments everywhere.

Miller, L. (1998). *Shocks to the system: Psychotherapy of traumatic disability syndromes.* New York: Norton.

National Institute of Corrections. (2010). *Hitting the wall: Dealing with stress in corrections.* Available at *http://nicic.gov/Library/024726.*—This 6½- hour course includes a lesson plan, participant's manual, ice-breaker exercises, a PowerPoint presentation, video vignettes, and participant handouts.

Regehr, C., & Bober, T. (2005). *In the line of fire: Trauma in the emergency services.* New York: Oxford University Press.—This book describes the consequences of trauma exposure for police officers, fire fighters, and paramedics. It offers suggestions for planning and evaluating intervention programs, developing and maintaining trauma response teams, and training first responders, their families, and mental health professionals.

Territo, L., & Sewell, J. (Eds.). (1999). *Stress management in law enforcement.* Durham, NC: Carolina Academic Press.

Toch, H. (2002). *Stress in policing.* Washington, DC: American Psychological Association.

★ *www.Safecallnow.org*: This nonprofit corporation provides crisis intervention and referral services to public safety employees and their families. The

24-hour confidential hotline at 206-459-3020 is staffed by current and former police officers.

★ *www.shiftwellness.org*: The Innocent Justice Foundation has partnered with the Department of Justice's Office of Juvenile Justice and Delinquency Prevention (OJJDP) and other criminal justice groups to develop on-site and online training programs to address the effects of exposure to child sexual abuse materials on law enforcement officers and their families. They also sponsor programs for mental health professions who work with individuals exposed to child pornography.

ORGANIZATIONS

The Police Psychological Services Section of the International Association of Chiefs of Police is an excellent resource. See the Resources tab of their web page (*www.theiacp.org/psych_services_section*) for a list of publications, links, and guidelines regarding fitness-for-duty (FFD) evaluations, officer-involved shooting (OIS) interventions, peer support, and preemployment psychological evaluations, and advice on consulting police psychologists. Membership is by application and is open only to psychologists.

The Society for Police and Criminal Psychology (*http://psychweb.cisat.jmu. edu/spcp*) encourages the scientific study of police and criminal psychology and the application of scientific knowledge to problems in criminal justice. It focuses on law enforcement, judicial, and corrections elements in criminal justice. There is an annual conference and membership includes the *Journal of Police and Criminal Psychology*.

There are over 50 functional competencies in the domains of assessment, intervention, consultation, and operations for psychologists who work with the first responder population. For more information, go to the American Board of Professional Psychology website (*www.abpp.org*) and click on "Police and Public Safety Psychology" under Member Specialty Boards.

★ Membership in the International Law Enforcement Educators and Trainers Association (*www.ileeta.org*) includes free periodicals, training resources, and tips. They sponsor an annual conference of law enforcement trainers in Chicago.

★ The International Critical Incident Stress Foundation (*www.icisf.org*) is a nonprofit, open-membership foundation whose mission is to provide leadership, education, training, consultation, and support to the emergency response professions. Their many publications and conferences are valuable resources for anyone interested in learning more about critical incident stress, peer support skills, or locating a critical incident stress management team in your area.

SHIFT WORK AND SLEEP DEPRIVATION

Alertness Solutions (*www.alertsol.com*).—Exercises on this website include free sleepiness scales and a sleep debt calculator. Founders, staff, and scientific advisors are sleep experts who work with public safety and transportation industry personnel.

Elliot, D., & Kuehl, K. (2007). *Effects of sleep deprivation on fire fighters and EMS responders.* Available from the International Association of Fire Chiefs at *www.iafc.org/Operations/content.cfm?ItemNumber=1331.*—This large study contains information about sleep management that is useful for all public safety workers plus a list of resources.

National Institute of Justice. *Officer work hours, stress and fatigue.* Available at *www.nij.gov/nij/topics/law-enforcement/officer-safety/stress-fatigue/welcome.htm.* Information about the causes and prevention of fatigue and its effects on performance and health, as well as links to online resources and research.

Rosa, R. R., & Colligan, M. J. (1997). *Plain language about shift work* (Publication No. 97-145). Washington, DC: National Institute for Occupational Safety and Health.

The Stanford Center for Sleep Sciences and Medicine (*www.stanfordhospital. org/clinicsmedServices/clinics/sleep*) is the premier center for sleep medicine research, treatment, and education.

Vila, B. (2000). *Tired cops: The importance of managing police fatigue.* Washington, DC: Police Executive Research Forum. Available at *www.policeforum. org/bookstore.*

REFERENCES

Aamodt, M., & Stalnaker, N. (2006). Police officer suicide: Frequency and officer profiles. Retrieved from *www.policeone.com/health-fitness/articles/137133-Police-Officer-Suicide-Frequency-and-officer-profiles/*.

ADA Amendments Act of 2008, Public Law 110-325, 122 Stat. 3553 (2008). Retrieved December 16, 2013, from *http://www.govtrack.us/congress/bills/110/s3406*.

Adler, A. B., Litz, B. T., Castro, C. A., Suvak, M., Thomas, J. L., Burrell, L., et al. (2008). A group randomized trial of critical incident stress debriefing provided to peacekeepers. *Journal of Traumatic Stress, 21*(3), 253–263.

Alcohol Policy Alliance. (2009). Firefighters, alcohol, and danger. Retrieved from *http://alcoholpolicy.org/2009/10/15/firefighters-alcohol-danger*.

American Academy of Family Physicians. (2011). *Mental health care services by family physicians* [position paper]. Retrieved January 21, 2012, from *www.aafp.org/online/en/home/policy/policies/m/mentalhealthcareservices.html*.

American College of Occupational and Environmental Medicine. (2012). *ACOEM guidance for the medical evaluation of law enforcement officers*. Retrieved January 21, 2012, from *www.acoem.org/LEOGuidelines.aspx*.

American Psychiatric Association. (2013). *Diagnostic and statistical manual of mental disorders* (5th ed.). Washington, DC: Author.

American Psychological Association. (2010). Ethical principles of psychologists and code of conduct. Retrieved from *www.apa.org/ethics/code/index.aspx*.

Americans with Disabilities Act of 1990, Public Law No. 101-336 § 2, 104 Stat. 327 (1991).

Anshel, M., Robertson, M., & Caputi, R. (2011). Sources of acute stress and their appraisals and reappraisals among Australian police as a function of previous experience. *Journal of Occupational and Organizational Psychiatry, 70*(4), 337–356.

Aronson, E. (1995). *The social animal.* New York: Freeman.

Asmundson, G. J. G., Stapleton, J. A., & Taylor, S. (2004). Are avoidance and numbing distinct PTSD symptom clusters? *Journal of Traumatic Stress, 17*(6), 467–475.

Ballenger J. F., Best, S. R., Metzler, T. J., Wasserman, D. A., Mohr, D. C., Liberman, A., et al. (2011). Alcohol use in male and female urban police officers. *American Journal of Addiction, 20*(1), 21–29.

Barlow, M. R., & Freyd, J. J. (2009). Adaptive dissociation: Information processing and response to betrayal. In P. F. Dell & J. A. McNeil (Eds.), *Dissociation and the dissociative disorders: DSM-V and beyond* (pp. 93–105). New York: Routledge.

Beck, A. (1993). *Beck Anxiety Inventory.* San Antonio, TX: Pearson.

Beck, A. (1998). *Beck Hopelessness Scale.* San Antonio, TX: Pearson.

Beck, A., Brown, G., Berchick, R. J., Stewart, B. L., & Steer, R. A. (1990). Relationship between hopelessness and ultimate suicide: A replication with psychiatric outpatients. *American Journal of Psychiatry, 147*(2), 190–195.

Beck A., Brown, G. K., & Steer, R. A. (1997). Psychometric characteristics of the scale for suicide ideation with psychiatric outpatients. *Behaviour Research and Therapy, 35*(11), 1039–1046.

Beck, A., & Steer, R. (1993). *Beck Scale for Suicide Ideation.* San Antonio, TX: Pearson.

Beck, A., Steer, R., & Brown, G. (1996). *Beck Depression Inventory—Second edition.* San Antonio, TX: Pearson.

Beck, J. S. (2011). *Cognitive behavioral therapy, 2nd ed: Basics and beyond.* New York: Guilford Press.

Beckner, V., & Arden, J. (2008). *Conquering post-traumatic stress disorder: The newest techniques for overcoming symptoms, regaining hope, and getting your life back.* Beverly, MA: Fair Winds Press.

Benedek, D., Friedman, M., Zatzick, D., Robert J., & Ursano, R. (2009). Practice guideline for the treatment of patients with acute stress disorder and posttraumatic stress disorder. Retrieved from *http://psychiatryonline.org/content.asp x?bookid=28&sectionid=1682793.*

Benner, A. (1982, August). *Concerns cops have about shrinks.* Paper presented at the annual meeting of the American Psychological Association, San Francisco, CA.

Benner, A. (1993, March). Editorial. *San Francisco Police Department Peer Support Group Newsletter,* p. 2.

Ben-Porath, Y. S., & Tellegen, A. (2008/2011). *MMPI-2-RF (Minnesota Multiphasic Personality Inventory-2 Restructured Form): Manual for administration, scoring, and interpretation.* Minneapolis: University of Minnesota Press.

Berninger, A., Webber, M., Cohen, H., Gustave, J., Lee, R., Niles, J., et al. (2010). Trends of elevated PTSD risk in firefighters exposed to the World Trade Center disaster: 2001–2005. *Public Health Reports, 125*(4), 556–566.

Best, S., Artwohl, A., & Kirschman, E. (2011). Critical incidents. In J. Kitaeff (Ed.), *Handbook of police psychology* (pp. 491–508). New York: Routledge.

Binder, E. B., Bradley, R. G., Liu, W., Epstein, M. P., Deveau, T. C., Mercer, K.

B., et al. (2008). Association of FKBP5 polymorphisms and childhood abuse with risk of posttraumatic stress disorder symptoms in adults. *Journal of the American Medical Association, 299*(11), 1291–1305.

Bisson, J. I., McFarlane, A. C., Rose, S., Ruzek, J. I., & Watson, P. J. (2009). Psychological debriefing for adults. In E. B. Foa, T. M. Keane, M. J. Friedman, & J. A. Cohen (Eds.), *Effective treatments for PTSD: Practice guidelines from the International Society for Traumatic Stress Studies* (2nd ed., pp. 83–105). New York: Guilford Press.

Blumenthal, J. A. (2007). Psychosocial training and cardiac rehabilitation. *Journal of Cardiopulmonary Rehabilitation and Prevention, 27,* 104–107.

Bonifacio, P. (1991). *The psychological effect of police work: A psychodynamic approach.* New York: Plenum Press.

Borum, R., & Philpot, C. (1999). Therapy with law enforcement couples: Clinical management of the high-risk lifestyle. In L. Territo & J. Sewell, *Stress management in law enforcement* (pp. 169–185). Durham, NC: Carolina Academic Press.

Boxer, P. A., & Wild, D. (1993). Psychological distress and alcohol use among fire fighters. *Scandinavian Journal of Work, Environment, and Health, 19*(2), 121–125.

Breslau, N. (2002). Epidemiologic studies of trauma, posttraumatic stress disorder, and other psychiatric disorders. *Canadian Journal of Psychiatry, 41*(10), 923–929.

Brewster, J., Wickline, P. W., & Stoloff, M. L. (2010). The Rorschach comprehensive system in police psychology. In P. Weiss (Ed.), *Personality assessment in police psychology: A 21st century perspective* (pp. 188–226). Springfield, IL: Charles C. Thomas.

Brick J., & Pohereckky, L. A. (1983). Ethanol–stress interaction: Biochemical findings. *Psychopharmacology, 74,* 81–84.

Briere, J. (1992). *Child abuse trauma: Theory and treatment of the lasting effects.* Newbury Park, CA: Sage.

Briere, J. (2001). *Detailed assessment of posttraumatic stress.* Lutz, FL: Psychological Assessment Resources.

Briere, J. (2002). *Multiscale Dissociation Inventory.* Odessa, FL: Psychological Assessment Resources.

Briere, J., & Scott, C. (2006). *Principles of trauma therapy: A guide to symptoms, evaluation and treatment.* Thousand Oaks, CA: Sage.

Briere, J. (2011). *Trauma Symptom Inventory–2.* Odessa, FL: Psychological Assessment Resources.

Briere, J., Weathers, F. W., & Runtz, M. (2005). Is dissociation a multidimensional construct? Data from the Multiscale Dissociation Inventory. *Journal of Traumatic Stress, 18*(3), 221–231.

Brown, J., & Campbell, E. (1994). *Stress and policing: Sources and strategies.* Chichester, UK: Wiley.

Brown, P. J., Read, J. P., & Kahler, C. W. (2003). Comorbid PTSD and substance use disorders: Treatment outcomes and role of coping. In P. C. Ouimette & P. J. Brown (Eds.), *Trauma and substance abuse: Causes, consequences, and treatment of comorbidity* (pp. 171–190). Washington, DC: American Psychological Association.

Bugental, J. (1987). *The art of psychotherapy.* New York: Norton.

Burke, R. J., & Mikkelsen, A. (2006). Police officers over career stages: Satisfaction and well being. *Europe's Journal of Psychology, 2*(1). Retrieved from *http:// ejop.psychopen.eu/article/view/314/222.*

Cahill, S. P., Foa, E. B., Hembree, E. A., Marshall, R. D., & Nacash, N. (2006). Dissemination of exposure therapy in the treatment of posttraumatic stress disorder. *Journal of Traumatic Stress, 19*(5), 597–610.

Calhoun, P. S., McDonald, S. D., Guerra, V. S., Eggleston, A., Beckham, J. C., & Straits-Troster, K. (2010). Clinical utility of the Primary Care-PTSD screen among U.S. veterans who served since September 11, 2001. *Psychiatry Research, 178*(2), 330–335.

California Public Employees' Retirement System. (2010). State employers' industrial disability cost report: 2009/2010 fiscal year. Retrieved December 21, 2012, from *www.calpers.ca.gov/eip-docs/about/pubs/employer/2010-idr.pdf.*

Cann, A., Calhoun, L. G., Tedeschi, R. G., Taku, K., Vishnevsky, T., Triplett, K. N., et al. (2010). A short form of the Posttraumatic Growth Inventory. *Anxiety, Stress and Coping: An International Journal, 23*, 127–137.

Carlan, P. E., & Nored, L. S. (2008). An examination of officer stress: Should police departments implement mandatory counseling? *Journal of Police and Criminal Psychology, 23*(8), 8–15.

Carlier, I. V. E., van Uchelen, J. J., Lamberts, R. D., & Gersons, B. P. R. (1998). Disaster-related posttraumatic stress in police officers: A field study of the impact of debriefing. *Stress Medicine, 14*, 143–148.

Carlier, I. V. E., Voerman, A. E., & Gersons, B. P. R. (2000). The influence of occupational debriefing on post-traumatic stress symptomatology in traumatized police officers. *British Journal of Medical Psychology, 73*, 87–98.

Chemtob, C., Tolin, D., van der Kolk, B., & Pitman, R. (2000). Eye movement desensitization and reprocessing. In E. B. Foa, T. M. Keane, & M. J. Friedman (Eds.), *Effective treatments for PTSD: Practice guidelines from the International Society for Traumatic Stress Studies* (pp. 333–335). New York: Guilford Press.

Clark, D. W., White, E. K., & Violanti, J. M. (2012, May). Law enforcement suicide: Current knowledge and future directions. *Police Chief, 79*, 48–51.

Cochrane, R., Tett, R., & Vandecreek, L. (2003). Psychological testing and the selection of police officers: A national survey. *Criminal Justice and Behavior, 30*(5), 511–537.

Colcombe, S., & Kramer, A. F. (2003). Fitness effects on the cognitive function of older adults: A meta-analytic study. *Psychological Science, 14*, 124–130.

Corneil, W. (1995). Traumatic stress and organizational strain in the fire service. In L. Murphy, J. Hurrell Jr., S. Sauter, & G. Keita (Eds.), *Job stress interventions* (pp. 185–198). Washington, DC: APA Press.

Cukor, J., Spitalnick, J., Difede, J., Rizzo, A., & Rothbaum, B. (2009). Emerging treatments for PTSD. *Clinical Psychology Review, 29*(8), 715–726.

Culpepper-Richards, K. (1998). Effect of a back massage and relaxation intervention on sleep in critically ill patients. *American Journal of Critical Care, 7*(4), 288–299.

Cunningham, M. (2003). Impact of trauma on social work clinicians: Empirical findings. *Social Work Journal 48*, 451–458.

Cyber-porn held responsible for increase in sex addiction. (2000, January 26). *Washington Times*. Retrieved from *http://washingtontimes.com/news/2000/jan/26/20000126-010843-1665r/?page=all*.

Dahlsgaard, K., Beck, A., & Brown, G. (1998). Inadequate response to therapy as a predictor of suicide. *Suicide and Life Threatening Behavior, 28*(2), 197–204.

Danieli, Y. (1994). Trauma to the family: Intergenerational sources of vulnerability and resilience. In J. Reese & E. Scrivner (Eds.), *Law enforcement families: Issues and answers* (pp. 163–175). Washington, DC: U.S. Government Printing Office.

Davidson, A., & Moss, S. (2008). Examining the trauma disclosure of police officers to their partners and officers' subsequent adjustment. *Journal of Language and Social Psychology, 27*, 51–70.

Davey, J. D., Obst, P. L., & Sheehan, M. C. (2000). The use of AUDIT as a screening tool for alcohol use in the police work-place. *Drug and Alcohol Review, 19*(1), 49–54.

Davis, J. L., & Wright, D. C. (2007). Randomized clinical trial for treatment of chronic nightmares in trauma-exposed adults. *Journal of Traumatic Stress, 20*(2), 123–133.

Dawson, D. A., Grant, B. F., Stinson, F. S., Chou, P. S., Huang, B., & Ruan, W. J. (2006). Recovery from DSM-IV alcohol dependence. *Alcohol Research and Health, 26*(2), 131–142.

Delaney, R., & Scheiber, D. (2008). *Covert: My years of infiltrating the mob*. New York: Union Square Press.

Derogatis, L. R. (1994). *Symptom Checklist-90-R: Administration, scoring and procedures manual*. Minneapolis, MN: NCS Pearson.

Deslandes, A., Moraes, H., Ferreira, C., Veiga, H., Silveria, H., Mouta, R., et al. (2009). Exercise and mental health: Many reasons to move. *Neurobiology, 59*, 191–198.

Devilly, G. J., & Spence, S. H. (1999). The relative efficacy and treatment distress of EMDR and a cognitive behavioural trauma treatment protocol in the amelioration of posttraumatic stress disorder. *Journal of Anxiety Disorder, 13*, 131–157.

Devilly, G. J., Gist, R., & Cotton, P. (2006). Ready! Fire! Aim! The status of psychological debriefing and therapeutic interventions: In the work place and after disasters. *Review of General Psychology, 10*, 318–345.

Dowd, S. M., Vickers, K. S., & Krahn, D. (2004). Exercise for depression: It really does help—here's how to get patients moving. *Current Psychiatry, 3*(b), 10–20.

Edwards, C. E., & Murdock, N. L. (1994). Characteristics of therapist self-disclosure in the counseling process. *Journal of Counseling and Development, 72*, 384–389.

Engel, L., & Ferguson, T. (2004). *Imaginary crimes: Why we punish ourselves and how to stop*. Lincoln, NE: Authors Choice Press.

Enright, R. D. (1996). Counseling within the forgiveness triad: On forgiving, receiving forgiveness, and self-forgiveness. *Counseling and Values, 40*(2), 107–126.

Erdelyi, M. H. (1990). Repression, reconstruction, and defense: History and integration of the psychoanalytic and experimental frameworks. In J. E. Singer (Ed.), *Repression and dissociation* (pp. 1–31). Chicago: University of Chicago Press.

Erickson, K. L., & Kramer, A. F. (2009). Aerobic exercise effecs on cognitive and neural placticity in older adults. *Brittish Journal of Sports Medicine, 43,* 22–24.

Everett, L., Worthington, E. L., Van Oyen Witvliet, C., Pietrini, P., & Miller, A.J. (2008). Forgiveness, health, and well-being: A review of evidence for emotional versus decisional forgiveness, dispositional forgivingness, and reduced unforgiveness. *Journal of Behavioral Medicine, 30*(4), 291–302.

Ewing v. Goldstein, 120 Cal. App. 4th 807 (2004).

Fagan, M., & Ayers, K. (1981).The life of a police offcer: A developmental perspective. *Police and Law Enforcement, 4,* 5–13.

Falsetti, S. A., & Resnick, H. S. (1997). Frequency and severity of panic attack symptoms in a treatment seeking sample of trauma victims. *Journal of Traumatic Stress, 4,* 683–689.

Family and Medical Leave Act of 1993, Public Law 103-3, 197 Stat. 6 (1993). Retrieved December 16, 2012, from *www.govtrack.us/congress/bills/103/hr1.*

Farnsworth, J. K., & Sewell, K. W. (2011). Fear of emotion as a moderator between PTSD and firefighter social interactions. *Journal of Traumatic Stress, 24*(4), 444–450.

Fay, A. (2002). The case against boundaries in psychotherapy. In A. A. Lazarus & O. Zur (Eds.), *Dual relationships and psychotherapy.* New York: Springer.

Fay, J., Kamena, M. D., Benner, A., Buscho, A., & Nagle, D. (2006). *Emergency responder exhaustion syndrome (ERES): A perspective on stress, coping and treatment in the emergency responder milieu.* Unpublished manuscript.

Federal Bureau of Investigation. (2011, October 24). FBI releases preliminary statistics for law enforcement officers killed in 2010. Retrieved from *www.fbi. gov/news/pressrel/press-releases/fbi-releases-preliminary-statistics-for-law-enforcement-officers-killed-in-2010.*

Figley, C. R. (1999). Police compassion fatigue (PCF): Theory, research, assessment, treatment, and prevention. In J. Violanti & D. Paton (Eds.), *Police trauma: Psychological aftermath of civilian combat* (pp. 37–53). Springfield, IL: Charles C. Thomas.

Finn, P. (2000). *Addressing correctional officer stress: Programs and strategies.* Washington, DC: National Institute of Justice, U.S. Department of Justice. Retrieved from *www.ncjrs.gov/pdffiles1/nij/183474.pdf.*

Finn, P., & Tomz, J. E. (1997, March). *Developing a law enforcement stress program for officers and their families.* Washington, DC: National Institute of Justice. Retrieved from *www.nij.gov/pubs-sum/163175.htm.*

Foa, E. B., Hembree, E. A., & Rothbaum, B. O. (2007). *Prolonged exposure therapy for PTSD: Emotional processing of traumatic experiences: Therapist guide.* New York: Oxford University Press.

Foa, E. B., Keane, T. M., & Friedman, M. J. (Eds.). (2000). *Effective treatments for PTSD: Practice guidelines from the International Society for Traumatic Stress Studies.* New York: Guilford Press.

Foa, E. B., Keane, T. M., Friedman, M. J., & Cohen, J. A. (2009) Introduction. In E. B. Foa, T. M. Keane, M. J. Friedman, & J. A. Cohen (Eds.) *Effective treatments for PTSD: Practice guidelines from the International Society for Traumatic Stress Studies* (2nd ed., pp. 1–22). New York: Guilford Press.

Ford, J. D. (1999). Disorders of extreme stress following war-zone military trauma: Associated features of posttraumatic stress disorder or comorbid but distinct syndromes? *Journal of Consulting and Clinical Psychology, 67*(1), 3–12.

Furr, R., & Funder, D. (1998). A multimodal analysis of personal negativity. *Journal of Personality and Social Psychology, 74*(6), 1580–1591.

Gaska, C. W. (1980). *The rate of suicide, potential for suicide, and recommendations for prevention among retired police officers.* Unpublished doctoral dissertation, Wayne State University, Detroit, Michigan.

Geller, J. D., & Farber, B. A. (1997, August). *Why therapists do and don't disclose.* Paper presented at the annual meeting of the American Psychological Association, Chicago.

Gershon, R. (2000). *Law enforcement and family support: "Project Shields"* (National Institute of Justice final report no. 97-FS-VX-0001). Retrieved from *www.ncjrs.gov/rr/vol2_2/18.html.*

Gerson, R. (2002). Work stress in aging police officers. *Journal of Occupational and Environmental Medicine, 44*(2), 160–167.

Ghahramanlou-Holloway, M., Cox, D. W., Fritz, E. C., & George, B. (2011). An evidence- informed guide for working with military women and veterans. *Professional Psychology: Research and Practice, 42,* 1–7.

Gilmartin, K. M. (2002). *Emotional survival for law enforcement.* Tucson, AZ: E-S Press.

Gist, R., & Devilly, G. J. (2002). Post-trauma debriefing: The road too frequently travelled. *Lancet, 360,* 741–742.

Goenjian, J. B., Steinberg, A., Dandekar, U., Noble, E., Walling, D., & Schmidt, D. (2012). Association of TPH1, TPH2, and 5HTTLPR with PTSD and depressive symptoms. *Journal of Affective Disorders, 140*(3), 244–252.

Goldfried, M. R., Burckell, L. A., & Eubanks-Carter, C. (2003). Therapist self-disclosure in cognitive-behavioral therapy. *Journal of Clinical Psychology, 59,* 555–568.

Gottman, J. (1999). *The seven priniciples for making marriage work.* New York: Crown.

Graff, F. A. (1986). The relationship between social support and occupation stress among police officers. *Journal of Police Science and Administration, 14*(3), 178–186.

Greenberg, L. S. (2011). *Emotion-focused therapy.* Washington, DC: American Psychological Association.

Greene, L. (1997, October). Uplifting resilient police families: A logic model to reduce stress and identify protective factors. *Police Chief,* pp. 70–71.

Greene, L., & Kirschman, E. (2001). On-line education, resources and support for law enforcement families, final report (Document No. 186749). Washington, DC: U.S. Department of Justice.

Greene, P., Kane, D., Christ, G., Lynch, S., & Corrigan, M. (2006). *FDNY Crisis counseling: Innovative responses to 9/11 firefighters, families, and communities.* Hoboken, NJ: Wiley.

Hackett, D. P., & Violanti, J. M. (2003). *Police suicide: Tactics for prevention.* Springfield, IL: Charles C. Thomas.

Halpern, J., Maunder, R. G., Schwartz, B., & Gurevich, M. (2012). Identifying, describing and expressing emotions in paramedics. *Journal of Trauma Stress, 25*(1), 111–114.

Hamer M., & Chida Y. (2009). Physical activity and risk of neurodegenerative disease: A systematic review of prospective evidence. *Psychological Medicine, 39*(1), 3–11.

Harris, A. H., Luskin, F. M., Benisovich, S. V., Standard, S., Bruning, J., Evans, S., et al. (2006). Effects of a group forgiveness intervention on forgiveness, perceived stress, and trait anger: A randomized trial. *Journal of Clinical Psychology, 62*(6), 715–733.

Harris, M. B., Baloglu, M., & Stacks, J. R. (2002). Mental health of trauma-exposed firefighters and critical incident stress debriefing. *Journal of Loss and Trauma, 7*, 223–238.

Hays, P. (2007). *Addressing cultural complexities in practice: Assessment, diagnosis, and therapy.* Washington, DC: American Psychological Association.

Hays, T. (1994, September 28). Daily horrors take heavy toll on New York City police officers. *The News*, pp. 2A–3A.

Health Insurance Portability and Accountability Act of 1996, Public Law 104-191, 110 Stat. 1936 (1996). Retrieved December 16, 2012, from *www.govtrack.us/congress/bills/104/hr3103*.

Heiman, M. F. (1975). The police suicide. *Journal of Police Science and Administration, 3*, 267–273.

Hem, E., Berg, A., & Ekeberg, O. (2001). Suicide in police—A critical review. *Suicide and Life-Threatening Behavior, 31*(2), 224–233.

Hitchcock, J. H., Weiss, P. A., Weiss, W. U., Rostow, C. D., & Davis, R. D. (2010). The future of personality assessment research in police psychology: What's next and what do we need? In P. A. Weiss (Ed.), *Personality assessment in police psychology: A 21st century perspective* (pp. 279–296). Springfield, IL: Charles C. Thomas.

Hochschild, A. (with Machung, A.). (2012). *The second shift: Working families and the revolution at home.* New York: Penguin.

Hogan, J. (2011). The challenges of moving into middle management: Responses from police officers. *Journal of Police and Criminal Psychology, 26*(2).

Honig, A., & Samo, D. G. (2007, October). *Best practices for preventing law enforcement suicide: Recommendations from the joint IACP and Joyce Foundation Great Lakes Summit on Gun Violence.* Paper presented at the IACP Police Psychological Services Section Conference, New Orleans, LA.

Honig, A., & Sultan, S. (2004). Reactions and resilience under fire: What an officer can expect. *Police Chief, 71*, 54–60.

Horowitz, M. J. (1994). Does repression exist? Yes. *Harvard Mental Health Letter, 11*(1), 4–6.

Horowitz, M. J. (2011). *Assessment-based treatment of post traumatic stress disorders.* Sausalito, CA: GreyHawk Publishing.

Howe, M. L., Courage, M. L., & Peterson, C. (1994). How can I remember when "I" wasn't there: Long-term retention of traumatic experiences and emergence of the cognitive self. *Consciousness and Cognition, 3*(3/4), 327–355.

International Association of Chiefs of Police. (2011). Addressing sexual offenses and misconduct by law enforcement: Executive guide. Retrieved from

*www.theiacp.org/PublicationsGuides/ContentbyTopic/tabid/216/Default.
aspx?id=1463&v=1.*

The internet porn "epidemic": By the numbers. (2010, June 17). *The Week.* Available at *http://theweek.com/article/index/204156/the-internet-porn-epidemic-by-the-numbers.*

Jaffe v. Redmond, 518 U.S. 1 (1996).

Joseph, P., Trevisan, M., Violanti, J., Donahue, R., Andrew, M., Burchfiel, C., et al. (2009). Police work and subclinical atherosclerosis. *Journal of Occupational and Environmental Medicine, 51,* 700–707.

Kamena, M. D., Gentz, D., Hays, V., Bohl-Penrod, N., & Greene, L. (2011). Peer support teams fill an emotional void in law enforcement agencies. *Police Chief, 78,* 80–84.

Katschnig, H., & Amering, M. (1998). The long-term course of panic disorder and its predictors. *Journal of Clinical Psychopharmacology, 18*(6)(Suppl. 2), 6S–11S.

Keane, T. M., Buckley, T. C., & Miller, M. W. (2003). Forensic psychological assessment in PTSD. In R. I. Simon (Ed.), *Posttraumatic stress disorder in litigation* (pp. 119–140). Washington, DC: American Psychiatric Publishing.

Keenan, P., & Royle, L. (2008). Vicarious trauma and first responders: A case study utilizing eye movement desensitization and reprocessing (EMDR) as the primary treatment modality. *International Journal of Emergency Mental Health, 9*(4), 291–298.

Kemeny, M., Foltz, C., Cavanagh, J., Cullen, M., Giese-Davis, J., Jennings, P., et al. (2012). Contemplative emotion training reduces negative emotional behavior and promotes prosocial responses. *Emotion, 12*(2), 338–350.

Kirschman, E. (2004). *I love a fire fighter: What the family needs to know.* New York: Guilford Press.

Kirschman, E. (2007). *I love a cop: What police families need to know* (rev. ed.). New York: Guilford Press.

Kitaeff, J. (Ed.). (2011). *Handbook of police psychology.* New York: Routledge.

Klinger, D. (2006). *Into the kill zone: A cop's eye view of deadly force.* San Francisco: Jossey-Bass.

Knox, S., Hess, S. A., Petersen, D. A., & Hill, C. E. (1997). A qualitative analysis of client perceptions of the effects of helpful therapist self-disclosure in long-term therapy. *Journal of Counseling Psychology, 44,* 274–283.

Koch, B. (2010). The psychological impact on police officers of being first responders to completed suicides. *Journal of Police and Criminal Psychology, 25*(2), 90–99.

Kosten, T. R., & Krystal, J. H. (1988). Biological mechanisms in posttraumatic stress disorder: Relevance for substance abuse. In M. Gallenter (Ed.), *Recent developments in alcoholism* (Vol. 6, pp. 49–68). New York: Plenum Press.

Kroll, J. (2007). No-suicide contracts as a suicide prevention strategy. *Psychiatric Times, 24*(8). Retrieved from *www.psychiatrictimes.com/articles/no-suicide-contracts-suicide-prevention-strategy.*

Kulka, R. A., Schlenger, W. E., Fairbank, J. A., Hough, R. L., Jordan, B. K., Marmar, C. R., et al. (1990). *Trauma and the Vietnam War generation: Report of findings from the National Vietnam Veterans Readjustment Study.* New York: Brunner/Mazel.

Laguna, L., Linn, A., Ward, K., & Rupslaukyte, R. (2010). An examination of authoritarian personality traits among police officers: The role of experience. *Journal of Police and Criminal Psychology, 25*(2), 99–104.

Langewiesche, W. (2003). *American ground: Unbuilding the World Trade Center.* New York: NorthPoint Press.

Larson, S. L., Eyerman, J., Foster, M. S., & Gfroerer, J. C. (2007). *Worker substance use and workplace policies and programs* [DHHS Publication No. SMA 07-4273]. Rockville, MD: Substance Abuse and Mental Health Services Administration, Office of Applied Studies.

Lawler, K. A., Younger, J. W., Piferi, R. L., Jobe, R. L., Edmondson, K. A., & Jones, W. H. (2005). The unique effects of forgiveness on health: An exploration of pathways. *Journal of Behavioral Medicine, 28*(2), 157–167.

Liddle, B. J. (1997). Gay and lesbian clients' selection of therapists and utilization of therapy. *Psychotherapy, 34,* 11–18.

Lieberman, J., III. (2003). The use of antipsychotics in primary care. *Primary Care Companion Journal of Clinical Psychiatry, 5*(Suppl. 3), 3–8.

Linden, J., & Klein, R. (1988). Police peer counseling—an expanded perspective. In J. T. Reese & J. Horn, (Eds.), *Police psychology: Operation assistance* (pp. 241–244). Washington DC: Federal Bureau of Investigation.

Lindsay, V., & Shelley, K. (2009). Social and stress-related influences of police officers' alcohol consumption. *Journal of Police and Criminal Psychology, 24*(2), 87–92.

Liptak, J., & Leutenberg, E. (2008). *Substance abuse and recovery workbook.* Duluth, MN: Whole Person Associates.

Loo, R. (1999). Police suicide: The ultimate stress reaction. In J. Violanti & D. Paton (Eds.), *Police trauma: Psychological aftermath of civilian combat* (pp. 37–53). Springfield, IL: Charles C. Thomas.

Loomis, C. C. (2011). Psychologists' role in identifying and treating sleep disorders. *California Psychologist, 44*(6), 6–9.

Lowery, K., & Stokes, M. A. (2005). Role of peer support and emotional expression on posttraumatic stress disorder in student paramedics. *Journal of Traumatic Stress, 18*(2), 171–179.

Ludwig, D., & Kabat-Zinn, J. (2008). Mindfulness in medicine. *Journal of the American Medical Association, 300*(11), 1350–1352.

Luskin, F. (2002). *Forgive for good.* San Francisco: Harper.

Lynch, M., Littleton, J., McKernan, R. M., Duncan, M. J., McMillan, T., & Campbell, I. C. (1983). Alpha adrenoceptor number and function in rat cortex after ethanol and immobilization stress. *Brain Research, 288,* 145–159.

Mallow, A. J. (1998). Self-disclosure: Reconciling psychoanalytic psychotherapy and Alcoholics Anonymous philosophy. *Journal of Substance Abuse Treatment, 15,* 493–498.

Maxfield, L. (2002). Eye movement desensitization and reprocessing treatment of post-traumatic stress disorder. In C. R. Figley (Ed.), *Brief treatments for the traumatized* (pp. 148–169). Westport, CT: Greenwood Press.

McCann, L. I., & Pearlman, L. A. (1990). Vicarious traumatization: A framework for understanding the psychological effects of working with victims. *Journal of Traumatic Stress, 3*, 131–149.

McCoy, S. P., & Aamodt, M. G. (2010). A comparison of law enforcement divorce rates with those of other occupations. *Journal of Police and Criminal Psychology, 25*(1), 1–16.

McCubbin, H., Thompson, A., & McCubbin, M. (1996). *Family assessment: Resiliency, coping and adaptation—Inventories for research and practice.* Madison: University of Wisconsin System.

McFarlane, A. C. (1998). The aetiology of posttraumatic stress disorders following a natural disaster. *British Journal of Psychiatry, 152*, 116–121.

McGinnis, J. H. (1985). Career development in municipal policing. *Canadian Police College Journal, 9*(2), 154–206.

McMorris, T., Davranche, K., Jones, G., Hall, B., Corbett, J., & Minter, C. (2009). Acute incremental exercise, performance of central executive task, and sympathoadrenal system and hypothalamic–pituitary–adrenal axis activity. *International Journal of Psychophysiology, 73*(3), 334–340.

McNally, R. J. (1999). Research on eye movement desensitization and reprocessing (EMDR) as a treatment for PTSD. *PTSD Research Quarterly, 10*(1), 1–7.

Medina, J. J. (2008). *Brain rules: 12 principles for surviving and thriving at work, home, and school.* Seattle, WA: Pear Press.

Mercer, K. B., Orcutt, H. K., Quinn, J. F., Fitzgerald, C. A., Conneely, K. N., Barfield, R. T., et al. (2012). Acute and posttraumatic stress symptoms in a prospective gene x environment study of a university campus shooting. *Archives of General Psychiatry, 69*(1), 89–97.

Miller, L. (2006a). Practical police psychology: Intimacy and family. Retrieved September 8, 2006, from *www.policeone.com.*

Miller, L. (2006b). *Practical police psychology: Stress management and crisis intervention for law enforcement.* Springfield, IL: Charles C. Thomas.

Miller, L. (2006c). Sex, lies and police work. Retrieved October 10, 2006, from *www.policeone.com.*

Miller, L. (2007a). Line-of-duty death: Psychological treatment of traumatic bereavement in law enforcement. *International Journal of Emergency Mental Health, 9*(1), 13–23.

Miller, L. (2007b). Police families: Stresses, syndromes, and solutions. *American Journal of Family Therapy, 35*(1), 21–40.

Miller, W. R., & Rollnick, S. (2002). *Motivational interviewing: Preparing people for change* (2nd ed.). New York: Guilford Press.

Mitchell, J. (2003). Crisis intervention and CISM: A research summary. Retrieved from *www.icisf.us/images/pdfs/rar/Crisis%20Intervention%20and%20 CISM%20-%20%20A%20Research%20Summary.pdf.*

Moffitt, K. (1994). Depression and memory narrative type. *Journal of Abnormal Psychology, 103*(3), 581–583.

Mueser, K. T., Noordsy, D. L., Drake, R. E., & Fox, L. (2003). *Integrated treatment for dual disorders: A guide to effective practice.* New York: Guilford Press.

Murphy, K. (2012, April 25). Army encourages new way of looking at PTSD. *Los Angeles Times.* Retrieved from *http://articles.latimes.com/2012/apr/25/ nation/la-na-army-ptsd-20120425.*

National Institute on Alcohol Abuse and Alcoholism. (2003). Recommended alcohol questions. Retrieved from *www.niaaa.nih.gov/research/guidelines-and-resources/recommended-alcohol-questions*.

Nelson, Z. P., & Smith, W. E. (1970). The law enforcement profession: An incident of high suicide. *Omega, 1*, 293–299.

Neylan, T. C., Brunet, A., Pole, N., Best, S. R., Metzler, T. J., Yehuda, R., et al. (2005). PTSD symptoms predict waking cortisol levels in police officers. *Psychoneuroendocrinology, 30*, 373–381.

Niederhoffer, A. (1978). *The police family: From station house to ranch house.* Lexington, MA: Lexington Books.

North, C., Tivis, L., McMillen, J., Pferrerbaum, B., Cox, J., Spitznagel, E. L., et al. (2002). Coping, functioning, and adjustment of rescue workers after the Oklahoma City bombing. *Journal of Traumatic Stress, 15*(3), 171–175.

O'Hara, A. F., & Violanti, J. M. (2009). Police suicide: A comprehensive study of 2008 national data. *International Journal of Emergency Mental Health, 11*(1), 17–23.

Otto, M. W., & Smits, J. A. J. (2011). *Exercise for mood and anxiety: Proven strategies for overcoming depression and enhancing well-being.* New York: Oxford University Press.

Palleson, S., Mitsem, M., Kvale, G., Johnsen, B., & Molde, H. (2005). Outcome of psychological treatments of pathological gambling: A review and meta-analysis. *Addiction, 100*, 1412–1422.

Parnell, L. (2007). *A therapist's guide to EMDR: Tools and techniques for successful treatment.* New York: Norton.

Parnell, L. (2008). *Tapping in: A step-by-step guide to activating your healing resources through bilateral stimulation.* Boulder, CO: Sounds True.

Paton, D., Violanti, J. M., Burke, K., & Gerhke, A. (2009). *From recruit to retirement: A career-length assessment of posttraumatic stress in police officers.* Springfield, IL: Charles C. Thomas.

Paton, D., Violanti, J., & Schmuckler, E. (1999). Chronic exposure to risk and trauma: Addiction and separation issues in police officers. In J. Violanti & D. Paton (Eds.), *Police trauma: Psychological aftermath of civilian combat* (pp. 37–53). Springfield, IL: Charles C. Thomas.

Peeters, M., Montgomery, A., Bakker, A., & Schaufeli, W. (2005). Balancing work and home: How job and home demandws are related to burnout. *International Journal of Stress Management, 12*(1), 43–61.

Petry, N., Ammerman, Y., Bohl, J., Doersch, A., Gay, H., Kadden, R., et al. (2006). Cognitive-behavioral therapy for pathological gamblers. *Journal of Counseling and Clinical Psychology, 74*(3), 555–567.

Pierce, H., & Lilly, M. (2012). Duty-related trauma exposure in 911 telecommunicators: Considering the risk for posttraumatic stress. *Journal of Traumatic Stress, 5*(25), 1–5.

Piggott v. City of New York. (2011). NY Slip Op 51212(U). Decided on June 15, 2011, Supreme Court, Kings County Ash, J. Published by New York State Law Reporting Bureau pursuant to Judiciary Law § 431.

Pokorny, A., Miller, B., & Kaplan, H. (1972). The brief MAST: A shorthanded version of the Michigan Alcoholism Screening Test. *American Journal of Psychiatry, 129*, 342.

Price-Sharps, J. (2011, October). *A new approach to couples counseling.* Presentation to the Society for Police and Criminal Psychology, Chicago.

Rajaratnam, S., Barger, L., Lockley, S. W., Shea, S. A., Wang, W., Landrigan, C. P., et al. (2011). Sleep disorders, health, and safety in police officers. *Journal of the American Medical Association, 306*(24), 2643–2742.

Raskind, M., Peskind, E., Kanter, E., Petrie, E., Radant, A., Thompson, C., et al. (2003). Reduction of nightmares and other PTSD symptoms in combat veterans by Prazosin: A placebo controlled study. *American Journal of Psychiatry, 160,* 371–373.

Regehr, C., & Bober, T. (2005). *In the line of fire: Trauma in the emergency services.* New York: Oxford University Press.

Resick, P. A., Monson, C. M., & Chard, K. M. (2008). *Cognitive processing therapy: Veteran/military version.* Washington, DC: Department of Veterans Affairs. Available at *http://depts.washington.edu/hcsats/PDF/research/Cognitive%20Processing%20Therapy%20Manual%208.08.pdf.*

Reynolds, G. (2012, April 28). Don't just sit there. *New York Times,* Sunday Review.

Rizzo, A., Reger, G., Gahm, G., Difede, J., & Rothbaum, B. O. (2009). Virtual reality exposure therapy for combat-related PTSD. In P. J. Shiromani, T. Keane, & J. E. LeDoux, (Eds.), *Post-traumatic stress disorder: Basic science and clinical practice* (pp. 375–400). New York: Humana Press.

Robins, L. N. (1993). Vietnam veterans' rapid recovery from heroin addiction: A fluke or normal expectation? *Addiction, 88,* 1041–1054.

Roland, J. (2010, September). *Developing and maintaining successful peer support programs in law enforcement agencies.* Paper presented at the annual conference of the Society for Police and Criminal Psychology, Honolulu, HI.

Rudofossi, D. (2007). *Working with traumatized police officer-patients.* Amityville, NY: Baywood.

Russell, M., Martier, S. S., Sokol, R. J., Mudar, P., Bottoms, S., Jacobson, S., et al. (1994). Screening for pregnancy risk-drinking. *Alcoholism: Clinical and Experimental Research, 18,* 1156–1161.

Sapolsky, R. M. (1998). *Why zebras don't get ulcers: An updated guide to stress, stress-related disease, and coping.* New York: Freeman.

Satir, V. (1983). *Conjoint family therapy.* Palo Alto, CA: Science & Behavior Books.

Saunders, J. B., Aasland, O. G., Babor, T. F., de la Fuente, J. R., & Grant, M. (1993). Development of the Alcohol Use Disorders Identification Test (AUDIT): WHO Collaborative project on early detection of persons with harmful alcohol consumption—II. *Addiction, 88,* 791–804.

Schauer, M., Neuner, F., & Elbert, T. (2011). *Narrative exposure therapy: A short-term treatment for traumatic stress disorders.* Cambridge, MA: Hogrefe Publishing.

Schutte, K. K., Nichols, K. A., Brennan, P. L., & Moos, R. H. (2003). A ten-year follow-up of older former problem drinkers: Risk of relapse and implications of successfully sustained remission. *Journal of Studies on Alcohol, 64*(3), 367–374.

Seaward, B. L. (2012). *Managing stress: Principles and strategies for health and well-being* (7th ed.). Sudbury, MA: Jones & Bartlett.

Sedlmeier, P., Eberth, J., Schwarz, M., Zimmermann, D., Haarig, F., Jaeger, S., et al. (2012). The psychological effects of meditation: A meta-analysis. *Psychological Bulletin, 138,* 1139–1171.

Serafino, G. (2010). Fundamental issues in police psychological assessment. In P. A. Weiss (Ed.), *Personality assessment in police psychology: A 21st century perspective* (pp. 29–55). Springfield, IL: Charles C. Thomas.

Shakespeare-Finch, J., & Enders, T. (2008). Corroborating evidence of posttraumatic growth. *Journal of Traumatic Stress, 21*(4), 421–424.

Shapiro, F. (2001). *Eye movement desensitization and reprocessing: Basic principles, protocols and procedures.* New York: Guilford Press.

Shapiro, F. (2007). EMDR, adaptive information processing, and case conceptualization. *Journal of EMDR Practice and Research, 1*(2), 68–87.

Shapiro, F., & Maxfield, L. (2002). EMDR: Information processing in the treatment of trauma. *In Session: Journal of Clinical Psychology, 58,* 933–946.

Sharpless, B. A., & Barber, J. P. (2011). A clinician's guide to PTSD treatments for returning veterans. *Professional Psychology: Research and Practice, 42*(1), 8–15.

Shulman, K. R., & Jones, G. E. (1996). The effectiveness of massage therapy intervention on reducing anxiety in the workplace. *Journal of Applied Behavioral Science, 32*(2), 160–173.

Sidhu, K. S., Vandana, P., & Balon, R. (2009). Exercise prescription: A practical effective therapy for depression. *Current Psychiatry, 8*(6), 39–51.

Simi, N. L., & Mahalik, J. R. (1997). Comparison of feminist versus psychoanalytic/dynamic and other therapists on self-disclosure. *Psychology of Women Quarterly, 21,* 465–483.

Simms, J. A., Haass-Koffler, C., Bito-Onon, J., Li, R., & Bartlett, S. E. (2012). Mifepristone in the central nucleus of the amygdala reduces yohimbine stress-induced reinstatement of ethanol-seeking. *Neuropsychopharmacology, 37,* 906–918.

Simon, J. C. (1990). Criteria for therapist self-disclosure. In G. Stricker & M. Fisher (Eds.), *Self-disclosure in the therapeutic relationship* (pp. 207–225). New York: Plenum Press.

Smart, R. G. (1988). Comments by Dr. Reginald Smart (Addiction Research Foundation, Toronto). *British Journal of Addiction, 83,* 892–893.

Smith, B. (2012). Inappropriate prescribing. *APA Monitor on Psychology, 43*(6), 36.

Smith, D. (2011, January 24). Entering 2011 in a "conspiracy of safety." PoliceOne.com. Available at *www.policeone.com/Officer-Safety/articles/3227758-Entering-2011-in-a-conspiracy-of-safety/.*

Southworth, R. (1990). *Taking the job home.* Unpublished manuscript. Available at *http://textfiles.com/law/jobhome.law.*

Stathopoulou, G., Powers, M., Berry, A., Smits, J., & Otto, M. (2006). Exercise interventions for mental health: A quantitative and qualitative review. *Clinical Psychology: Research and Practice, 13,* 1179–1193.

Stone, A. V. (1995). Law enforcement psychological fitness for duty: Clinical issues. In M. I. Kurke & E. M. Scrivner (Eds.), *Police psychology into the 21st century* (pp. 109–132). Hillsdale, NJ: Erlbaum.

Sue, D. W., & Sue, D. (2008). *Counseling the culturally diverse.* Hoboken, NJ: Wiley.

Tarasoff v. Regents of the University of California, 17 Cal. 3d 425, 551 P.2d 334, 131 Cal. Rptr. 14 (Cal. 1976).

Tedeschi, R. G., & Calhoun, L. G. (1995). *Trauma and transformation: Growth in the aftermath of suffering.* Thousand Oaks, CA: Sage.

Tedeschi, R. G., & Kilmer, R. P. (2005). Assessing strengths, resilience, and growth to guide clinical interventions. *Professional Psychology: Research and Practice, 36,* 230–237.

Terr, L. (1988). What happens to early memories of trauma? A study of twenty children under age five at the time of documented trauma events. *American Academy of Child and Adolescent Psychiatry, 27,* 96–104.

Terr, L. (1991). Childhood traumas: An outline and overview. *American Journal of Psychiatry, 148,* 10–20.

Thompson, G., & Jenkins, J. (2004). *Verbal judo: The gentle art of persuasion.* Colorado Springs, CO: Alive Communications.

Toch, H. (2002). *Stress in policing.* Washington, DC: American Psychological Association.

Tuohy, A., Knussen, C., & Wrennall. M. (2005). Effects of age on symptoms of anxiety and depression in a sample of retired police officers. *Psychology and Aging, 20*(2), 202–221.

USA Patriot Act (Uniting and Strengthening America by Providing Appropriate Tools Required to Intercept and Obstruct Terrorism Act of 2001), Public Law No. 107-56 § 224, 115 Stat. 272 (2001). Retrieved November 28, 2012, from *www.gpo.gov/fdsys/pkg/PLAW-107publ56/pdf/PLAW-107publ56.pdf.*

U.S. Bureau of Labor Statistics, U.S. Department of Labor. (2012). Injuries, illnesses, and fatalities. Retrieved January 3, 2013, from *http://www.bls.gov/iif.*

U.S. Census Bureau. (2012). Law enforcement, courts, and prisons. Retrieved from *www.census.gov/compendia/statab/2012/tables/12s0330.pdf.*

Vaillant, G. E. (2005). Alcoholics anonymous: Cult or cure? *Australian and New Zealand Journal of Psychiatry, 39,* 431–436.

van der Kolk, B. A., & van der Hart, O. (1991). The intrusive past: The flexibility of memory and the engraving of trauma. *American Imago, 48*(4), 425–454.

van Dierendonck, D., Gaarssen, B., & Visser, A. (2005). Burnout prevention through personal growth. *International Journal of Stress Management, 12*(1), 62–77.

van Liempt, S., Vermetten, E., Geuze, E., & Westenberg, H. (2006). Pharmacotherapeutic treatment of nightmares and insomnia in posttraumatic stress disorder: An overview of the literature. *Annals of the New York Academy of Sciences, 1071,* 502–507.

Vila, B. (1996). Tired cops: Probable connections between fatigue and the performance, health and safety of patrol officers. *American Journal of Police, 15*(2), 51–92.

Vila, B. (2000). *Tired cops: The importance of managing police fatigue.* Washington, DC: Police Executive Research Forum.

Vila, B. (2009). Sleep deprivation: What does it mean for public safety officers? *National Institute of Justice Journal, 262,* 26–30.

Vinogradov, S., & Yalom, I. D. (1990). Self-disclosure in group psychotherapy. In G. Stricker & M. Fisher (Eds.), *Self-disclosure in the therapeutic relationship* (pp. 191–204). New York: Plenum Press.

Violanti, J. M. (1983). Stress patterns in police work: A longitudinal study. *Journal of Police Science and Administration, 11*(2), 211–216.

Violanti, J. M., Burchfiel, C. M., Miller, D. B., Andrew, M. E., Dorn, J., Wactawski-Wende, J., et al. (2006). The Buffalo cardio-metabolic occupational police stress (BCOPS) pilot study: Methods and participant characteristics. *Annals of Epidemiology* 16(2), 148–156.

Violanti, J., Charles, L. E., Hartley, K., Mnatsakanova, A., Andrew, M., Fekedulegn, D., et al. (2008). Shift-work and suicide ideation among police officers. *American Journal of Industrial Medicine, 51*(10), 758–768.

Violanti, J. M., & Drylie, J. J. (2008). *Copicide: Concepts, cases, and controversies of suicide by cop.* Springfield, IL: Charles C. Thomas.

Violanti, J. M., Vena, J. E., Marshall, J. R., & Petralia, S. (1996). A comparative evaluation of police suicide rate validity. *Suicide & Life-Threatening Behavior, 26,* 79–85.

Visher, E., & Visher, J. (1996). *Therapy with stepfamilies.* New York: Routledge.

Waitzkin, H., & Magana, H. (1997). The black box in somatization: Unexplained physical symptoms, culture, and narratives of trauma. *Social Science Medicine, 45*(6), 811–825.

Walsh, F. (1999). *Strengthening family resiliency.* New York: Guilford Press.

Wedding, D. (1987). Substance abuse in Vietnam veterans. *AAOHN Journal, 35,* 74–76.

Weir, H., Stewart, D. M., & Morris, R. G. (2012). Problematic alcohol consumption by police officers and other protective service employees: A comparative analysis. *Journal of Criminal Justice, 40,* 72–82.

Weiss, D. S. (2007). The Impact of Event Scale: Revised. In J. P. Wilson & C.S. Tang (Eds.), *Cross-cultural assessment of psychological trauma and PTSD* (pp. 219–238). New York: Springer.

Whelan, J. P., Steenbergh, T. A., & Meyers, A. W. (2007). *Problem and pathological gambling.* Cambridge, MA: Hogrefe.

White, E., & Honig, A. (1995). Law enforcement families. In M. Kurke & E. Scrivner (Eds.), *Police psychology into the 21st century.* Hillsdale, NJ: Erlbaum.

White, M., & Epston, D. (1990). *Narrative means to therapeutic ends.* New York: Norton.

Wilk, J. E., West, J. C., Narrow, W. E., Rae, D. S., & Regier, D. A. (2005). Economic grand rounds: Access to psychiatrists in the public sector and in managed care. *Psychiatric Services, 56*(4), 408–410.

Wilson, J. A. B., Onorati, K., Mishkind, M., Reger, M. A., & Gahm, G. A. (2008). Soldier attitudes about technology-based approaches to mental healthcare. *Cyberpsychology and Behavior, 11,* 767–769.

Winzelberg, A., & Humphreys, K. (1999). Should patients' religiosity influence clinicians' referral to 12-step self-help groups?: Evidence from a study of 3,018 male substance abuse patients. *Journal of Clinical and Consulting Psychology, 67,* 790–794.

Woolley, S. (2007). The revolution in couples therapy. *The California Psychologist, 40*(1), 12–15.

Yehuda, R., & McFarlane, A. C. (1995). Conflict between current knowledge about posttraumatic stress disorder and its original conceptual basis. *American Journal of Psychiatry, 152*(12), 1705–1713.

INDEX